www.wadsworth.com

wadsworth.com is the World Wide Web site for Wadsworth and is your direct source to dozens of online resources.

At wadsworth.com you can find out about supplements, demonstration software, and student resources. You can also send e-mail to many of our authors and preview new publications and exciting new technologies.

wadsworth.com
Changing the way the world learns®

Learning Skills
for College
and Life

David L. Watson
University of Hawai'i at Manoa

with Malia Watson

WADSWORTH

★

™

THOMSON LEARNING

Australia • Canada • Mexico • Singapore • Spain • United Kingdom • United States

WADSWORTH

THOMSON LEARNING ™

Executive Manager: Elana Dolberg
Assistant Editor: MJ Wright
Project Editor: Cathy Linberg
Print Buyer: Barbara Britton
Permissions Editor: Joohee Lee
Production Service: Delgado Design

Text and Cover Designer: Delgado Design, Inc.
Copy Editor: Linda Stern
Cover Image: Richard Price/FPG
Compositor: Delgado Design
Text and Cover Printer: Malloy Lithographing

Wadsworth/Thomson Learning
10 Davis Drive
Belmont, CA 94002-3098
USA

For more information about our products, contact us:
Thomson Learning Academic Resource Center
1-800-423-0563
http://www.wadsworth.com

International Headquarters
Thomson Learning
International Division
290 Harbor Drive, 2nd Floor
Stamford, CT 06902-7477
USA

UK/Europe/Middle East/South Africa
Thomson Learning
Berkshire House
168-173 High Holborn
London WC1V 7AA
United Kingdom

Asia
Thomson Learning
60 Albert Street, #15-01
Albert Complex
Singapore 189969

Canada
Nelson Thomson Learning
1120 Birchmount Road
Toronto, Ontario M1K 5G4
Canada

Library of Congress Cataloging-in-Publication Data
Watson, David L.,
    Learning skills for college and life /
David Watson with Malia Watson.
      p. cm.
Includes bibliographical references and index.
ISBN 0-534-56161-6 (alk. paper)
1. Study skills--Handbooks, manuals, etc.
2. Life skills--Handbooks, manuals, etc. I.
Watson, Malia. II. Title.
LB2395 . W39 2000
371.3'028'1--dc21   00-043761

For Dear Abby

Brief Table of Contents

Detailed Table of Contents

Part VIII **Lifelong Learning**   307

Preface

To achieve academic success, students need to acquire, develop, and practice vital learning skills and strategies. *Learning Skills for College and Life* aims to provide the required knowledge and the practice needed for students to reach their full potential as college students as well as life-long learners.

Often students find that their tried and true study strategies fail them when employed to meet the new challenges of their college academic endeavors. As a result of such difficulties, some students experience anxiety and disappointment about their academic performance but do not know how to improve or change their study habits. My career has focused on teaching college students how to accomplish self-change in the area of personal adjustment. Using some concepts from psychology, this book aims to teach students not only what to change, it guides the student through the difficult process and personal challenge of how to change.

Here are a few ways my text guides students to improved learning skills:

- Chapters start with an outline and a set of questions students can answer, my adaptation of the SQ part of Robinson's famous SQ3R procedure, encouraging valuable self-reflection.

- All the material presented for students to learn has been shown by research to actually work to improve study skills.

- Each chapter has built-in opportunities to practice the ideas, with many suggestions on how to slowly and realistically develop them into good academic habits.

- Chapters contain many real-life cases and examples using real students in real situations that students can relate to.

As instructors, we want to avoid the old tradition of "teach and hope" that the students benefit from what we teach. This requires us to do more than simply transmit information. We need to provide practice in the learning skills we teach, and follow students' progress to encourage continued use of the skills. Thus in my book I include many practice exercises, called **Skill Builders**, and many opportunities to be reflective of the process of skill building, called **Think Pieces**.

- **Skill Builders,** present in every chapter, provide opportunities for planning and gaining practice in developing important skills.

- **Think Pieces,** also present in every chapter, aim to produce mindful practice of learning skills, accomplished through self-reflection and monitoring of skills development.

Even the best students, research shows, do not know and use all the learning strategies available, and the average student does not know or use many of them. Most instructors know students who do not seem willing to put in the time and effort needed. We need to motivate them to succeed.

There is an explicit motivational theory behind this book, the value x expectancy theory ("value by expectancy"). It is used extensively in modern research and has much research to support it. The basic idea is that humans are motivated to approach goals by two variables: the value the goal has for them, and their estimation of their chances of attaining the goal. In the text I explicitly attempt to show students the value of good grades for them, by tying grades to other goals they have in life, and teach them that, no matter what their previous school experience has been, they can reach their goal.

Acknowledgements

Several people helped me as I was writing this book. Many thanks to my excellent graduate students, Rosiana (Nani) Azman, Kelly Chang, and Shane Cobb-Adams, who contributed substantial ideas that I used in the text and who were very helpful in preparing the Instructor's Manual. Special thanks to Andrew Greene and Audrey Kawaoka, who ably served as library assistants during the whole process. I received excellent editorial advice from Elana Dolberg and Sally Cobau of Wadsworth.

Thank you to the following reviewers: Pamela Backes, Keene State College; Jeanne Higbee, University of Georgia; Linda Kleeman, Lewis and Clark Community College; James Kole, Clarion University; Clarence J. Landry, Rockford College; Alice Lenning, University of Oklahoma; Jodi Levine, Temple University; Patricia Malinowski, Finger Lakes Community College; Lisa Portwood, University of Oklahoma; Barbara Sherman, Liberty University; and Betty Smith, University of Nebraska-Kearney.

My dear wife, Abby Brown-Watson, to whom this book is dedicated, helped me think of solutions to many writing problems as the book developed, and was very supportive throughout. Now can we go birding?

Most of all, thanks to the hundreds of undergraduate students who carried out all the real learning skills projects used as cases and examples in the book. Here in Hawaii they were a very diverse group of folks, but they were united by the experience of beginning college and wanting to cope well with the new challenges. They are quoted on many pages, though of course disguised. Thanks to all of you.

David L. Watson
Honolulu

About the Author

David L. Watson received his Ph.D. in psychology from Yale University in 1963. His first book (1972), with Roland Tharp, was *Self-Directed Behavior: Self-Modification for Personal Adjustment,* now in its eighth edition. This book is frequently referred to as a "classic" in psychology. In it Watson laid out a set of scientifically tested ideas to enable readers to change important aspects of their own behavior.

In *Learning Skills for College and Life* Watson continues this tradition of "giving psychology away" by teaching readers what and how to change in their academic and working lives.

Watson is a Fellow of the American Psychological Association and Charter Fellow of the American Psychological Society. His other books include *Psychology: What It Is and How to Use It, Here's Psychology, Social Psychology: Science and Application,* and *Psychology: An Introductory Textbook.* Watson has two grown children, Dan and Malia, and lives in Hawaii with his wife, Abby, with whom he frequently goes birding around the world.

Part I

Getting Started

Students who do well in school have work habits that others do not. They use learning strategies others don't use, or they use them more often. This book shows you the learning strategies they use, and shows you how to develop these strategies as habits. We cover

- What to change
- How to change

If you want to improve your academic success, this book tells you the best areas to work on and gives you tools to make changing as easy as possible. The focus is on strategies for greater efficiency, but the book won't urge you to work harder. Our motto is "Work smarter, not harder."

The book is both for those people who need only a little work to become really fantastic students and for those who need a lot of work to ensure college success.

What will you learn?

There are several sets of learning skills you could practice, if you need to improve. The book covers them all:

1. Time management—managing your life
2. Basic skills such as holding the right attitudes, working with others, taking notes, concentrating in class and out, and thinking critically
3. Reading skills, with an emphasis on reading like an expert
4. Study techniques and memorizing, with some surprising news
5. Test-taking skills—getting ready and getting calm
6. Verbal skills—such as improving vocabulary and writing
7. Preparation for lifelong learning

You might need only a little work here and there to be excellent, or you might need to focus heavily on several of these skills to become excellent. Either way, by practicing the habits laid out in this book, you can become an excellent student.

Chapter 1

School's Hidden Agenda: Learning Strategies

PREVIEW WITH QUESTIONS TO ANSWER

NOTE: Every chapter starts with a list like this. It outlines what will come and raises questions for which you can find answers as you read. You will learn better when you see the outline first and when you search for answers as you read.

School's Hidden Agenda

- What is the hidden agenda?
- Is school learning important? Do grades in school matter?
- What are learning strategies?

Examples of Learning Strategies

- How does the use of learning strategies help, and lack of them hurt?

How Effective Are Learning Strategies?

- Do learning strategies really help? Can people learn them?

The Need for Planning and Practice

- Why are planning and practice important?
- What learning skills should you practice?

Do You Want to Do This?

- How do your life goals relate to the skills taught in this book?

School's Hidden Agenda

There is a hidden agenda in schools, a set of skills you are supposed to learn but which no one ever points out to you. "Good" students learn these skills and do well in school, even though they may not be aware of the skills

**QUESTIONS TO ANSWER
AS YOU READ:**

Note: At the beginning of each
segment of each chapter, there
are questions to answer as you
read. Don't skip these. You will
learn better if you are searching
for answers as you read.

- What is the hidden agenda?
- Is school learning important?
- Do grades in school matter?
- What are learning strategies?

they have learned. Struggling students do *not* learn the skills well, and that is why they struggle. Many students learn the skills partially, but not completely.

This agenda is so hidden that even many instructors cannot say what it is. They can see the difference between "good" students and struggling ones, but cannot tell you what causes that difference. This is as if a mechanic said, "This car runs faster than that one," but could not tell you why. Perhaps one car is well tuned, but the other is not. One car might even have the brake on.

Educational psychologists have been studying the differences between smoothly running students and those whose engines knock. We now know what produces the smoothness. We can tell you what skills "good" students learn that others do not. The best part is *we can teach you how to develop these skills in yourself to give your academic engine a tune-up.* The agenda is no longer hidden.

Schooling Is Not Just Subject Matter

Some people think of education as simply the transmission of information. The instructor or textbook writer knows a lot about her area and tells some of it to you. You memorize this information, and that's your education. We do need to learn specific knowledge—who was Macbeth? how does a stereotype affect our perception?—because we use that information in our thinking.[1] A person with a college education is expected to know more than a person with a high school education. But we need more than just information.

In college, you don't just learn facts to use in your thinking, *you learn skills.* In the process of getting an A.A. or a B.A., you might learn, for example, to turn your work in on time, or to do your best job the first time because there isn't any extra credit work to make up for deficiencies.

Learning does not stop when you get your A.A or B.A. Far from it. You may have an A.A. in business, but you are not ready to run a large store. You may have a B.A. in psychology, but you are not ready to do psy-

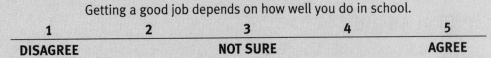

THINK PIECE 1.1   Do grades in school matter?

What do you believe about this? Respond to the following statement by circling the number below it that reflects your opinion.

Getting a good job depends on how well you do in school.

1	2	3	4	5
DISAGREE		NOT SURE		AGREE

More than one-third of high school students in the Chicago area disagreed with this statement.[2] Are they right? Are grades unimportant?

chotherapy. We have to keep on learning, building on what we have already learned. All of adult life involves learning.

Life is full of learning. One of the professors who reviewed this book in its early stages said, "A growing person is always a freshman at something. Me, I'm a freshman at golf."

Do grades in school matter?

Casey, a freshman, confided, "I know teachers want us to make good grades, but I don't see the point. It's too hard, and frankly, grades don't make that much difference. I got all the way through high school without cracking a book, and I got in here, didn't I? So what's the point of grades?"

Is Casey right? If grades do *not* matter, there is little point in working to get good grades. Therefore, there would be little point in trying to develop the skills that help you get good grades.

It depends on what grades you are talking about.

High school students are indirectly encouraged to believe that grades are not important. After all, students get promoted each year no matter what their grades are. They can graduate with very low grades. And they can almost always get into some college no matter what their grades were in high school. Even D's will get them in. All these facts encourage some students to believe that grades are *not* important, that grades don't matter.

But college is a new ball game. Suddenly, what was not important becomes important. You may be able to get *into* college with low grades, but you cannot get *out of* college with them. Making a good grade in college is more challenging than doing so in high school. You may pass in high school with low effort, but you will not in college. In college, standards go up.

Some students are the victim of a sort of cruel kindness. We believe in an America that gives everyone a second chance. Even if your grades in high school are low, you can get into college. That is our national kindness. Unfortunately, this encourages people to believe that grades are unimportant. But college is where the new ball game begins, and without anyone warning you. The rules are changed, but no one tells you. That is our cruelty. You get set up to believe grades are unimportant; then suddenly they become very important.

Why are grades in college important? It's not the grade *itself* that is important. What is important is the *effort and skill* you have to develop and use to get the good grade. Making an A in math, for example, requires effort plus several skills: getting yourself to do the homework, studying the concepts, understanding and remembering them, and doing well on the tests. What the grade tells future employers is not merely that you know a lot of math, but that you have the skills necessary to get a good grade in math. You have self-management skills.

That is why grades in college are important. Employers today are looking for people with skills. They feel that many high schools are not doing a good job teaching the skills they are looking for.[3] The job is left up to colleges. You didn't need the skills in high school, but you will need them in college, and you will need them in your work later.

Learning skills

"Learning skills," or "learning strategies," are a set of knowledge and skills that make learning easier. People with good learning skills know how to control their behavior, thoughts, emotions, and motivation to make learning easier and more effective.[4]

The hidden agenda in schooling is that you do *not* just learn important subject matter such as literature or science. You learn strategies for controlling yourself, for maintaining your willpower, for keeping up your endurance over long periods of time.[5] You learn how to get the job done even though it is difficult. An important learning event in college is not just writing some huge term paper, but learning to plan ahead and budget your time and overcome boredom and fatigue. Once you have learned these skills, you use them for the rest of your life.

In his book on the changes that are coming in the world of work, John Naisbett, an economist, concluded, "In a world that is constantly changing, there is no one subject or set of subjects that will serve you for the foreseeable future, let alone for the rest of your life. The most important skill to acquire now is *learning how to learn*."[6]

QUESTION TO ANSWER
AS YOU READ:

■ How does the use of learning strategies help, and lack of them hurt?

Examples of Learning Strategies

Brooke, a second-semester freshman, is surprised when her instructor in developmental psychology announces that in three weeks the class will have a "take-home, open-book" exam covering the first five chapters of the textbook. Brooke has never had a take-home exam before. Her first thought is "Wow, that's going to be easy. I can just look up answers in the book."

After class, Brooke realizes that the test will have different questions than she is used to dealing with. "He's not going to ask us to regurgitate material," she thinks. "That would be stupid when we can just copy stuff out of the book. What kinds of questions is he going to ask, then?"

She thinks, "I need to ask him about this." She approaches the instructor after the next lecture and asks what kinds of questions will be on the exam. She doesn't ask for specific questions, of course, but tries to get a feeling for the type of question. His answer: "They will ask you to apply the material."

Brooke realizes that she does not have to memorize the material, but she does need to know what it is and where it is located in the text, so she can flip to it if she needs it while taking the exam. Brooke begins to read the text, focusing on making some notes on the major ideas and also noting where the material occurs in the five chapters.

All this while, Brooke has been trying to imagine what kinds of questions will be on the exam. She decides one question might be, "Give examples from your own childhood of the three principles listed in Chapter 4." She thinks of this because she has noticed that the professor keeps emphasizing relating the material in the course to the students' own lives. Now she has one general question, but she figures that she needs more.

Brooke decides she will finish all the reading for the first time by the Wednesday before the test. She also decides to do all her studying in the school library, which is very quiet and where she will be free of interruptions.

Brooke calls a friend who is in the class to discuss the exam with her. She wants to know how her friend is preparing for the exam. Her friend has some good ideas, which Brooke makes a note to use herself.

In the last two days leading up to the exam, Brooke sees she is getting bored with all this preparation, so she takes a break and goes hiking with a friend for several hours. She also reminds herself of the importance of this exam: Doing well in the course, Developmental Psychology, is essential for her because she wants to be a teacher.

Here is a list of the learning skills Brooke demonstrated in this two-week period:

- Brooke wonders what kinds of questions will be asked on the exam.

- She asks her professor about the kinds of questions and tries to imagine questions.

- She prepares practice questions.

- She plans how she needs to learn the material and adapts her usual approach to the new situation of a take-home exam.

- She remembers what the professor seems to emphasize.

- At the end of the first week, she reviews what she has done, revises her plans a bit, and sets goals for the next week.

- She consults with a friend and uses some of her ideas.

- She copes with the boredom of an all-study week.

- She reminds herself how important this work is to her.

Brooke makes good grades. Not everyone is so fortunate. Let's consider a second case of someone in Brooke's class. Brooke used many learning strategies that this person did not use.

> When Chad heard the news that there was to be an "open book, take-home exam," he thought, "Whoa! How easy can this get?" Then he didn't think any more about the exam. He figured he could read the material when the instructor gave out the questions. He said to himself, "I know I can read five chapters over the weekend, so I will just read his questions, then read the parts of the chapters that cover them and write out the answers."
>
> Two weeks later, leaving class after picking up the exam, Chad was stunned. He didn't understand one of the questions, and it was not obvious to him how to look up the answers to the others. But Chad hung out with his friends the rest of the day and began a weekend in which many distractions came up—a movie, a cute girl, a serious talk with a buddy about life. By the time the take-home exam was due, Chad had managed to answer only two of the four questions. Not surprisingly, he failed the test.

Many students fall somewhere in between Brooke's excellent performance and Chad's poor performance. There are many stages in the development of learning skills. For many of us, there are a few tricks yet to be learned, a few steps yet to be taken to attain excellence.

Going from high school to college is a rough transition for some people because they have not learned all the skills they need.[7] One of your tasks in college is to find out where you are weak and to strengthen that part. Brooke, for example, tried to figure out what the test questions would be, and she also set goals for herself. Chad, on the other hand, neglected to plan ahead. He didn't think about the test at all and did not budget his work time to prepare for it. He overestimated the ease of the exam. He allowed himself to be distracted from his work. These are typical problems for students who don't do well in school.

A problem with Chad's low grade is that he may begin to think of himself as someone who *cannot* do college work. If the pattern continues, at some point he may think, "Maybe college is not for me. I guess I'm just not quite smart enough." That would be a shame, because Chad really isn't *deficient*. But he was *inefficient*.

Your effectiveness in school is affected not only by your intelligence, but by the strategies you use and your self-awareness of your own behavior. Chad may or may not have known the material, but he did not analyze the task, didn't use learning strategies, and did not seem to believe that effort helps. What could Chad have done to be efficient?

So-called good students use learning strategies, while underachieving students do not. If Chad had used learning strategies, as Brooke did, he would have had very different results. At all levels of school, from elementary up, good students use learning strategies much more than underachieving students.[8] They may have learned these from their parents, they may have learned these at school; they may even have figured them out for themselves. It is not that the good students are smarter. They are more efficient. They use learning strategies that the other students do not.

That raises an interesting possibility. Can Chad, at this late date, make himself a successful student by learning to do the things successful students do? What about most of us, who are more skilled than Chad but not yet perfect students? Can we improve by developing more or better learning skills?

QUESTIONS TO ANSWER AS YOU READ:

- Do learning strategies really help?
- Can people learn them?

How Effective Are Learning Strategies?

Students can learn learning strategies at any age, and doing this does help them in school.[9] In fact, a wide variety of improvements follows the increased use of learning strategies.[10] Here is some evidence to support that statement.

For many years, instructors at the University of Michigan have been teaching a course, Learning to Learn, that teaches learning strategies. Topics covered include learning from textbooks, learning in lectures, and test taking. The instructors made comparisons between students who enrolled in the course and students enrolled in the usual Introduction to Psychology course, who were *not* taught learning strategies. The students who learned the learning skills improved their grade point averages (GPA) compared to the others. They also lowered the anxiety they felt when taking tests.[11] The more the students used learning strategies from the course, the better they did, and the better they felt about their abilities as students.[12]

Learning these skills or getting better at them will help you graduate from college. A study at the University of Texas found that on the average only about 55 percent of students who start college finish. But when the students took a course that taught them the learning skills covered in this book, 71 percent graduated.[13] That means that if there were 1,000 students in the freshman class, at graduation four years later there would be 710 of the original students instead of 550—a difference of 160. Those "extra" graduates are probably pretty happy they improved their skills. And these percentages don't include the number who improved their GPA, with all the advantages that go with a higher GPA.

Even the best students benefit from the addition of learning strategies. At Texas Tech University in Lubbock, Dr. William Lan taught a group of graduate (post-B.A.) students to use advanced learning strategies in a challenging statistics course and compared their performance to the performance of other graduate students who did not learn the strategies.[14] The students learned to teach themselves to study material they didn't know, instead of reviewing material they already knew. Lan found that those students who learned and used the techniques did better in the statistics course than those who did not.

Learning strategies don't help only struggling students, then; they help *all* students. A struggling student might have to work on basic skills, but even an advanced student can expect improvement if she works on polishing her skills. This book is for all students, not just those who are at risk.

When do these ideas *not* work? We don't know the complete answer to that yet. But we do know one situation when they *don't* work: when you don't use them. If you over estimate your learning ability, or think college is easy, you may try to work without using these learning strategies, and if you do that, you lower your chances for success.

The Need for Planning and Practice

QUESTIONS TO ANSWER AS YOU READ:

■ Why are planning and practice important?

■ What learning skills should you develop?

The only way to become a better student is to plan and practice to be a better student. Good habits, as well as bad, are developed through practice. You can read everything in this book, and even do well on a test on the material but if you don't *use* the ideas to make changes in your life, you could still do poorly in school.

Skills are based on knowledge, but they are developed through planning and practice. If you had a theoretical knowledge of how to play the piano, for example, but did not practice, you could not reasonably expect to improve your skill. The same is true for the learning skills you will read about here. The book provides the information, but you develop the skills through planning and practice. Here's an example of planning and practice.

Jordan started a self-change project directed at his studying. He began by keeping a record of how much time he studied each chapter in the text. He also kept track of how much of this time he was actually studying, as opposed to dealing with distractions. "I found I wasn't studying 'smart,'" he reported. "My habit of studying in the living room made me susceptible to many distractions, including the TV, the telephone, and my girlfriend. These not only interrupted my train of thought, but meant that some of the time I wasn't thinking about the text at all.

"So, I began studying in my room alone. But I ran into a new distraction. All my life, when I'm stressed, I cut my nails and spend a lot of time doing that to calm myself. Now this was distracting me from studying. So, I made a conscious effort to keep my nails from distracting me and told myself I would work on them after I finished studying. At the end of four weeks, I was making A's on the weekly psychology quizzes."

Jordan now turned to the broader time management issue of how he was spending his entire working day.

"For three days I kept track of everything I did, blocked off in thirty-minute periods. I noticed a lot of things. First, I tend to study too late at night. I often don't begin until 9:00 P.M., and I am usually exhausted. I have plenty of free time during the day, but I procrastinate. I usually get my school work done at the last minute, and there are plenty of other, extracurricular things I would like to get done, but never do.

"I planned to schedule study periods, with starting and stopping times, during the day instead of at night. Probably, I'll study from 4:30 to 6:30. I scheduled my chores too. I wrote all of this down and made it a contract with myself."

After a few days Jordan noted that on Friday afternoon he was in the mood for socializing and just couldn't make himself study at 4:30. So he made changes in his schedule to take that into account. He did note, too, that scheduling his chores made it much more likely he would do them, which made him and his girlfriend feel better.

Instead of just hoping he would change, Jordan had a plan for change, and he practiced the habits he wanted to develop. He

- Observed his own study behavior.

- Set goals for change.

- Moved forward in small steps.

- Dealt with the mistakes that he made.

- Changed the environment to support the study behavior he wanted.

Planning with Think Pieces and Skill Builders

Each chapter in this book has sections, called Think Piece or Skill Builder, which contain exercises to get you started on an academic self-improvement project for that topic. The purpose of the Think Pieces and

Skill Builders is to structure your planning and practice so you get off on the right foot, and continue well. You can start increasing your skill at any level, from beginner to advanced.

Most students carry out several academic self-improvement projects while working through this book. A student might carry out a time management project that applies to all his courses and at the same time be doing a project to improve his test taking in one course that has many tests. Later in the semester, the same student will be working to improve his vocabulary and doing a project to improve his classroom note taking.

You should do each project long enough to make the new skill a habit. That means you need to practice the new skill for several weeks. How long you do the project is affected by the level of skill you begin with. If you are already pretty good at some topic, all you'll need is some polishing, but if you are pretty much a beginner, you will need more time practicing.

What kinds of changes should you make?

Research with the students at the University of Michigan showed that the more skills you develop, the better your improvement in school will be.[15]

There are two levels of skill you might want to work on. First, there are the ones you are already good at, but would enjoy improving, much as a pretty good gardener might take a course in advanced gardening. Second, there are the ones you are *not* good at, and perhaps they are painful for you, but these are also skills that you need to develop. Choose some skills to develop because it will be fun, but choose some because they will strengthen you at weak points. Use Skill Builder 1.1 to decide what needs attention.

Do You Want to Do This?

QUESTION TO ANSWER AS YOU READ:

- How do your life goals relate to the skills taught in this book?

Is there a risk that doing the exercises in this book will shake you out of your comfortable niche in life, make you work harder than you want to work? *No.* If you work any harder, it will be because you think it is worthwhile for you. Remember our motto, "Work smarter, not harder."

We all want to be comfortable. What are your other goals in life? Martin Ford[16] suggests four categories of goals that most of us strive for in life:

1. Experiencing positive emotions such as happiness or relaxation.
2. Maintaining positive self-evaluations.
3. Feeling connected to others; caring for and feeling accepted by others.
4. Being physically active and energetic.

Your skills inventory

Which learning strategies and skills should you work on while you read this book? You are probably already good at some, but for others you may need practice. For each skill listed here, rate yourself on the continuum below the skill by placing a ✓ somewhere on the line. If you really don't know your skill level, place a *?* at the edge.

Be honest with yourself. No one will see this except you.

A. Time management skills (Chapters 2, 3, and 4)

1. Not wasting time; spending time on important things

LOW SKILL LEVEL	INTERMEDIATE	HIGH SKILL LEVEL

2. Avoiding procrastination

LOW SKILL LEVEL	INTERMEDIATE	HIGH SKILL LEVEL

3. Coping with stress

LOW SKILL LEVEL	INTERMEDIATE	HIGH SKILL LEVEL

B. Basic skills and attitudes (Chapters 5, 6, and 7)

1. Overcoming negative attitudes about college work

LOW SKILL LEVEL	INTERMEDIATE	HIGH SKILL LEVEL

2. Using study groups

LOW SKILL LEVEL	INTERMEDIATE	HIGH SKILL LEVEL

3. Going to class, paying attention, and participating

LOW SKILL LEVEL	INTERMEDIATE	HIGH SKILL LEVEL

4. Talking to instructors

LOW SKILL LEVEL	INTERMEDIATE	HIGH SKILL LEVEL

5. Knowing and using a good note-taking system

LOW SKILL LEVEL	INTERMEDIATE	HIGH SKILL LEVEL

6. Thinking critically

LOW SKILL LEVEL	INTERMEDIATE	HIGH SKILL LEVEL

Your skills inventory

C. Reading Skills (Chapters 8, 9, and 10)

1. Reading college textbooks to extract the main ideas

| LOW SKILL LEVEL | INTERMEDIATE | HIGH SKILL LEVEL |

2. Knowing how to increase your reading skills

| LOW SKILL LEVEL | INTERMEDIATE | HIGH SKILL LEVEL |

3. Knowing how to use different reading strategies—skimming, looking for main ideas; and so on

| LOW SKILL LEVEL | INTERMEDIATE | HIGH SKILL LEVEL |

4. Using college libraries and computers

| LOW SKILL LEVEL | INTERMEDIATE | HIGH SKILL LEVEL |

D. Studying Skills (Chapters 11, 12, 13 and 14)

1. Dealing with distractions and concentrating while studying

| LOW SKILL LEVEL | INTERMEDIATE | HIGH SKILL LEVEL |

2. Knowing and using the most effective study techniques, such as self-explanation and elaboration

| LOW SKILL LEVEL | INTERMEDIATE | HIGH SKILL LEVEL |

3. Using systems to organize your studying, such as summarizing or the SQ3R system

| LOW SKILL LEVEL | INTERMEDIATE | HIGH SKILL LEVEL |

4. Knowing how and when to mark your texts

| LOW SKILL LEVEL | INTERMEDIATE | HIGH SKILL LEVEL |

E. Test-taking skills (Chapters 15, 16, and 17)

1. Being well prepared for tests

| LOW SKILL LEVEL | INTERMEDIATE | HIGH SKILL LEVEL |

2. Avoiding cramming

| LOW SKILL LEVEL | INTERMEDIATE | HIGH SKILL LEVEL |

S K I L L   B U I L D E R   1.1

Your skills inventory

3. Staying calm during tests

| LOW SKILL LEVEL | INTERMEDIATE | HIGH SKILL LEVEL |

4. Dealing with objective tests or essay tests efficiently

| LOW SKILL LEVEL | INTERMEDIATE | HIGH SKILL LEVEL |

F. Verbal skills (Chapters 18, 19, 20, and 21)

1. Writing

| LOW SKILL LEVEL | INTERMEDIATE | HIGH SKILL LEVEL |

2. Speaking before groups

| LOW SKILL LEVEL | INTERMEDIATE | HIGH SKILL LEVEL |

3. Increasing your vocabulary

| LOW SKILL LEVEL | INTERMEDIATE | HIGH SKILL LEVEL |

4. Improving your spelling

| LOW SKILL LEVEL | INTERMEDIATE | HIGH SKILL LEVEL |

How do these four life goals relate to getting better at the learning skills taught in this book? Ask yourself, "If I work to get better at one of the learning skills taught in this book, how will that relate to the major life goals I have?"

Michelle is considering working on her time management. She asks herself, "How will becoming more skilled at time management affect those four life goals?" She writes out her thoughts:

"If I work on my time management skills, . . . My grades may improve.

That would give me more options about my career, because some careers require pretty high GPAs to get in.

I won't feel so frantic when deadlines come around.

As a result, my health at those times might get better.

I will feel more in control of my life. (I'll have to be careful not to become too controlled.)

THINK PIECE 1.2   Life goals and learning strategies

If increasing your school skills leads to achieving some of your important life goals, would the effort be worthwhile?

Pick several different skill areas covered in this book, and write down ways in which developing each skill might help you with your life goals, using Ford's list of life goals. If you do *not* think these skills will benefit you, fine. But if they will, it would be a shame to miss out on them because at first you didn't think of their advantages, so spend a few minutes on this exercise. Really think about your life to try to see connections.

Here is a list of the skills covered in this book:

- Time management skills
- Basic skills and attitudes
- Reading skills
- Study skills
- Test-taking skills
- Verbal skills
- Life-long learning skills

Michelle, above, provides an example of how time management relates to her life goals. Fill in the blank at the beginning of each item with the name of the skill you chose.

1. Skill: _____

How is it related to my life goals? _____

_____

_____

_____

_____

_____

_____

_____

_____

2. Skill: _____

How is it related to my life goals? _____

_____

_____

THINK PIECE 1.2   Life goals and learning strategies

_____

_____

_____

_____

_____

_____

3. Skill: _____

How is it related to my life goals? _____

_____

_____

_____

_____

_____

_____

4. Skill: _____

How is it related to my life goals? _____

_____

_____

_____

_____

_____

_____

_____

I'll probably get more exercise done, which will help me feel less stressed.

I might have a better social life, because I will plan social events more."

She sees that at least two, perhaps three, of her life goals can be furthered by working on time management. That makes the effort seem worthwhile to her, so she embarks on a time management project.

Try these ideas; then evaluate them. Maybe you'll like them, maybe you won't. You can always go back to your old ways if you don't like what you are learning here. A woman who was successfully learning these skills after a lifetime of mediocre school performance commented on the fact that some of the approach here was unexpected. "I always wanted to be a good student, but never was. Now I am. I guess if you want something you never had, you have to do something you've never done."

Adela M. was a thirty-something woman who had come to the United States from Mexico. She was tall, attractive, dark-haired, and full of energy. She radiated excitement. Her eyes sparkled, and she was always smiling. She was still having problems with English pronunciation, and when she talked excitedly, the words got jumbled. She really loved being in college, was doing *very* well, and was making plans for a professional career. "You know what I love about this learning skill stuff?" she said. "It helps me get an education. I *love* getting educated. For me, being educated saves me from a life of poverty, a life of boredom, and a life of dependence."

What might learning skills do for you?

Part II

Time Management:

Time Management: How to Control Your Time and Life

Time management, for some people, evokes a negative attitude. For them it implies an obsessive concern with time, keeping a stopwatch on themselves, not allowing themselves to have fun, always working, nose to the grindstone. That's not the way it is at all. Actually, good time management makes you feel better. You might schedule two hours for studying and then for the rest of the day enjoy no schedule at all—and without having anything hanging over your head. As you become better at managing your time, you might have more fun, not less. Self-discipline gives you freedom. You feel as if you are using your life well.

We are *not* talking about learning to work harder. Remember, our motto is "Work smarter, not harder." The whole idea of good time management is to control your time well enough to do the things you want do, to do things that fit with your important life goals.

The advantages of time management are powerful:

- Better grades
- More self-confidence
- Less stress

Here's the evidence to support that statement.

People who develop good time management make better grades. A research study at the University of Texas, Austin, showed that students with poor time management skills made 56 percent of the D's and F's in one class, while those with good time management skills made 69 percent of the A's and B's.[1] In the same class, students who improved their time management skills showed improvements in their grade point average (GPAs), *often by as much as one full grade,* for example, moving from a 2.2 to a 3.2. Being good at time management is more important than your SAT score in its effect on your grades in college.[2]

Students who use good time management also feel more self-confident.[3] Tytus, an excellent student, wrote, "Learning to be a self-regulated learner can reduce stress-related problems and create a happier and more fulfilling life." Research supports this idea.

Students who do *not* manage their time show *more* signs of stress— getting sick, for example—toward the end of each semester.[4] The ones who manage their time feel *less stress* day to day and are sick less often. Procrastination is stressful. It actually makes you sick and/or depressed or both.

Chapter 2

Your Goals for Your Life

PREVIEW WITH QUESTIONS TO ANSWER

Managing Time to Achieve Your Life Goals

- What are the advantages and disadvantages of more carefully managing your time?

How You Spend Your Time Now

- Does keeping a record of your use of time help you gain control of your life?
- What is reactivity?

What Your Records Tell You

- What opportunities for change do you find in your records?

Goal Setting: How You Would Like to Spend Your Time

- What are the characteristics of effective goals?
- What kinds of goals should you set for your time management?

Managing Time to Achieve Your Life Goals

In a report for one of his classes, Jason wrote, "When looking over my records of how I spend my time, it hit me that I don't spend enough time studying. My priorities seem kind of messed up. I am more worried if I miss a good day of biking or softball than finishing up some homework due for the following day. I am at a point in my life where I need to make a decision. Either I work now for a couple of years and enjoy the rest of my life with a good job, or I have all the fun I can handle now, and struggle later with a job I detest. So I feel like I need to buckle down and take care of business by becoming more time efficient."

**QUESTIONS TO ANSWER
AS YOU READ:**

- What are the advantages and disadvantages of more carefully managing your time?

Jason is right. The single most important thing you can learn in college is good time management. That's because *time management is life management.* Your life, after all, consists in the passing of time. If you gain control of your time, you gain control of your life.[1] You can spend your life in ways that are important to you, doing things that you value, seeking goals that you desire.

People are often ambivalent about their schoolwork. They might want the advantages of being a good student, but also like the advantages of not working too hard. Dieters face a similar problem. Their long-term goal is to lose weight, but that conflicts with their short-term goal of minimizing hunger or feeling full. Whenever this kind of conflict occurs, it is very easy to put off the long-term goal in favor of the short-term one. You may want to lose weight, but even more strongly you want to eat.

The goal that is closer in time almost always has a stronger effect on us. For example, talking with your friends right now will often win out over studying for a test, which fits the long-term goal of getting a good grade. Short-term goals are usually stronger unless we do something to increase the power of the more distant goal.[2]

To deal with this problem, make a list of the advantages and disadvantages of controlling your time.

For example, under advantages you might list:

- Make better grades

- Feel I'm using my time well

- Get a better job in the future

- Feel less stress

Under disadvantages you might list:

- Less time to be with my friends

- Less time to have fun

- Danger of becoming a loner, unpopular

People who make such lists actually have a better chance of successfully bringing their use of time under control.[3] Making the list helps you keep all your goals in mind—both the long-term and short-term goals. This enables you to find a balance between them. "Well, I don't have to be with my friends much less, and I do want to get more schoolwork done."

How Do You Spend Your Time Now?

**QUESTIONS TO ANSWER
AS YOU READ:**

- Does keeping a record of your use of time help you gain control of your life?

- What is reactivity?

How well do you use your time now? Some people have a pretty good idea, while others do not.

THINK PIECE 2.1   Advantages and disadvantages of time management

If you are not sure whether or not you want to do the work of time management, making a list like this will help you decide. List here the long- and short-term advantages and disadvantages of improving your time management.

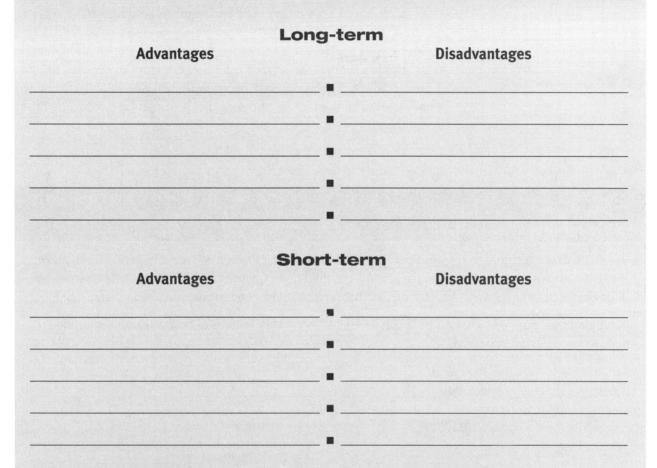

Long-term

Advantages		Disadvantages
_____	■	_____
_____	■	_____
_____	■	_____
_____	■	_____
_____	■	_____

Short-term

Advantages		Disadvantages
_____	■	_____
_____	■	_____
_____	■	_____
_____	■	_____
_____	■	_____

Sometimes it is possible to minimize the disadvantages while keeping the advantages. For example, you might be able to see your friends as much as you do now, but also be able to do some time management, by cutting down on wasted time. You don't miss the wasted time, but you do more schoolwork and get to be with your friends just as much as before. Spending some time thinking about this helps. Look for ways to keep your advantages while eliminating the disadvantages. Your ideas:

_____

_____

_____

_____

_____

Robin, a graduate student in English, knows how she spends many of her hours: in class or studying. But even she feels that there are hours she does not spend particularly well. "I think there are several hours in each day that I don't use well. I end up chatting with people, having a coffee, or messing around. I'd like to spend my time in a more organized way, because there is a lot I want to accomplish."

Many of us pass hours each day *not* doing things that are of high value to us. Robin's highest values, for example, are working on her master's degree, reading, exercising, and being with her new husband, but she spends a lot to time on none of those. "I sort of mess around some of the time," she says.

S K I L L   B U I L D E R   2.1

Daily time record

Use this daily time record to keep track of every half hour of your time for a three-day period. First, make copies of this blank record to use on the second and third days. Choose days which are fairly typical. The three days before finals week, for example, are not typical, so it will not be helpful to use them.

Don't start trying to make changes until you have your three days' records of how you spend your time now. You need that information.

Date: _____ Name: _____

Time	Activity	Time	Activity
6:00 – 6:30 A.M. _____		6:00 – 6:30 P.M. _____	
6:30 – 7:00 _____		6:30 – 7:00 _____	
7:00 – 7:30 _____		7:00 – 7:30 _____	
7:30 – 8:00 _____		7:30 – 8:00 _____	
8:00 – 8:30 _____		8:00 – 8:30 _____	
8:30 – 9:00 _____		8:30 – 9:00 _____	
9:00 – 9:30 _____		9:00 – 9:30 _____	
9:30 – 10:00 _____		9:30 – 10:00 _____	
10:00 – 10:30 _____		10:00 – 10:30 _____	

How do you spend your time? Do you spend most of it doing things that are truly important to you, in a way that fits your personal values? You may think you know the answer, but using Skill Builder 2.1 will give you a much clearer picture.

If you are as well organized as Robin, you probably don't need this step. She already knew how she spent her time. But for many students this is a very helpful, even necessary, step to getting organized.

Keep careful records

Your beliefs about how you spend your time now and the actual truth may *not* be the same. Some students are really surprised to see how they are actually spending their time. You need a reliable picture of yourself.

SKILL BUILDER 2.1

Daily time record

10:30 – 11:00 _____	10:30 – 11:00 _____
11:00 – 11:30 _____	11:00 – 11:30 _____
11:30 – 12:00 NOON _____	11:30 – 12:00 MIDNIGHT _____
12:00 – 12:30 P.M. _____	12:00 – 12:30 A.M. _____
12:30 – 1:00 _____	12:30 – 1:00 _____
1:00 – 1:30 _____	1:00 – 1:30 _____
1:30 – 2:00 _____	1:30 – 2:00 _____
2:00 – 2:30 _____	2:00 – 2:30 _____
2:30 – 3:00 _____	2:30 – 3:00 _____
3:00 – 3:30 _____	3:00 – 3:30 _____
3:30 – 4:00 _____	3:30 – 4:00 _____
4:00 – 4:30 _____	4:00 – 4:30 _____
4:30 – 5:00 _____	4:30 – 5:00 _____
5:00 – 5:30 _____	5:00 – 5:30 _____
5:30 – 6:00 _____	5:30 – 6:00 _____

Make an entry every hour

Don't wait until the end of the day to fill out your form. It is too easy to forget. Don't estimate your time spent doing things. It is tempting to estimate because then you do not have to think about the project. But the whole point is to get you to think about how you spend your time, and you want to be sure you know how you truly do. People who make estimates are often far off the truth.[4]

Tell yourself the truth

If you spend six hours a day watching TV, you need to admit this to yourself. Then you can ask, is that how I want to spend my life? If so, great. If not, you need to admit to yourself what you are doing so you can work on changing.

Be sure you keep the records

If you don't have your record form with you, you can still jot down the time and how you are spending it. Enter the information in the record form later.

> George, in the college library, realizes he has left his daily time record in his notebook in his room. So he writes down in the margin of the notebook he has with him, "11:00 to noon, in the library." When he gets back to his daily time record, he makes the entry.

Reactivity

If you keep a record of how you spend your time, you may spend your time differently than you would if you were not keeping a record. You become more conscientious because you are paying attention. This is fairly common and is known in psychology as reactivity.[5] Your use of time "reacts" to your observing of yourself.

If you do not value some act, keeping a record of it will *not* increase how often you do it. But if you do value it, recording the act may lead you to do it more.[6] The recording provides you with feedback about how your actions match your values. By itself, this reactivity effect is not enough to lead to important changes, but it can help.

QUESTION TO ANSWER AS YOU READ:

■ What opportunities for change do you find in your records?

What Your Records Tell You

There are important things to be learned from keeping records of how you spend your time.

Robin, the graduate student, discovered that by allowing other students to drop by her desk for a chat each day, she ended up spending more than two hours a day in conversation that really was not that important to her. "I love people," she noted, "and don't want to be antisocial, but I'm letting others control how I spend my time."

Paul, a sophomore, wrote, "I thought I was spending my daily schedule pretty well, but. . ." Here are Paul's records for a typical day (not counting sleeping).

8:00 – 8:30	Wake up; shower; brush teeth; etc.
8:30 – 9:00	Get ready for class; eat breakfast
9:00 – 9:30	Walk to geology
9:30 – 10:00	In class
10:00 – 10:30	In class till 10:20
10:30 – 11:00	Walk back to my dorm
11:00 – 11:30	Go over notes
11:30 – 12:00	Watch TV
12:00 – 12:30	Watch TV
12:30 – 1:00	Go out to lunch
1:00 – 1:30	Walk to psych class
1:30 – 2:00	In class
2:00 – 2:30	In class; out at 2:20
2:30 – 3:00	Watch TV at dorm
3:00 – 3:30	Watch TV
3:30 – 4:00	Watch TV
4:00 – 4:30	Sleep
4:30 – 5:00	Sleep
5:00 – 5:30	At dorm talking to guys
5:30 – 6:00	Study
6:00 – 6:30	Lift weights
6:30 – 7:00	Lift weights
7:00 – 7:30	Run
7:30 – 8:00	Play basketball
8:00 – 8:30	Shower
8:30 – 9:00	Eat dinner
9:00 – 9:30	Try to study
9:30 – 10:00	Study
10:00 – 10:30	Watch the news
10:30 – 11:00	Talk on the phone
11:00 – 11:30	Watch TV
11:30 – 12:00	Watch TV
12:00 – 12:30	Sleep

"I discovered that I wasted a lot of time," Paul said. "I found out that I *do* watch a lot of TV. I also discovered that right after school I just do nothing."

These are typical comments. After keeping records of their use of time, students often say things like "My time doesn't seem to be my own" or "I had no idea I was watching so much TV!" or "I'm learning I can't sit in bed to study. I always fall asleep" or "I'm shocked at how much time I waste."

Some people, of course, spend their time very well, but even they can benefit from keeping a record of how they spend it.

Ruth, a mother of three, ran a small business and took courses in college on the side. Even she found that keeping track of how she spent her time helped her plan her use of time better. "All my hours are full," she wrote in her report, "so the last thing I want to do is add more hours of work. But I did find that I could get some of the hours to do double duty. For example, two times a week I take my daughter to soccer practice. I've been just drifting around the edge of the field during that time, talking to the other parents, not spending the time particularly well. But I realized I could be studying during that time, so now I take my textbook along and read while I wait for my daughter."

Goal Setting: How You Would Like to Spend Your Time

QUESTIONS TO ANSWER AS YOU READ:

■ What are the characteristics of effective goals?

■ What kinds of goals should you set for your time management?

Goal setting has been studied extensively, and there are helpful ideas about how to set goals effectively. Research shows that if you follow these procedures, you are more likely to reach your goals.[7]

Focus your goals on the process you go through to increase your study time, not on the final goal

Your final, important goal may to be have better grades, be more self-confident, or feel less stress. But the thing to do now is focus on how you spend your time.[8] By controlling your time, you will reach those goals.

THINK PIECE 2.2   **Opportunities for change**

When they keep records of how they spend their time, many people find some things they want to change. They would like to spend their time a bit differently. They set new goals.

Look at your record of how you spent your time in the days on which you kept a record. Do you see any opportunities for change here? Almost everyone does, if only a small change like the one Ruth made. Look over your records, think about them, and write down here changes you might like to make in how you use your time.

_____

_____

_____

_____

_____

_____

The goals you set for yourself should be

- Slightly challenging . . .
  but definitely attainable.

- Rather specific . . .
  but flexible.

This leads to some suggestions.

Set your first goal only a little bit above where you are now performing

Suppose your records show that typically you study three hours per week. If you want to increase your studying, your first goal might be to study three and a half hours.

Start with low goals, just above where you have been performing, and slowly increase your goals as you progress.

> Pam keeps records for several days and sees that on average she studies about five hours per week. "That's pretty good," she thinks; but she would like to do more. She sets her goal for next week: five and a half hours. She then keeps records to see if she makes this goal. She does, so now she raises the level to six hours per week. Again, she keeps records to see if she can do it, and again she succeeds. Now she raises her desired level to seven hours. But it is a distracting week, with a lot of socializing and a football game, and her records show she studied only five and a half hours that week. "I'm pushing too fast," she thinks, and for the next week she asks herself to study only five and a half hours.

Notice how Pam's goal was challenging but attainable, and how it was very specific. Notice also that she remained flexible and changed the level when that was indicated.

Sometimes a student says "I'm only studying a couple of hours a week, and you tell me in the beginning I should increase study time only an hour more? That's not enough. I'm going to increase it to twelve hours per week." Lots of luck. Almost certainly the student will run into frustration and disappointment and drop the whole project. Most people are just not capable of that kind of drastic change. As the old Chinese proverb goes, "A journey of a thousand miles begins with a single step."

Your long-term goal may be much higher than your present level, but the way to get there is one small step at a time.

Of course, you should challenge yourself. Don't just take one step and stop. If you set challenging but attainable goals, you will try harder. But

SKILL BUILDER 2.2

Goal Setting

Use this form to work out your time-use goals.

A. Set your final goal.

Hours a week you currently spend studying

_____ (from your record keeping):

Example: Penny keeps records for three days and finds that she studies an average of one hour each school day, or about five per week.

Your first goal. How many hours a week do you think you would like to spend studying?

_____

B. Gradually increase the time you spend each week.

Start near your current level, and take small steps upward. Take as many steps as you need to reach your final goal, but keep focused on the process of getting there, not the final goal.

1. For your first step, just fill out where you are now and the (small) increase you will make.

   Current level: _____ Next step upward: _____

2. Don't do this next step until you have done the first step for a week. You may intend, for example, to increase by a half hour each week, but you cannot accurately project very far into the future because you cannot be sure what will happen. So, even though your long-term goal may be several hours ahead, plan for only one step at a time. This approach will help you avoid feeling overwhelmed by the distance you propose to travel.

   New level:_____ Next step upward:_____

   Example: Penny works out the following schedule.

   > Current level: 5 ½ hours
   > Next step upward: 6 hours

   This works fine, so she increases.

   > Current level: 6 hours
   > Next step upward: 6 ½ hours

3. Repeat this process one unit at a time until you reach your final goal. Fill out only one step here each week.

   New level: _____ Next step upward: _____

   New level: _____ Next step upward: _____

   New level: _____ Next step upward: _____

   New level: _____ Next step upward: _____

   New level: _____ Next step upward: _____

   New level: _____ Next step upward: _____

   New level: _____ Next step upward: _____

   New level: _____ Next step upward: _____

   New level: _____ Next step upward: _____

   New level: _____ Next step upward: _____

4. Remember to stay flexible. You may have to revise several times. Pauses and setbacks will occur. Make adjustments in your goals when they do.

   Example: In the third week Penny only studies five hours, so she decides that her schedule is too steep. She revises it.

   > Week 1: 5 hours
   > Week 2: 5 hours 15 minutes
   > Week 3: 5 hours 30 minutes

   She continues to increase her study time by 15 minutes each week.

5. Keep on revising; never give up.

   Example: The new plan works for Penny until the ninth week, when she tries too big a step—she tries to increase by a full hour—so she cuts down the size of the required step. After a full semester, she levels off.

you should give yourself a good chance of succeeding. If you try but do not succeed, that means you challenged yourself too much and need to make adjustments.

If your level of studying is so low you are in danger of flunking out of school, then of course you should challenge yourself as much as you can right away. But the challenges must be attainable. If you try for a very high level but do *not* succeed, cut back to a level at which you *can* succeed. It is far better to take one successful small step than to fail trying to take a giant step.

Planning to Meet Your Goals

PREVIEW WITH QUESTIONS TO ANSWER

Strategies for Change
- What strategies can you use so that situations encourage the time-use behavior you want?

Supporting Your Time Management
- How do record keeping and practice support your time management?
- What should be your attitude about making mistakes?
- How can you reward sticking to your schedule?
- How can you use self-talk to guide your time-management behavior?

Problem Solving to Improve Plans
- How do you use problem solving to revise your plans?

Planning to meet your goals is far better than just hoping success will happen. Hoping for change can be like hoping you will lose weight. Losing weight might happen by chance, but it is much more likely to happen if you plan for it. People who diet successfully make all sorts of plans: to control their eating, increase their exercise, resist or avoid temptation, and so on. Planning is as important in time management as it is in dieting.

Students who only read about time management are much less likely to accomplish it than those who make plans to fit the ideas into their daily lives.[1] The goal of this book is *not* just to teach you some ideas and hope you find use for them in your life. The goal is to enable you to reach your life goals. For that we need plans.

Good intentions are not enough. You need to use strategies to fit the ideas into your life.

QUESTION TO ANSWER
AS YOU READ:

■ What strategies can you use so
that situations encourage the
time-use behavior you want?

Strategies for Change

There are several steps you can take to encourage good time management.

Schedule regular study periods with clear starting and stopping times

It is a mistake to wait until you "feel like" studying, and then do it. You have scheduled classes, for example, so why shouldn't you have scheduled study times?

> Jack sees that each afternoon he is finished with classes by 3:30, so he schedules a study time for that period.

Don't schedule huge study sessions

One hour at a time is a good rule to follow. If you schedule huge sessions, (1) you're cramming, and that minimizes your chances of learning well, and (2) you are likely to get bored and not use the session well.

Have a written schedule

You probably write down your class schedule, just to keep from forgetting it. You should have a written study schedule too. For example:

11:30 – 12:30	History class
12:30 – 1:30	Lunch
1:30 – 2:30	Psych class
2:30 – 3:30	Study in library

Use Skill Builder 3.1 to plan your weekly schedule. The chart has a space for every hour of the day, but that does *not* mean that you will schedule your time for every hour of the day. There should be lots of open times to do whatever you want. And, you can schedule enjoyable activities as well as schoolwork:

Friday, 9:00 P.M.   Concert with Juan

Besides helping you manage your study time, written schedules help you to be punctual. You've probably already learned that even your friends can get upset if you are not on time. "Where were you? I've been waiting an hour!" Patricia, age twenty-eight, said, "When I was a teenager I was often late, but pretty soon I realized it was rude of me to keep others waiting. I was wasting their time." If you write into your schedule times that you've agreed to meet someone, it becomes easier to be on time:

Wednesday, 1:00 P.M.   Coffee with Haley

Make a list of things to do each day and week

Lists are a reminder. If you don't make the list, you are less likely to do the things on it. Here's a sample of Vaughn's list:

> To do today:
> Check library for material for term paper
> See Prof. Lindsay
> Study for math test

As he accomplishes each of these goals, Vaughn checks off the item on his list.

Use a weekly planner

Skill Builder 3.1 is a weekly planner. You can also buy these in many forms in a bookstore or office supply store. The typical weekly planner has schedule and planning sheets for every week of the year, allowing you to plan out days, weeks, and months. Buying a planner is one of the best investments in your education you can make.

If you've never used a weekly planner, try going over one with another student. You can show each other how you are using the planner to plan your work, class, and study time. You can get ideas from each other. "I never thought of that: you're scheduling in times to call your mom. Good idea!" How much you plan is, of course, entirely up to each of you, so you shouldn't comment on that. At first, just get used to the process.

Written schedules work only if you follow them. Once you make your written schedule, check it now and then to see what you should be doing.

> One student confessed he writes a written schedule for most weeks, but then never looks at it. He just drifts through the week and, of course, is just drifting through his life.

Plan by the week, and prioritize your work

> Ruth, the well-organized working mom, wrote, "Each Sunday night I sit down to plan the coming week. I write in my classes and my scheduled study times, and I make some notes on what I need to do in those times—and I'm organized for the week."

Make a copy of Skill Builder 3.1, the daily and weekly time planning sheet, to draw up your weekly plans. Use your to-do list for ideas on what to schedule and when.

Prioritize your work. If you have a history test on Friday, a scheduled study hour earlier in the week could be devoted to history, but if you have

SKILL BUILDER 3.1

Daily and weekly time-planning sheet

Make copies of these blank sheets to make changes in your scheduled steps each week. Make any changes in the form that you want.

Write all your weekly scheduled events on the sheets. Include class times, work times, and scheduled study times.

Follow the goal-steps you worked out in Skill Builder 2.2.

If you are gradually changing how you spend your time, your scheduled study times this week will be different from those for next week.

Sunday		Monday		Tuesday		Wednesday	
Time	Activity	Time	Activity	Time	Activity	Time	Activity
6:00		6:00		6:00		6:00	
6:30		6:30		6:30		6:30	
7:00		7:00		7:00		7:00	
7:30		7:30		7:30		7:30	
8:00		8:00		8:00		8:00	
8:30		8:30		8:30		8:30	
9:00		9:00		9:00		9:00	
9:30		9:30		9:30		9:30	
10:00		10:00		10:00		10:00	
10:30		10:30		10:30		10:30	
11:00		11:00		11:00		11:00	
11:30		11:30		11:30		11:30	
12:00		12:00		12:00		12:00	
12:30		12:30		12:30		12:30	
1:00		1:00		1:00		1:00	
1:30		1:30		1:30		1:30	
2:00		2:00		2:00		2:00	
2:30		2:30		2:30		2:30	
3:00		3:00		3:00		3:00	
3:30		3:30		3:30		3:30	
4:00		4:00		4:00		4:00	
4:30		4:30		4:30		4:30	
5:00		5:00		5:00		5:00	
5:30		5:30		5:30		5:30	
6:00		6:00		6:00		6:00	
6:30		6:30		6:30		6:30	
7:00		7:00		7:00		7:00	
7:30		7:30		7:30		7:30	
8:00		8:00		8:00		8:00	
8:30		8:30		8:30		8:30	
9:00		9:00		9:00		9:00	
9:30		9:30		9:30		9:30	
10:00		10:00		10:00		10:00	
10:30		10:30		10:30		10:30	
11:00		11:00		11:00		11:00	
11:30		11:30		11:30		11:30	

SKILL BUILDER 3.1

Daily and weekly time-planning sheet

Thursday		Friday		Saturday	
Time	**Activity**	**Time**	**Activity**	**Time**	**Activity**
6:00	_____	6:00	_____	6:00	_____
6:30	_____	6:30	_____	6:30	_____
7:00	_____	7:00	_____	7:00	_____
7:30	_____	7:30	_____	7:30	_____
8:00	_____	8:00	_____	8:00	_____
8:30	_____	8:30	_____	8:30	_____
9:00	_____	9:00	_____	9:00	_____
9:30	_____	9:30	_____	9:30	_____
10:00	_____	10:00	_____	10:00	_____
10:30	_____	10:30	_____	10:30	_____
11:00	_____	11:00	_____	11:00	_____
11:30	_____	11:30	_____	11:30	_____
12:00	_____	12:00	_____	12:00	_____
12:30	_____	12:30	_____	12:30	_____
1:00	_____	1:00	_____	1:00	_____
1:30	_____	1:30	_____	1:30	_____
2:00	_____	2:00	_____	2:00	_____
2:30	_____	2:30	_____	2:30	_____
3:00	_____	3:00	_____	3:00	_____
3:30	_____	3:30	_____	3:30	_____
4:00	_____	4:00	_____	4:00	_____
4:30	_____	4:30	_____	4:30	_____
5:00	_____	5:00	_____	5:00	_____
5:30	_____	5:30	_____	5:30	_____
6:00	_____	6:00	_____	6:00	_____
6:30	_____	6:30	_____	6:30	_____
7:00	_____	7:00	_____	7:00	_____
7:30	_____	7:30	_____	7:30	_____
8:00	_____	8:00	_____	8:00	_____
8:30	_____	8:30	_____	8:30	_____
9:00	_____	9:00	_____	9:00	_____
9:30	_____	9:30	_____	9:30	_____
10:00	_____	10:00	_____	10:00	_____
10:30	_____	10:30	_____	10:30	_____
11:00	_____	11:00	_____	11:00	_____
11:30	_____	11:30	_____	11:30	_____

THINK PIECE 3.1   Your to-do list

Try planning by the week, but with flexibility. Here is a blank to-do list for a week to practice with. Copy this to use for several weeks. Once a week fill in all the to-do lines for the week; then each day make additions or deletions. When you do something on the list, joyously scratch it off.

Prioritize your work by assigning *1* to the most important items.

To do this week:

_____

_____

_____

_____

_____

_____

_____

_____

Example: Here's Vaughn's to-do list for the full week.

1. Check library for material for term paper
   Begin reading and making notes for term paper
   See Prof. Lindsay
1. Study for math test
   Study for history test next week

He assigns the highest priority to getting started on the term paper and studying for the math test.

Each day, you should have a to-do list as well, so that by the end of the week you have done all the things on your weekly list. On the first day of the week, Vaughn picks three of the items on this weekly list to work on. As you make up your daily list, check your high-priority items from the weekly list to be sure you are doing them.

To do today:

_____

_____

_____

_____

_____

_____

an English paper due Friday, you would want to spend that time working on the paper. What you schedule in your planner each week will depend on what is on the top of your to-do list that week.

Plan over the whole term or semester

Use a long-term planner to get an overview of all the tasks you will have to accomplish in the entire semester. Any weekly planner you buy will have spaces to write down plans for the entire term, giving you a semester at a glance. List important due dates, test dates, and any other important information. You can also list birthdays, holidays, important social occasions, bills coming due, and so on. This allows you to look ahead to make plans each week. It is much easier to prioritize your work each week, for example, if you have the big picture in mind.

> Brooke, whom you met in Chapter 1, showed the benefits of long-term planning when she prepared for her take-home exam in developmental psychology. She knew she had a test coming in two weeks and budgeted her time to prepare for it.
>
> Brooke made notes to herself on what to do to prepare a to-do list:
>
> > Ask Prof. what kinds of questions will be on the exam.
> > Begin reading the five chapters.
> > Talk to fellow student about what questions to expect.
>
> She began reading the material and set a goal to finish all the preliminary reading by Wednesday of the week before the exam. As she progressed, she coped with some boredom.
>
> By planning ahead like this, Brooke did very well on the exam.

When planning, simply ask yourself, What do I need to do? How much time do I have to do it? What steps should I take to be ready? Then make a to-do list.

Skill builder 3.2 is a long-term planner for your whole academic year.

Supporting Your Time Management

Time management doesn't just happen; you have to do things to help it. Here are some steps to take.

Keep records of how well you stick to your schedule

Are you actually succeeding in gaining control over your time? To answer this, you need to keep records. One of the easiest ways to keep track of

QUESTIONS TO ANSWER AS YOU READ:

- How do record keeping and practice support your time management?

- What should be your attitude about making mistakes?

- How can you reward sticking to your schedule?

- How can you use self-talk to guide your time management behavior?

SKILL BUILDER 3.2

Long-term planner from ___/___ to ___/___

Week	Monday	Tuesday	Wednesday	Thursday	Friday	Saturday	Sunday
__/__-__/__							
__/__-__/__							
__/__-__/__							
__/__-__/__							
__/__-__/__							
__/__-__/__							
__/__-__/__							
__/__-__/__							
__/__-__/__							
__/__-__/__							
__/__-__/__							
__/__-__/__							
__/__-__/__							
__/__-__/__							
__/__-__/__							
__/__-__/__							
__/__-__/__							
__/__-__/__							
__/__-__/__							
__/__-__/__							
__/__-__/__							
__/__-__/__							
__/__-__/__							
__/__-__/__							
__/__-__/__							
__/__-__/__							
__/__-__/__							

Example Part of Juan's planner looks like this:

	Monday	Tuesday	Wednesday	Thursday	Friday	Saturday	Sunday
3/18 – 3/24	Chem. lab report		English paper due		Psych quiz	Concert	
3/25 – 3/31	No chem. lab		Student council mtg.		Psych quiz	Go home	

how well you stick to your schedule is to (1) have a written schedule and then (2) simply check off the hours as you use them.

> James makes a ✔ when he does what he intended for each of his scheduled hours, so he can take a quick look at his schedule to see how he's doing:

	Monday	Tuesday	Wednesday	Thursday	Friday
10:00–11:00 A.M.	Study ✔	Class ✔	Study	Class ✔	Study ✔

> He sees he didn't study Wednesday as he intended. He needs to figure out why. If he found that each Wednesday he didn't study as he wanted, he would want to deal with whatever problem was coming up.

You should be able to stick to about 80 percent of your scheduled hours. If you're not doing that, start at a lower level and/or lower the steps until you *can* stick to your schedule 80 percent of the time. Then gradually build up from there.

Keeping these records is important. It is pointless to schedule events each week and then not know whether you are meeting your goals. It is very easy to delude yourself about this, so be sure to keep a record as a reality check.

Avoid studying when you are tired or sleepy

It's common to see students' records like these:

9:00 – 9:30 P.M.	Trying to study (but I'm sleepy)
9:30 – 10:00	Studying, but fell asleep; not sure when
10:00 – 10:30	Watching the news (I'm gradually going to sleep)

You will study better when your brain is fresher and you have more energy. Your school and work schedule may make it impossible to study much during the daytime, but find hours when you are fresh, not tired or sleepy, to do schoolwork. Even when they have the time, some students procrastinate, putting off the dreaded studying until the end of the day. By then they are too tired to do a good job. If you are not used to studying during the daytime, try gradually increasing how much you do it.

Be prepared to practice, and expect to make mistakes

Time management is a skill, and learning any skill requires practice. During practice you sometimes make mistakes. You must be prepared to practice, and you should expect to make mistakes.[2] You might schedule yourself to study math from 3:00 to 3:30 on Monday, but then when the time comes, you watch TV or talk to your friend on the phone. This kind of slip is *very* common.

Don't get discouraged and quit the whole plan. Making mistakes simply means you need more practice. You understand this for learning to play the piano. If you hit a wrong note, it means you need more practice. You are going to hit some sour notes when practicing time management, too.

Even if you make many slips, that does not mean you can't do this. It means that your goal level is too high. You are trying to schedule more of your time than fits your current level of skill. The trick is to schedule just enough of your time that you can stick to your schedule most of the time, then to gradually move up from there. If you're making a lot of slips, reschedule with an easier goal, setting the first level at a step you're sure you can do without mistake. Then gradually move up from there.

Don't schedule a dull life; make room for fun

Sometimes you meet a student who has scheduled nearly every hour in her life. Alicia, for example, filled up her schedule from the moment she got up in the morning until the time she went to sleep. She was even thinking about trying to cut down on her sleep. After a few months of this, she was near collapse. "I hate my schedule," she said.

Give yourself a break. Leave room for fun or for having nothing on the schedule at all. The point, after all, is to work smarter, not harder. Alicia wasn't really living up to her values by sacrificing all her happiness to work.

Use enjoyable things to reward sticking to your schedule

You can use any activity that you often do, such as watching a favorite TV program, as a *reward* for taking some step in your time management schedule. *First, do the scheduled work, then take the reward.* Sarah, for example, loves the TV show *Seinfeld*. She arranges her schedule so that first she does some studying and then she rewards herself with *Seinfeld*. Any activity you love can be used as a reward—going for a hike, taking a bubble bath, reading, playing a computer game, socializing, surfing the Web, anything.

Schedule the work *before* doing the thing you love to do, then don't let yourself do the favorite thing *until* you've done the work. This is called *reinforcing* the studying with the TV watching. It works well, because any act you reinforce is more likely to be repeated. By rewarding the scheduled work, you reinforce it as a habit.

If you didn't do the scheduled work, but took the reward anyway, then studying would not be reinforced. Make sticking to the schedule easy to do, so you can both do the work and get the reward. Start with a low goal, do the work, then get the reward. "Tonight all I have to do is fifteen minutes extra studying; then I get to watch *Seinfeld*." Gradually increase the level of the goal you have to reach before taking the reward.

Reward yourself with mental pats on the back

"Hey, that was great. I scheduled an hour to work on my term paper, and I did it!" Successful students tend to say things like this to themselves to reinforce their desired activities.[3] It's smart to reward yourself with these positive statements, because you won't get rewarded by anyone else for small positive steps, yet you need to take them. You might be rewarded in the long run with a better grade, but that is many weeks away. In the meantime, if you do a good job sticking to your schedule, tell yourself so: "Good job."

Some people balk at the idea of rewarding themselves with self-talk. It seems false or vain. But it's not. To admit when you did a good job, when you improved, is to be honest with yourself. As soon as you accomplish what you scheduled yourself to do, remind yourself, "I did it. I did a good job."

Guide your behavior with self-directions

Whenever you are tempted to spend your time in some way you don't want, try reminding yourself of your goals. Remind yourself of the good things that will happen if you do what you intended and wanted to do. You might be stressed, distracted, or frustrated, and for a time forget your long-term goals, but with self-directions you can remind yourself of the path you want to take.

> Sherri, who was on probation because she was going to too many parties and not studying enough, had worked out a plan to study one hour each night of the school week, then socialize on the weekends.
>
> After a few days, however, her old party friends tempted her. "Sherri, there's a party in C dorm tonight. Let's go." Sherri was very tempted to go, but to do so would violate her plan to work an hour. "I can't go," she reminded herself, "until I've done my hour's work. If I don't buckle down and do some schoolwork, I'm going to flunk out. First, do the work; then go to the party."

People who successfully make difficult changes often use self-talk to guide themselves through tempting situations,[4] as Sherri did. In fact, self-talk is one of the best techniques for self-control. The dieter says to himself, "Don't start eating chips. If you do, you'll eat a ton of them. Move away from the chips." Students can guide themselves toward their important goals in the same way. "Don't turn on the TV. If you do, you'll watch too long. Move away from the TV."

If you have not been in the habit of doing this kind of self-controlling talk, try to practice it. Habits are developed through practice, and you can be sure you are practicing if you keep track of your practice. Keep track of each time you use self-directing statements.

THINK PIECE 3.2   Putting the ideas into operation

1. Reward studying. Make a list of things you like to do that you could use to reinforce studying. The activities have to be under your control, so you can earn them by studying, and you have to be willing to earn them only if you do the scheduled work.

   Activities:

   _____ ▪ _____ ▪ _____

   _____ ▪ _____ ▪ _____

   Now work out the rule you will follow. "If I do the scheduled studying, then I will gain the reward of [the activity] _____ "

   Example John's rule is "If I study Monday from 4:00 P.M. to 5:00, then I get to watch Monday night football. Don't start the football until I have done the hour's studying."

2. Give yourself mental pats on the back. Think of several rewarding things you can say to yourself when you finish a job you have scheduled or when you stick to a scheduled time for work. When you have done the good work, remind yourself with one of these statements.

   _____

   _____

   _____

3. Guide yourself with self-directions. Think of directions you can give yourself to guide you through times when you are tempted *not* to stick to your schedule. Remind yourself of your goals. It is easier to overcome temptation if you remind yourself of those goals. Create the self-directions now to have them handy when temptation arises.

Problem Solving to Improve Plans

QUESTION TO ANSWER AS YOU READ:

▪ How do you use problem solving to revise your plans?

When people first start a time management plan, they often do not think of everything, and problems develop. For example, Jenny wants to have a regular study schedule, but her job has variable hours and she never knows from week to week when she will have to work. She needs to do a bit of problem solving.

Using problem solving is a crucial step in developing your time management. You are almost certainly going to run into problems when you try to bring aspects of your life more under your own control. There may be events that conflict with your schedule or people who interfere, or you might make mistakes. Regardless of your situation, the one thing you can be sure of is that there will be problems. These need not be stumbling blocks, however, if you use problem solving to overcome them.

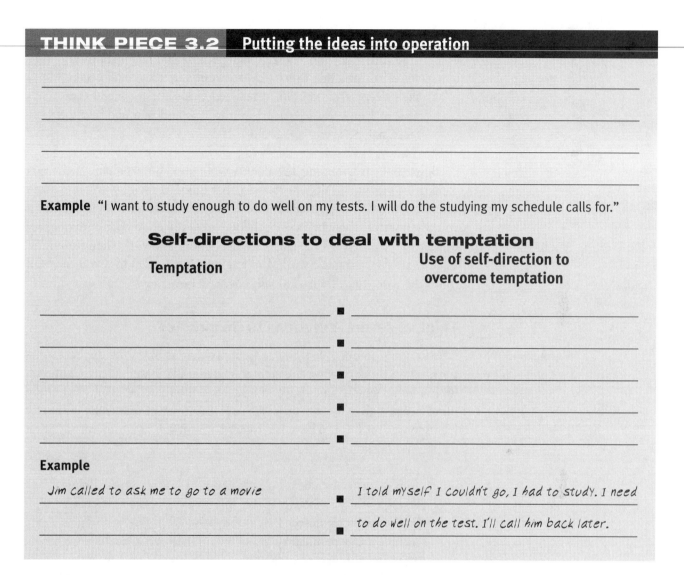

THINK PIECE 3.2   Putting the ideas into operation

Example "I want to study enough to do well on my tests. I will do the studying my schedule calls for."

Self-directions to deal with temptation

Temptation		Use of self-direction to overcome temptation

Example

| Jim called to ask me to go to a movie | ■ | I told myself I couldn't go, I had to study. I need |
| | ■ | to do well on the test. I'll call him back later. |

In problem solving there are two things to consider.[5]

1. What are the details of the problem?
2. How many solutions to the problem can you think of?

Examine the details of the problem

By dealing with the details, you can often solve the problem.

John can't study because of the noise in his dorm, so he moves his study place to the library.

Lani often doesn't do the study work she scheduled for herself because her close friend calls every evening and they talk too long. She discusses this with her friend, and they agree Lani will call as soon as the scheduled hour is finished.

Debbie at first schedules a study hour every afternoon at 1:30. But she soon realizes that because she has intramural volleyball practice every day at noon and then eats lunch, she's sleepy around 1:30. "I realized I would always feel that way, so I moved the study hour to 2:30 and planned just to relax, maybe even nap, at 1:30."

Sometimes rearranging the details will solve the problem. If there is something you like to do, or often do, that interferes with your time management, you can use it to reinforce time management. For example, if you often watch TV when your schedule says you should be studying, try using the TV to reward the studying. First, do some work; then watch TV as a reward for doing the work. Start at such a low level that you can't fail to do the work first, then gradually increase how much you do.

Think of several solutions to the problem

The first solution people think of for a problem is often *not* the best solution. If you think of several different solutions, you are likely to come up with a better one. Lani, above, might have thought, "Well, I can't study more because that messes up my friend's evening phone calls." A better solution was for Lani to have her cake and eat it too, by studying and then calling her friend.

Jean, a varsity basketball player, wrote, "I knew I wasn't doing enough of my schoolwork, and that I can't flunk courses even if it is basketball season. I set a study schedule for myself, which included the mandatory study hall varsity athletes have to attend, and I kept records of how much I did what I intended to do. Not much. I tried listing the details: Why don't I do the intended study work? I feel I am just too damned busy. I have practice every day, study halls and classes—and I am trying to keep a relationship going. It's too much. I thought of several solutions: dump my boyfriend, dump the team, or take occasional 'mental health' days when I don't do much at all. I decided this latter plan was best, but I put a twist on it. I allowed myself to take a mental health day off if I had done the scheduled work I intended to do the previous week. That worked well, and I even kept my boyfriend, which is cool."

Here are common reasons why people run into problems when they try time management.

- Not practicing enough, so the new habit isn't forming.

- Not allowing long enough for the practice to have an effect (giving up too soon).

- Not using enough different strategies.

- Taking too large steps; not using gradual approximations to a goal.

- Underestimating how long a task such as writing a term paper will take.

- Not keeping records of actual time use.

- Not believing you can actually control your time.

- Not using problem solving, so the details defeat the task.

Try working with others to solve your problems in time management. The general approach is the same: list all the details of the problem; and try to think of many solutions to the problem; then choose one or more solutions. Talking a problem over with others can be a big help, because they may see details you miss or think of solutions you don't see.

THINK PIECE 3.3   Problem solving

Most people run into problems as they work out a time-management program. To best solve problems,

- Make a list of the details.
- Try to think of several different solutions.

Try this when you run into a problem.

1. Write the problem: _____

_____

2. List the details:

_____   ▪   _____

_____   ▪   _____

_____   ▪   _____

3. List possible solutions:

_____   ▪   _____

_____   ▪   _____

_____   ▪   _____

4. Choose a solution (may be a combination of the above): _____

_____

_____

Chapter 4

Taking Action

PREVIEW WITH QUESTIONS TO ANSWER

Dealing with Procrastination
- How can fixing problems with goals help with procrastination?
- What can you do to deal with temptation?
- What is bootstrapping?

Stress Proofing
- What is the two-step process to stress-proof yourself?

Can You Gain Greater Control over Time?
- Can you, and will you, do the work outlined in these three chapters?

Your Final Plan
- What are the two rules for a successful plan for change?
- What is your self-contract?

Dealing with Procrastination

June had a big test coming on Monday. She meant to begin studying for it several days ahead, but somehow never got around to it. So she had to cram like crazy Sunday night and Monday morning. She was stressed-out and didn't do very well on the test.

Sound typical? Many students have problems with procrastination. Fortunately, there are steps you can take to cope with this monster.

If you begin to organize your time, you will automatically cut down on procrastination. Without realizing it, you've been reading about how to cope with procrastination. Do the steps outlined in the preceding chapters: Set goals and

QUESTIONS TO ANSWER AS YOU READ:

- How can fixing problems with goals help with procrastination?
- What can you do to deal with temptation?
- What is bootstrapping?

subgoals, and work out strategies to encourage the time-use behaviors that you want. Each of the strategies will help you cope with procrastination.

Procrastination, for example, can be caused by a lack of short-term goals. One step under goal setting is to break large goals into small subgoals, and then to work out strategies to reach these. Students sometimes say, "I have this huge term paper to do, but I keep putting off starting on it."

For situations like this, break the big task into a set of smaller tasks; then begin work on one of the smaller tasks. Forget the whole term paper, just begin by doing some library work, for example. That subgoal becomes your only goal for the moment. Schedule a starting and a stopping time: "Tuesday evening at 6:30 I'm going to the library to do one hour's work on the stuff I have to read for the paper." The scheduled starting time is good because it gets you going, and the scheduled stopping time is good because then you don't feel overwhelmed by the task ahead.

Suppose you have to do some boring assignment, and you've been putting it off. Here are a couple of tricks: Use rewards heavily ("As soon as I finish I'm going to buy myself a giant ice cream cone!"), and break the assignment into a series of small tasks, so you can do each one pretty quickly. Schedule each task for a convenient time; then finish the tasks one by one and reward yourself for doing so.

Sometimes we dread things more than they are worth dreading. Try doing the worst or most difficult task first, so that it doesn't hang over your head. If it's a small job, over quickly, you'll feel good to get it out of the way. Doing that difficult task is like having an injection: You may dread it, but it is rarely as bad as you feared it would be, and it is soon over.

Keeping your goals in your mind

> Jason said, "When I first started trying to control my use of time, I was often really tempted just to throw over the whole thing and go play ball. But I discovered I could talk myself out of that. I'd say to myself, 'No, come on. You really *do* want to do well in school. So give up a little ball now in exchange for better grades and a better job later.'"

Your long-term goals call for some schoolwork now, but your short-term goals lead you elsewhere. This is a common problem. If this happens too often, you won't be able to meet your longer-term goals. Try reminding yourself of the long-term goals. A dieter, for example, might say to herself, "Well, the chocolate would taste good now, but I want to lose a pound this week, so I won't have any." Here are some other examples of how people remind themselves of their goals:

> "When John calls for his usual chat, I'll say, 'Hey, it's great you called. Can I call you back? I'm in the middle of some important schoolwork right now, and I promised myself I'd finish.'"

"If I schedule thirty minutes study time, but before the time is up I'm thinking 'This is boring,' I'll say to myself, 'You scheduled only thirty minutes because you were sure you could do that much. Don't bail out now. It's only ten minutes until you've met your goal. So, keep it up.'"

"If I start thinking, 'I've got to go make some coffee,' before my time is up, I'll tell myself, 'No, not yet. You told yourself you would go twenty minutes before stopping, and the time is not up yet.'"

Bootstrapping

This technique is helpful for overcoming procrastination. *Bootstrapping* involves the following:

1. Divide your work on some large task into very small time units, then do one small unit.
2. After doing each tiny unit, ask yourself, "Do I want to continue, or not?"
3. If you want to continue, do another unit.
4. If not, do one more unit and then quit.

Suppose you have to do a big paper or study for a big test, but you've been procrastinating. Commit yourself to doing only ten minutes' work on the goal. If that is too much, start with seven minutes of work. Start with a level of work so low that you cannot fail to do it, a level so low you would be embarrassed to admit to anyone that you couldn't do it. Then schedule and do the seven minutes. At the end of the first unit of time, ask yourself, "Do I want to continue or not?" If you want to continue, do seven more minutes; then ask again. If you do *not* want to continue, do seven more minutes and then stop.

You should be able to start this process at least 90 percent of the time. If you don't start, it means your time unit is too large. Make it so small you cannot fail to start. Keep a record of the times you successfully start. It doesn't matter if you do one or several units.

A young woman who wanted to be a writer used this technique to get herself to write. She had been putting off writing again and again. Then she became frustrated because she was putting it off. "My new rule was, Write for fifteen minutes, writing anything at all. At the end of that time, I could quit if I did fifteen more minutes, or I could continue. I could stop at the end of any period, provided I did one more period before I stopped. This worked really well for me, and pretty soon I had overcome my writer's block."

THINK PIECE 4.1   Problems with goals and how to fix them

Problem 1 Sometimes you will be tempted to give in to a short-term goal instead of pursuing the long-term goal that you really want. Prepare self-directions to guide yourself through temptation by reminding yourself of the advantages of your long-term goal.

Example "No, I really do want to get better grades, so I will stick to my schedule now."

Use your own words and feelings here to write some self-directions.

_____

_____

_____

Keep a record of using these self-reminders to encourage yourself to stick to your schedule. Put a ✓ and the date when you used a self-reminder.

_____ ■ _____ ■ _____ ■ _____ ■ _____

_____ ■ _____ ■ _____ ■ _____ ■ _____

_____ ■ _____ ■ _____ ■ _____

Problem 2 Procrastination can be due to lack of small steps toward a final goal. First, identify your final goal.

Example Do a term paper. Work out details for dealing with each subgoal. Final goal:

_____

Next, break your final goal into subgoals.

Example Find materials, read, make notes, organize notes, draft an outline, begin writing, revise.

Subgoal (small step)		Starting and stopping time
_____	■	_____
_____	■	_____
_____	■	_____
_____	■	_____
_____	■	_____
_____	■	_____
_____	■	_____

Repeat this procedure as necessary. Don't just allocate one time slot if the subgoal requires several time periods.

Example If you think you will need three hours' work in the library, allocate three different hours to reach that subgoal.

THINK PIECE 4.1 Problems with goals and how to fix them

Second start and stop time	Third start and stop time
_____ ■	_____
_____ ■	_____
_____ ■	_____
_____ ■	_____
_____ ■	_____
■	_____

Problem 3 Some procrastination is due to boring goals. For example, you have to do a report, but the subject bores you. To get yourself to do these, break them into small steps, and reward yourself immediately for doing each step. Schedule these here.

Boring Goal: _____

Small step	Reward
_____ ■	_____
_____ ■	_____
_____ ■	_____
_____ ■	_____
_____ ■	_____
_____ ■	_____

Use more steps if you need them.

Schedule the bootstrapping just as you would a regular study period. For example:

Thursday, 4:00 P.M.,　Begin bootstrapping algebra
Friday, 1:00 P.M.,　　Bootstrap algebra again
Saturday, 4:30 P.M.,　Bootstrap algebra

This technique gets you started because the starting steps are so low you can't fail to reach them, *and* it encourages you to continue a little bit, because you feel as though the process is under your control. You can stop after any unit without guilt as long as you do one more.

SKILL BUILDER 4.1

Bootstrapping to overcome procrastination

To bootstrap, decide on the unit of time you will work and then schedule the work.
After each unit, decide to continue or to stop. If stop, do one more unit.

A. Task One

Task to bootstrap: _____

Size of the (small) time unit: _____

Scheduled time to begin: _____

Example: "I'm going to bootstrap work on my term paper. The time unit will be fifteen minutes. I will begin at 4:30 P.M. this Thursday."

Record keeping

1. Place a ✓ if you began as scheduled: _____

2. If you decided to stop after the first unit but did one more unit before stopping, place a ✓: _____

3. If you decided to continue, place a ✓ for each time you decided to continue:

   _____ _____ _____ _____ _____

4. Once you decided to stop, and did one more unit, place a ✓: _____

5. Repeat this procedure until you are working adequately on the project.

If you don't have all ✓s , use a smaller unit of time, and reschedule. Begin again.

B. Task Two

Task to bootstrap: _____

Size of the (small) time unit: _____

Scheduled time to begin: _____

Record keeping

1. Place a ✓ if you began as scheduled: _____

2. If you decided to stop after the first unit but did one more unit before stopping, place a ✓: _____

3. If you decided to continue, place a ✓ for each time you decided to continue:

   _____ _____ _____ _____ _____

4. Once you decided to stop, and did one more unit, place a ✓: _____

5. Repeat this procedure until you are working adequately on the project.

If you don't have all ✓s , use a smaller unit of time, and reschedule. Begin again.

Working with others

Try consulting with others about your bootstrapping procedures, particularly if you are having any difficulties. Describe your task, the size of the units you are using, and the procedure you are following. Explain the bootstrapping procedure if the people you're consulting don't know it. Then just listen to their advice on how to make it work for you. Write here ideas you get from this consultation:

_____

_____

_____

_____

_____

_____

Stress Proofing

QUESTION TO ANSWER AS YOU READ:

■ What is the two-step process to stress-proof yourself?

Some stress in college is inevitable. There are going to be tests coming up, term papers due, the pressures of your other work, sometimes a bad grade, arguments with a friend, and not enough sleep. You need to minimize the disturbing effects of stress, however; for if you do not control it, it will interfere with the quality of your schoolwork and can even make you sick.[1]

All students have to face important tests, due dates for term papers, the pressures of work, and so on, but not all students are equally stressed-out by those pressures. Some people control the stresses of student life better than others. They *stress-proof* themselves. How do they do that?

Stress proofing yourself involves two steps:

1. Controlling the events that cause your stress reaction.
2. Controlling the stress reaction itself.

These are two separate, but important, elements in stress proofing.

Step One: Controlling the external causes of stress

Some people think of stressful events as the catastrophe that occurs occasionally in our lives, such as breaking up with a loved one. These events are stressful, but *more stressful* are the little things that occur over and over.[2] Even though you may not cry, over the long run it is harder on you to be constantly late for class than it is to break up with a boyfriend or girlfriend. This is why procrastination is so hard: It can occur over and over, and wear us out.

Try to reduce the problems you have to deal with. Because each individual stressful event may be small, it is easy to let a recurring stressor run on and on. But that is a mistake. It can make you frantic. If there are little hassles that occur over and over, try to figure out ways to make them disappear. For example, getting to class on time reduces stress. Not procrastinating in your studying does, too.

To eliminate external causes of stress, use the problem-solving approach outlined in Chapter 3: List the details of your problem, and think of many solutions to it.

> David felt constantly stressed, so he listed the events of the days that were stressing him. Two that came up over and over were the frequent nagging he got from his boss at work and his constant sleepiness. David listed the things he could do about the boss: quit the job, transfer to another shift, always greet the boss with a smile, tell him off, and so on. He decided to do two things: Always smile, hoping to disarm the man, but also try to find a place on another shift.

THINK PIECE 4.2   What stresses you?

What are the events that stress you? List here the details, and look for solutions by changing the details. Think of many solutions; then choose some to put into operation. The goal is to control events so that little, but stressful, events do not occur over and over.

Details of the stress:

_____

_____

_____

_____

Possible solutions:

_____

_____

_____

_____

Solutions chosen:

_____

_____

_____

_____

David's list of things he could do about being sleepy was short: Get more sleep. Then he listed actions he could take to accomplish that.

Talk over your stresses with friends. The social support you get can have two effects: It gives you ideas on how to deal with the stress, and by itself, it has a calming effect. When people are under stress but feel they are supported by others and are members of a group, they are less likely to become ill as a result of the stress.[3] The people most important to you are the ones who are most likely to help you cope.

Who could you talk with to solve problems that lead to stress?

_____

_____

Step Two: Controlling your reaction to the stress

Stress is worse for some people than others. Some stay calm while preparing for tests or meeting a deadline while others get stressed-out. What's the difference?

People who stay calm work at staying calm. They tell themselves how to react to a stressor; they don't let their negative emotions gain the upper hand.

> When David's boss was rude, for example, David said to himself, "Okay, stay calm. This does not have to upset me. The guy is acting stupidly, but that's his problem, not mine. Relax. Smile."

What kinds of things could you say to yourself to calm yourself when something upsetting occurs?

> Julie has just learned that she got a worse grade on the test than she expected. Her eyes start to tear up. But she thinks to herself, "Well, I knew this course was going to be hard. Getting upset is natural. It's frustrating. I'm still learning how to do this well. So, I won't get discouraged; I'll just prepare even better next time."

Think of situations in which you become stressed; then write out here self-instructions to stay calm and do something productive in those situations.

_____

_____

_____

You can also do things to calm yourself. Exercise is calming. It has two kinds of beneficial effects.[4] First, people who exercise regularly are less stressed-out when they confront a stressful event such as a test. Their heart rate and blood pressure, for example, go up less. Second, people who are in good aerobic condition recover from the effects of stress more quickly. They might get nervous for a moment, but recover more quickly. A person in good aerobic condition, then, might start to get nervous during a test, but would become less upset, and would get over the stress more quickly, than someone not in good condition.

If you are prone to getting nervous and not currently exercising, you need to calm down your body _via_ exercise. This will benefit your schoolwork. Use the same ideas for change you have already learned: Set goals, start low, move up slowly, schedule a time to do the exercise, keep records of sticking to your schedule, give yourself instructions, eliminate negative thoughts, and expect to have to practice a lot.

THINK PIECE 4.3   An exercise plan

Work out an exercise plan to help yourself stay calm. It does not have to be intense; walking is fine. Ideally, you should exercise three times per week. More exercise may have an even more calming effect, but be sure not to overdo it.

1. First goal (start low): _____

   Gradual (small) steps to increase: _____ _____ _____ _____

2. Schedule times to exercise.

Sunday	Monday	Tuesday	Wednesday	Thursday	Friday	Saturday
____ ■	____ ■	____ ■	____ ■	____ ■	____ ■	____
____ ■	____ ■	____ ■	____ ■	____ ■	____ ■	____
____ ■	____ ■	____ ■	____ ■	____ ■	____ ■	____
____ ■	____ ■	____ ■	____ ■	____ ■	____ ■	____

Keep records with a ✔ each time you exercise at the scheduled time. Repeat this each week.

3. If you are not living up to your schedule, reschedule. Use problem solving—think of the details, think of several solutions—to work out a new schedule.

   Example: "If I had someone to exercise with I'd be more likely to do it, so I'm going to look for an exercise buddy."

4. Work out self-instructions to encourage yourself to exercise:

   _____

   _____

Example: "This is a good way to spend my time. I'll be healthier and less nervous. So, go exercise!"

5. Work out rewards to gain for meeting your weekly schedule:

   _____

   _____

Example: "I won't let myself watch TV until I've done my scheduled exercise." "If I do it all week as scheduled, I'll treat myself to something good to eat on the weekend."

Some people have a hard time making themselves exercise, yet each time they take a test, they get nervous. Make yourself see the connection between lack of exercise and getting too nervous on tests. The exercise will calm you. Try it for a month. If you don't see that exercise makes you calmer, give it up.

Penny wrote in her report, "I can't believe how much exercise keeps me calm. I've always gotten fairly nervous when taking tests, but a month ago I started a pretty vigorous exercise program. Since then I've had three tests, and it is almost scary how much less nervous I have become. Nerve-wracking things come up on the tests, and I notice them, but I don't panic. I just keep on working and end up really remarkably calm. I feel like a different person."

Does caffeine—which you get from coffee, tea, cola drinks and even a little from chocolate—make you nervous? Caffeine has an interesting effect. If you are not already stressed, it does *not* make you feel stressed. But if something happens to make you feel stressed—a nasty shock on a test, for example—then caffeine exaggerates your body's stress reaction.[5] Your heart literally becomes jumpier during stress if it is full of caffeine. If you tend to get nervous on a test, for example, then you probably should avoid caffeine. If you take caffeine, you will get jumpier.

Some people use alcohol to relieve stress. This works in the short term, because you no longer focus on being upset. But it does not work in the long term, because (1) you do nothing about the situations causing the stress, (2) alcohol can cause other, stressful situations, and (3) taking alcohol one time does not change your emotional reaction when the stress occurs the next time.

Alcohol also has an interesting effect. If you learn something while under the influence of alcohol, you will probably not remember it when sober.[6] If you study for a test while drinking, then take the test sober, you will probably not do well because you will not remember a lot of the material you learned while full of alcohol. You should study sober if you are going to take the test sober.

Chapter 16 teaches two techniques to use to get calm while taking a test—meditation and muscle relaxation. You can use them to relax at any

THINK PIECE 4.4   Reducing stress

What can you do to reduce the stress in your life? What problems lead to stress?

_____

_____

What emotions need to be coped with?

_____

_____

THINK PIECE 4.5   **What can you control?**

For each of the questions below, estimate the chances that you will be able to do what you need to do. Make your estimates in terms of percentages. One hundred percent means you are certain you will do something. Fifty percent means you are not at all certain. Zero percent means you are certain you will *not* do the needed practice.

   This is a questionnaire for your eyes only, so be honest with yourself.

1. Will you keep a record of your use of time? (Chapter 2)

   Estimate: _____ percent

2. Will you set goals that are only a little above where you are now and that are flexible? (Chapter 3)

   Estimate: _____ percent

3. Will you arrange situations to encourage good use of time, such as using a written schedule, making lists of things to do, and planning by the week? (Chapter 3)

   Estimate: _____ percent

4. Will you encourage the desired time use behavior by keeping records as you go and being prepared to practice over and over? (Chapter 3)

   Estimate: _____ percent

5. Will you arrange the consequences to encourage good use of time, such as rewarding yourself for a good job, using self-directions to guide your actions, and revising your plan as the need arises? (Chapter 3)

   Estimate: _____ percent

time. If you are nervous while studying, for example, or stressed at work, use them.

   Use the exercises in this chapter to work out plans to stress-proof yourself. Stress can be reduced only if you try to control it.

Can You Gain Greater Control over Time?

QUESTION TO ANSWER AS YOU READ:

■ Can you, and will you, do the work outlined in these three chapters?

You might value a particular goal. But if you don't believe you can reach that goal, you won't try, even though you would love to be successful. Most of us, for example, would love an Olympic medal; but most of us believe that even if we worked very hard, we could *not* win one—so we don't try. Do you believe you can bring your use of time under your own control, or is accomplishing that goal like winning an Olympic medal?

   This book is structured so that *if* you do the exercises suggested, *then* you will develop the skills necessary to do well in college. If you do the practice, the grades will come. So, the crucial question is, Can you and will you do the suggested skill-building practice?

THINK PIECE 4.5   What can you control?

6. Will you take some of the steps outlined for dealing with procrastination? (Chapter 4)

   Estimate: _____ percent

7. Will you keep long-term goals in mind? (Chapter 4)

   Estimate: _____ percent

If, in all honesty, your estimates are not high, there are still things you can do.

First, ask yourself, Why is my estimate low for a particular question? Perhaps the idea expressed in the question seems unattractive to you, something you don't want to do. Ask yourself, If I could get better grades by doing that, is it worth it? Remember the idea is to try something and then evaluate it. You might not dislike an activity as much as you think. It might not be as much trouble as you think it is going to be. And doing it might be worth while because you could then do better in college.

Second, find parts of the three chapters you feel you can put into operation. If you make only a little progress in time management, that is still some progress. Often people find that when they begin with one part of a plan to improve their time management, other parts which at first seemed unattractive become easier to do later. Start with the parts you believe you can do, and see what happens.

Third, try discussing your feelings about this with another student, if you wish. Write out here the reasons why you gave any question a low estimate, and then talk over your thoughts with the other student:

_____

_____

_____

_____

_____

_____

If you do the practice in Chapters 2, 3, and 4, you will gain greater control over your use of time. If you don't, you may not. But you need to follow the steps in the chapters. Can you do that?

Your Final Plan

QUESTIONS TO ANSWER
AS YOU READ:

■ What are the two rules for a successful plan for change?

■ What is your self-contract?

Use several strategies, not just one or two

People who use several strategies are more likely to be successful in their efforts to change.[7] You could do several things at once: Keep records of your use of time, arrange situations to encourage good time management, commit yourself to plenty of practice, reward yourself for good behavior, use self-guiding talk to get through sticky situations, and use problem solving when difficulties arise.

Not only should you use a variety of techniques, you should use them for long enough to have an effect. When people fail to make changes in themselves that they wanted to make, it's usually not because the techniques fail. It is because they fail to use the techniques.[8] Keeping records for one day won't do it. Having a written schedule for one week isn't enough. People who change their own behavior practice these techniques over and over.

So, there are two rules:

1. Use a lot of techniques.
2. Persist for a long time.

Part of Colin's assignment in his psychology class was to keep track of how he used his time for three days. He was upset by the results. He had begun the project saying, "I suppose there is room for improvement in my time." But after three days of records, he was saying, "This is terrible. I really need to plan my time better." His first day of records, for example, which was two days before a big test in math, showed that he slept six hours, worked at his job five hours, watched TV for two hours, watched two videos for four more hours, socialized for two hours, and did miscellaneous other things for the rest of the time. No studying for the upcoming test. That of course led to cramming the next night. He got a C on the test. "It's terrible how I procrastinate," he said.

Colin decided he needed to schedule some time each day for studying. He set himself to study in the dorm one hour each evening. "This wasn't such a great plan, however, because there are just too many distractions in the dorm. It's noisy, people drop in all the time, the TV is on somewhere." He then moved his study place to the library. This was better, but he found that he too often fell asleep when he tried to read. Was the library too quiet?

"I have to face the fact that I'm not getting enough sleep. It seems funny, but if I scheduled sleep, it might actually help me study better. This could be a rationalization, but I don't think it is." So he set himself a time to go to sleep—midnight to 1:00 A.M. each night—and tried to stick with that, giving himself eight hours of sleep each night. This worked well, and he noted that not only did he feel better, but he was able to begin exercising and was able to stay awake during his scheduled study hours.

SKILL BUILDER 4.2

Your plan for change

A. Decide on your goal and subgoals

Goal: _____

_____

Subgoals: Refer to Skill Builder 2.2 in Chapter 2 for ideas.

_____	■	_____
_____	■	_____
_____	■	_____
_____	■	_____
_____	■	_____
	■	_____

B. Plan strategies to reach the subgoals

Strategies were dealt with in Chapter 3. Look back over them, and select several strategies that you would like to use. The more you use, the better.

1. _____

2. _____

3. _____

4. _____

5. _____

6. _____

7. _____

8. _____

C. Make a self-contract

Make a contract only if you are truly going to follow through. Write a statement like "I intend to do all the practice I am outlining for myself. I am willing to do this." Then sign and date your plan, which is now your self-contract.

_____

_____

_____

"Still, I need to study more. Five hours a week is not enough to get all B's." Colin took several steps to reach this goal. He had already been using a written schedule. Now he began to prepare a to-do list for each week. This allowed him to plan his time better. He scheduled extra hours, some in the morning, when he thought he would be fresher. "I passed a rule for myself: I could only watch videos, which I love, if I did the scheduled study hours each day. I also prepared a list of reminders to give myself. Like 'Come on, Colin, you scheduled an hour's study now. You really do want to make B's, so do the hour.'"

This new plan worked pretty well for Colin, but there were still a couple of problems. "One problem was that I skipped around a lot in what I was doing. I'd start on my math homework, then switch to psychology, then something else. This is inefficient, so I'm going to use my to-do list to schedule exactly what I should be working on. Another thing I've realized is that I spend a lot of time waiting for the bus and then riding to work. I'm going to start trying to do some of my school reading during this time."

At the end of his report, Colin noted that he was now studying eight hours per week and that his grades were improving. By using several techniques, persisting, and solving problems as they came up, Colin gained control over his use of time.

A self-contract

It helps to write out a detailed plan. Treat the plan as a contract with yourself, an agreement about what you will do. People who make out self-contracts that specify what they will do to change are more successful in carrying out their plans.[9]

Part III

Being There: Important Basics

If you were going on a four- or -five year expedition, you would want to be very sure you had all the equipment you needed, and that you possessed the skills for a successful adventure. It would be foolish to set out into the mountains or desert or on to the sea without the needed skills, or to try to limp along for years with underdeveloped skills. You might prepare a checklist, and go over it, to be sure you had everything you need, including important skills. Do we have flashlights? spare tires? Does everyone know first aid?

There are skills you need in your four or five years in college, too. In Part III we focus on basic skills you need: holding the right attitudes, working well with others, going to class, taking notes, participating, and thinking.

Skill 1 (Chapter 5): You need to have the right attitude and to understand how your beliefs about yourself and about learning can affect you.

Do you feel that college is an opportunity to develop yourself more fully, to become more, or do you worry that *you* are constantly being evaluated, that *your performance* is often evaluated?
The first _____ The second _____ A bit of both _____

How does this affect you?

Skill 2 (Chapter 5): You need to be able to use study groups effectively.

Can you? Yes _____ No _____ Not sure _____

Skill 3 (Chapter 5): You need to be able to talk with instructors, to seek their aid when it will help.

Can you? Yes _____ No _____ Not sure _____

Skill 4 (Chapter 6): You have to get yourself there, physically and mentally.

Do you almost always go to class?
Yes _____ No _____ Not sure _____

Do you know what to do to stay focused and interested
when you are in class?
Yes _____ No _____ Not sure _____

Skill 5 (Chapter 6): You need to take good notes in your classes, ones that will help you learn efficiently.

Do you think you take good notes in class, ones that help you study later?
Yes _____ No _____ Not sure _____

Skill 6 (Chapter 6): In order to benefit fully, you need to participate in your classes. You need to be active, not passive.

Do you participate in discussions in classes when that is appropriate?
Yes _____ No _____ Not sure _____

Skill 7 (Chapter 7): College is about thinking, and you need to be sure your thinking skills are well polished.

Do you ask questions in class?
Yes _____ No _____

Do you know how to get yourself to think about what
you are learning in class?
Yes _____ No _____ Not sure _____

Skill 8 (Chapter 7): You need to know how to solve problems and make decisions.

Are you practicing problem-solving and decision-making skills?
Yes _____ No _____ Not sure _____

Attitudes about Yourself and Others

The Skills-Development Attitude

QUESTIONS TO ANSWER AS YOU READ:

- What is the skills-development attitude? What are its benefits?
- How can you develop it in yourself?

On the night before his SAT test, very important for getting into college, José did a peculiar thing. He got very drunk and stayed out until three in the morning. He took the big test hung over and needing sleep. Similarly, the day before a major test in English, Kristen didn't study at all. She spent the day feeling depressed and watching TV and took the test totally unprepared.

José's and Kristen's actions are self-destructive. Why would they do what they did?

Trying to do well on a test is a double-edged sword for some people. If they do well after studying, they feel good; but if they do poorly, their poor performance has bad implications. "I studied a lot for my English test but only made a D. I'm dumb." If you *don't* study and make a D, that does *not* show you're dumb, because you took the test with a handicap.

Self-handicapping means putting obstacles in your own way to provide yourself with an excuse for *not* doing well. This is a strategy some people follow when their feelings of self-worth are threatened by something like an upcoming test.[1] If you don't do well on the test, failure does *not* challenge your self-worth, because you have the handicap to provide an excuse. "I wasn't ready, so failing doesn't show I am a loser."

Compare José and Kristen to Jack. When Jack was fifty, he decided to run a marathon. He trained hard and after six months was able to finish the twenty-six mile race in four hours and twenty-three minutes. "I'm thrilled," said Jack.

"But what about the winner?" someone asked. "He finished two hours ahead of you. What about the hundreds of others who finished ahead of you?"

"Oh, I don't care about them," replied Jack. "I just wanted to see if I could do it. And four hours twenty-three minutes is a good time for me." Jack does not feel his self-worth is challenged because of his slow time.

Jack does not compare his performance to other people's. He compares it to his own goal. Suppose José had thought as Jack did. "English is my second language, after all, and I am still in the learning stage. I don't read it as well as I speak it. This SAT is only going to show me where I am now, not where I am going to end up."

Skills development versus performance goals

If José thinks of the SAT as an indicator of his true worth, then the emphasis is on Jose's *performance* on the test.[2] A person with a *performance orientation* is concerned with questions like these:

- Will I look okay?

- How will I do?

- What will people think of me?

If, on the other hand, José thinks of the test as an indication of his current level of skill then the emphasis is on *skills development*. A person with a *skills development orientation* is concerned with questions like these:

- What will this show me I have learned so far?

- How have I improved?

The test results are feedback about how he's doing so far, but have no implications about his self-worth. Such people don't compare themselves with other people because others' scores are not relevant to their goals. They are like Jack, who did not care how others had run the marathon.

If you emphasize your skills development, you are more likely to get involved in your own learning process, use better study strategies, be interested in the material, and even accept a bit of a challenge.[3] If you emphasize performance goals, on the other hand, you are more likely to fear tests and not do as well on them. Making high grades is hard, and if that is your only goal, you can get discouraged. But improving from wherever you are now is possible, and if that is your goal, you can feel optimistic about success.

Encouraging a skills-development attitude

Did you ever listen to an interview with an athlete, for example, someone who has just won a big tennis tournament? Athletes often say things like "I just focused on doing my game plan" or "I just tried to execute." They mean they focused on doing the process and didn't worry too much about the score. If they do the process well, the score will follow. If they don't win, that only means they need more practice. That's the attitude you should develop about studying.

> Andrea is getting ready to study for a test. She first makes a little speech to herself, "I'm going to put some real effort into this. I'm going to predict some of the test questions. I'm not going to let myself even think about what kind of grade I might get." She keeps a reminder in her notebook: "Give myself instructions on what to do" and "Don't think about the grade; think about doing the work." She puts a check by this reminder each time she does it. She also keeps track of how long she practices—"Monday, 45 minutes"—and how many test questions she tried to predict—"4 questions fully predicted."

Self-directions like those Andrea used remind you what to do. Work out your game plan, and don't think about the score.

When you are working on your study skills, give yourself self-directions. The self-instructions you give yourself should remind you of two things.[4]

SKILL BUILDER 5.1

Practicing a skills-development attitude

A. Control your thinking

When you are managing your time, or in class, or in a study situation, follow three steps to encourage your skills-development attitude:

- Minimize competitive thinking.

- Tell yourself to put out effort.

- instruct yourself on specific strategies to use.

1. Compare your progress to your own goals, not to others' performance. Minimize thinking about grades. Write self-instructions to do this:

_____

_____

_____

_____

2. Write self-instructions to put out some effort when you begin to study or are in class:

_____

_____

_____

_____

Example: Jill is settling in to take notes in her geology lecture. She says to herself, "Okay, really concentrate and put your mind into this. Don't sweat grades now. Listen carefully, and try to get great notes."

Write a reminder to yourself to do this—perhaps on a three by five card—and keep it in front of you when you are managing your time or taking notes or encouraging yourself to think.

B. Analyze how you think

What's your orientation—skill or performance? Fill in these blanks:

1. If I do well on a test, it means...

_____

_____

_____

2. If I do poorly on a test, it means...

_____

_____

_____

Example: Jandra writes, "If I do well it means I'm lucky. If I do poorly, it means I'm dumb." What kind of orientation does that show?

Penn, on the other hand, writes, "If I do well, it means I studied enough. If I do poorly, it means I didn't." Who feels better, Jandra or Penn?

C. Analyze your courses

Do the courses you are taking encourage a skills-development attitude, or do some encourage a performance attitude? Think of all your courses:

1. In what courses can you work cooperatively with others?

_____

_____

2. In what courses do you have some control, for example, by having a choice of what to do?

_____

_____

SKILL BUILDER 5.1

Practicing a skills-development attitude

3. In what courses does the instructor seem to want you to understand the material, or want you to get interested in it?

_____

_____

4. Are there any courses graded on a curve?

_____

_____

5. Are there any courses in which the instructor overemphasizes grades or competition in the classroom?

_____

_____

6. Do some courses have too few tests so you can't get feedback about your improvement?

_____

_____

---

1. To put out some effort.
2. To use specific strategies.

If you want to ask thinking questions in class, for example, tell yourself what to do: "Okay, put some effort into this. Ask myself a question and let that lead to a question I can ask in class."

Here are some ideas on how to encourage yourself to have a skills-development attitude:

Compare yourself with yourself, not with other people. "This is good. Last week I only tried to ask two questions in class, but this week I asked four." Wherever you are in your level of skill, you start from there and try to get better.

Don't compete. Think like Jack the marathon runner, who didn't care how well or poorly others did. Compete only with yourself. "Next week I'm going to ask even more questions."

Don't think about grades for a while. Focus on getting yourself to put in the effort; practice skills such as time management or the other skills you will learn in this book. Your ultimate goal may be to raise your grades, but for now, concentrate on putting in the practice time and developing specific skills. Like the tennis player, just work on your game plan, and forget whether you're winning or not. Later you will win.

Don't focus on getting your schoolwork over quickly.[5] Skills-development is ongoing, so you should focus on putting in enough practice time—at time management, at note taking or thinking or other skills you will learn—to gain some benefit. The goal is *not* to get an assignment over with. The goal is to become an educated person.

Look for situations that encourage you to have a skills–development attitude instead of a performance orientation. Some instructors encourage you to think mainly of grades—a performance orientation—while others encourage a skills-development attitude.[6] Try to find classes

- Where you can work cooperatively with others.

- That give you some control, for example, by letting you choose the order in which you do things.

- With instructors who try to get you to truly understand, or who want to get you interested in the material.

Avoid situations that overemphasize a performance attitude. For example, avoid

- Instructors who grade "on a curve," making you compete with others for a grade.

- Instructors who emphasize competition in the classroom.

- Courses with only a few tests so you can't get frequent feedback about your skills improvement.

- Instructors who pay too much attention to grades.

Sometimes you don't have a choice, and you find yourself in a class that discourages a skills-development attitude. There may be little you can do about this. The important point is to realize that this is the nature of the class. It's the class's problem, not your problem. What happens in that class says nothing about you. Don't form any important attitudes about yourself as a result of your performance in the class.

Your Beliefs about Learning

The idea of a skills-development attitude shows how our beliefs can affect our interpretation of what happens. The same grade on a test could be seen as real progress or bad news, depending on your attitude.

Your beliefs about the nature of learning and how it happens also affect your interpretation of events in your school life. Answer these two questions by checking a number that indicates your agreement or disagreement:[7]

1. The ability to learn is inherited, not developed.

1	2	3	4	5
STRONGLY AGREE	AGREE	UNCERTAIN	DISAGREE	STRONGLY DISAGREE

QUESTIONS TO ANSWER AS YOU READ:

- What are your beliefs about how learning develops and how fast it should occur?

- What are the effects of your beliefs on how you work in school?

THINK PIECE 5.1   What do you believe?

Sometimes it is hard to know what belief we hold, unless we try to explain it to someone else. Explaining how we feel helps us get clear on how we feel. Try discussing these two beliefs with another student. Do you think learning skill is inherited? Do you think learning should be fast? How do you explain how you react to a less-than-perfect grade? If a poor grade tempts you to give up, then you may be showing one of the self-destructive beliefs outlined here. If a poor grade means you need to put out more effort and use better learning strategies, then you are showing a positive belief.

2. Learning happens quickly or not at all.

1	2	3	4	5
STRONGLY AGREE	AGREE	UNCERTAIN	DISAGREE	STRONGLY DISAGREE

Suppose a student checks 1 for both those questions. Then he gets a poor grade on a test. He believes that learning ability is inherited and that learning should happen quickly. He has just shown that even though he studied some, he did *not* learn the material on the test well. What are the implications? That he *cannot* learn this material. He studied a bit, but got nowhere. He believes that ability is inherited and learning should be fast. Therefore, there is no point in studying longer or using better learning strategies because he believes these actions won't help. The student's beliefs about learning will have a drastic effect on how he does in this course.

What are your beliefs about learning? If you tend to believe that learning should be easy and that learning ability is inherited, then taking a skills-development approach to college, doesn't make sense to you. Either you have the ability to do well in college or you don't. Either you will get the material pretty quickly, or you won't get it at all.

But it is not necessary to believe this way. You could believe that the ability to learn can be developed by developing learning skills. You could see that all the easy learning of school days is behind you and now comes the complex material that takes much practice to learn. These beliefs would lead to a skills-development attitude.

Try adopting the beliefs that learning can be improved if you use learning skills and that learning at the college level takes time.

Holding these beliefs has these implications:

- Developing learning skills will help your learning.

- You can develop these skills if you practice them.

- If you put out effort, you will learn.

- Different learning situations call for different strategies.

Learning Styles and Different Kinds of Intelligence

QUESTIONS TO ANSWER
AS YOU READ:

■ Are there different ways of being intelligent?

■ What are you good at?

Peter had to take a course in statistics and was dreading it because he had never been able to understand all the mathematical explanations he had been given in various other classes. But to his delight, when he took the course, he found that the instructor did not explain the statistics in terms of math. She explained statistics in terms of spatial relations, in terms of simple geometry. For example, Peter had tried unsuccessfully before to understand the idea of correlation, but when he heard the concept explained in terms of lines in three-dimensional space, he really understood it. He could think in terms of space, but not so well in terms of algebra.

Peter's experience is an example of what is called learning style, the idea that different people understand things in different ways. The divisions between different ways of learning, however, are not clear-cut, and there is considerable overlap in people's skills. The fact that Peter can learn statistics better when it is explained one way does not mean that he always thinks that way, or that he should always try to learn that way. Humans are complicated.

There are different ways of being intelligent, although theorists do not agree about just how many different ways there are. One well-known theory suggests three different kinds of intelligence—analytical, creative, and practical.[8] You don't have just one kind, although you may be better at one than another.

The instructors you encounter in college will have theories about what and how they should teach. One might emphasize creative intelligence, while another emphasizes the practical and a third, the analytical. Most activities require us to use all three kinds of intelligence. If you had to write a paper in a class, for example, you might use your analytical intelligence to think about what to write, your creative intelligence to think of an interesting way to write it, and your practical intelligence to get organized to do the writing on time and with a point of view your instructor would like.

College courses sometimes emphasize analytical intelligence because that is the college tradition, and that may be what many of your instructors are best at. Don't fall into the trap of thinking that you are not smart just because you are not terribly strong in analytical intelligence. That is only one way to be smart. If your strength lies in creative or practical intelligence, and if you are willing to work, you will succeed in life. Lawrence Sternberg, the author of the theory of intelligence you are reading about here, became the IBM Professor at Yale University, which is about as high as you can go in his field. Yet Sternberg was told by teachers in high school that he would probably never amount to much because he had scored only average on an IQ (intelligence quotient) test. That test measured only analytical intelligence, but Sternberg has shown that he is brilliantly creative, very practical and very hard working. Being a well-off, highly respected Yale professor isn't too bad an outcome in life.

Whenever you are learning, you should ask yourself, "Is this the best way for me to learn this?" What works best for one person will not necessarily be best for another. You might find that taking your class notes in words doesn't work for you as well as drawing lots of diagrams, but someone else might find just the opposite. Try making changes in how you learn to see what works best for you.

> Shayna has always studied by cramming the night before a test. She would read the material and then try to memorize it by writing it over and over. Finally, she asked herself "Is this the best way to learn this?" and the answer was "Probably not." She stopped cramming and tried to spread out her studying, but she also stopped writing material she did not understand over and over. Instead, she worked on understanding it. Later she found that if she made diagrams, she could understand some material even better.

This book is full of learning strategies you can use. Try them to see which work best for you, then build on the helpful ones. Like Lawrence Sternberg, find your strengths and make them greater.

Working with Others: How Should You Deal with Diversity?

QUESTIONS TO ANSWER AS YOU READ:

- What are the advantages of sometimes studying with others? How can you do this best?
- What is the best way to handle the diversity of people you encounter on campus?

In college you have opportunities to work with other students, instructors, and people different from any you have ever known. That's the beauty of college.

Study groups

There are several advantages to sometimes working with other students on your studies. Learning from another student is often just as effective as learning from an instructor, and there are lots more students available. Working with another student can keep you motivated—"I have to do this because I've got to explain it to Jim tonight!"—and it keeps your interest level high. You can learn how to study from seeing others do it, and you can develop better learning skills by noticing the example set by others.[9] For example, you might not think of keeping your notes in a certain way until you see how another student does it. Other people provide feedback and give us new ideas on how to do the work. Even more pertinent, you learn a subject better if you have to explain it to someone else. Ask your instructor: most of us feel we learned our subject matter best when we had to teach it to you students. Teaching others helps you learn better.[10]

There is one disadvantage to study groups: You can use them as a *source of distraction*, a way of substituting socializing for studying, so that you don't do much learning. A few people "just love" the idea of study groups because they think it means others will do the work for them, or that they will be able to just hang out. But of course that is not the point at all.

Students think of using study groups to prepare for tests, but there are many other ways to work with others in a group:

- Two students can meet after class to compare their notes from lectures, to see if they got all the main points, and incidentally to learn better note taking from each other.

- Students can edit and comment on each other's writing, on both the form of the writing and its content.

- Students can take turns reading a text to each other, remarking on the main ideas and incidentally teaching each other how to spot main ideas.

- Math or science students can review each other's problems solved and make suggestions for solving others, or try to solve difficult problems together, a good way to learn how others go about problem solving.

- Students can meet in a group to predict questions on an upcoming test.

- Students can assign topics from the text to each other and give short lessons on the topic to the others.

- Students can combine the results of their library searches.

- Students can meet after a test and review it, emphasizing what they need to do in order to do better next time.

- Students can work together, often in pairs, to develop weekly study plans, carrying out the procedures in Chapters 2, 3 and 4 together, to encourage each other to develop good time management skills.

You can construct multipurpose groups that meet several of these goals. Tamia's group, for example, first organized itself to study for a test, but the students continued in the group after that test with several goals: to prepare for the next test, to predict test questions, to go over tests afterwards to see how to take them better, and to solve problems in their difficult science course.

Best procedures for study groups

Don't have more than four or so people in the group.

Begin with a trial period, so you are not stuck if the group doesn't work out well.

Have an agreed-upon agenda for each meeting, so you don't waste a lot of time. "Next time let's make a list of the main ideas in chapter three and solve the problems at the end." Be sure all agree on the time and place of each meeting, as well as the agenda.

Be sure all the group members are doing their part. If someone does not, practice assertion by smilingly, politely saying something like "We all depend on each other to come to the group prepared, so please be prepared next time." Assign tasks to people, and be sure each person knows what he or she is supposed to do for the next meeting. "Sue, can you go over the first five pages of chapter three and review them for the rest of us? I'll take the next five."

Be sure the group spends most of the allotted time on the task. Of course, a bit of fun and socializing is good, but don't let that dominate the group's time. At the end of each hour, ask the group members to comment on how well they used their time together.

(You can see how participating in these groups gives you excellent training in leadership, a very helpful skill to have in the business world. Take a skills-development attitude about this: The more you practice, the better you will get at it.)

If group members explain material to each other, the person doing the explaining will learn the most. Therefore, once something is explained, other members should explain it again, to be sure they have learned it.

Ask each other generic questions like the ones listed in Chapter 7. For example, one group member could pick a topic and, to test the others, say "Explain why . . ." This should be a common procedure for your study group, because answering the generic questions greatly helps group members learn the material.[11] Contrast this procedure with a situation in which one group member explains an idea to the others, and the others just listen. Just listening is very passive and is not nearly as good a way of learning as answering generic questions.

Diversity on campus

Countries like the United States and Canada are made great by their diversity. They are plural nations made up of many different kinds of people, and that is a major source of their strength. For some students in the United States, college is a time when they first face America's great diversity, for in their earlier years they have lived and attended school in a less diverse environment. Now there are many different kinds of people in their classes, and they have to think of how to deal with everyone.

SKILL BUILDER 5.2

Setting up a study group

A. Write down the purpose of the group and list of its members.

Purpose of the group:_____

_____

Group members: _____

_____

B. Write an agenda for first meeting (if the group is multipurpose, there will be more than one item):

_____

_____

_____

C. List procedures you may use (for example, explanation, reading, generic questions, problem solving).

Write these down before the meeting:

_____

_____

_____

D. After the first meeting, evaluate how well the group functioned.

Note things you could do better next time.

Example: How much of the time do you estimate you spent on the group's task?

_____

_____

_____

_____

_____

_____

In our city there is a woman who is known for being able to deal with a great diversity of clients in her business. In any given hour she deals with men and women, young and old, and customers of as many as eight different ethnic backgrounds. Everyone likes her, and everyone feels appreciated by her. So it was with great interest that one read an article about her in the newspaper. "What is your secret to getting along with so many different ethnic groups, with so many different kinds of people?" she was asked.

"I just treat everybody as an individual, not like they were representative of some group," she replied.

That is the great secret: Treat people like individuals, not like stereotypes. A stereotype is an oversimplified, self-perpetuating way of thinking about people that puts them into categories and does not allow for individual variation. It is easy—too easy—to think in terms of stereotypes. For example, many people love to discuss how men act one way and women act another, as though the two sexes were completely different from each other, while in fact they are very much alike.

We have many stereotypes we can use in our thinking—about men, women, the old, and every ethnic group in the country. You can't think of a group about which there are no stereotypes, can you?

There are many problems with thinking in stereotypes.[12] First, stereotypes can be negative: "Men are aggressive." Second, stereotypes treat all members of a category as though they were just alike, ignoring the great differences that may exist between them. Some men are aggressive, but some are not at all, and others fall in between. Stereotypes often contain a tiny germ of truth, but it is greatly overgeneralized. Third, stereotypes tend to make us think there are great differences between our group and the stereotyped one. "They" are all alike, and "we" are not like them at all. But that may not be true. We might actually be quite a bit like "them" if we only knew. Finally, stereotypes tend to be self-perpetuating. We tend to notice when a person fits the stereotype, but fail to notice when another person does not. Worse, we may look for clues that a person fits the stereotype and ignore clues that point the other way.

Three factors help people overcome prejudice and stereotyped thinking:

- Pleasant, extensive contact between people of different groups who are of equal status.

- Cooperation between people of different groups working on tasks together.

- Knowledge about other groups.

If you want to reduce your own stereotyped thinking—and we are all sometimes guilty of stereotyped thinking—then engage in those three kinds of activities. If you want to encourage other people to reduce their stereotyped thinking, encourage those activities.

Talking to Instructors

Many college students go all the way through college, four or more years, and never have a conversation with an instructor outside class.[13] That is too bad, because research shows that the more a student talks to instructors in college, the higher his or her grades tend to be.[14] In fact, the students who *most* need help in college courses are *least* likely to visit their instructor, so they continue performing poorly.[15]

There are major advantages to talking to your instructors. You can clear up points you are confused about. You can find out what is important. You can develop your ideas more fully. You can show you are truly interested in the course. You can get advice or guidance on other issues. You can learn from them.

Given those advantages, why don't some students talk to their instructors? Because they see disadvantages. What are they?

> Ross has followed the same pattern throughout school: When he is confused about or doesn't know something, he lies low, says nothing, and does not raise his hand in class or call attention to himself in any way. Thus it seems foolish to him to go to an instructor for help, because that is the very time when he should be lying low.
>
> Joe is embarrassed at the thought of going to his instructor for help. "That's baby stuff," he thinks. "I ought to be able to get this on my own without shining up to the instructor."
>
> Tess wants to talk to her instructors, but fears they will act superior to her, patronize her, or make her feel small, so she avoids them.
>
> Marie did go to talk with one of her instructors, but later a classmate said to her, "Are you having a hard time in this course? I noticed you were talking to the instructor." Now Marie avoids talking to instructors for fear other students will think less of her.

Remember how people used to think the earth was flat, but they were all wrong? Same idea applies here. The facts are these:

- The students who do the *best* in a course, not the worst, are the ones who talk to the instructor.

- Talking to instructors is a sign of intellectual maturity, not immaturity, because it means you are interested in learning.

- When you are confused or don't know something you think you should know, that is the best time to talk to an instructor, because he or she can help you learn.

■ Most instructors want their students to talk to them and are unhappy if they don't. There are, of course, a few instructors who put students down, but they are the minority.

Talking to instructors, asking for help, is just another learning strategy. In fact, the more students use various learning strategies such as time management, the more likely they are to *also* use the strategy of talking to the instructor.

People who are willing to talk to their instructors, to seek their help, are demonstrating a skills-development attitude toward learning. They want to learn and know they have to put in more practice, so they go to the instructor for ideas about their practice. You probably wouldn't try to learn to play the piano without ever talking to a piano teacher, so why should you learn your various courses without talking to the instructor?

People who avoid talking to the instructor are showing the opposite of a skills-development approach—a performance evaluation approach. They think they will be evaluated and worry how they will look, and so they avoid talking to the instructor. If this describes you, try adopting a skills-development attitude, and go talk to the piano teacher.

Shayna had been somewhat friendly with two of her high school teachers, but since entering college had hardly spoken to any of her instructors. "But I need to talk to them, to get things straight, because right now I am confused about some stuff." She thought about her four instructors and decided to first approach Dr. Rettig, her general science teacher, because Shayna was confused about several things in that course and because Rettig seemed fairly friendly.

"I was hesitant to go talk to her, even though she often said, 'Come talk to me,' because I was afraid I'd appear uneducated. But one day someone said to me, 'That's a performance orientation, isn't it?' and I realized he was right, and I needed to have a skills-development orientation. So I decided to go talk to her.

"I planned two questions to ask her, one about plate tectonics and one about convergent evolution, plus a backup question in case I couldn't think of anything to say. For the first, I would say, 'Why are the plates moving?' and for the second, 'I don't understand this idea.'"

"I told myself to focus on saying the questions clearly and listening carefully to her answers, and not thinking about what kind of impression I was making.

"It worked pretty well. I got my answers, and also found she may be pretty cool, because she has Beatles posters on her walls."

SKILL BUILDER 5.3

Talking to instructors

A. Overcome any obstacles.

1. Does learning by talking with your instructor fit your goals, or will it help you reach your goals? How?

_____

_____

_____

_____

2. Which of your attitudes or beliefs might be an obstacle to your talking to an instructor?

   Example: You feel you should not call attention to yourself; you think it will be embarrassing; you fear you will look bad; you fear the possibility of being put down.

_____

_____

_____

_____

3. How might you overcome the obstacles by adopting a skills-development attitude?

_____

_____

_____

_____

B. Plan your approach.

The best plan is to pick whom you will talk to outside class, and then plan your talk so you don't feel flustered.

1. Which instructors do you think are interested in talking with you?

_____

_____

When talking to the instructor, it works best if you do _not_ think about yourself or the impression you may be making, but focus on the questions you ask and the answers to them.

Talking to instructors

2. Write self-instructions to do this:

_____

_____

_____

_____

3. What questions will you ask?

_____

_____

_____

_____

C. Write your goals.

The ideal goal would be for you to talk with an instructor, or ask for help, whenever it is needed. Can you set a goal like this?

Write self-instructions to do this:

_____

_____

_____

_____

D. Keep records.

Keep a record of talking with instructors when it is needed. Whom did you talk with? How did it go?

Date	Instructor	Comment
_____	_____	_____
_____	_____	_____
_____	_____	_____
_____	_____	_____

Chapter 6

Class Attendance, Note Taking, and Participation

PREVIEW WITH QUESTIONS TO ANSWER

Being there

- How frequently should you attend class, where should you sit, and what are the advantages of doing this?
- What should you do to be a good listener in a lecture? How do you get yourself to focus?

Taking notes

- How do you know what to write in your notes?
- What are the outline method and the Cornell system for note taking?

Participating in Class

- What can you do to make it easy to participate in class?

Being There

Going to class

The motto of a sci-fi comedy movie and the title of a book a few years ago was "Wherever you go, there you are." That's deep. It has implications: Where you are when you should be in class has a big effect on where you are going. If you go to most of your classes, your destination is a lot easier to reach than if you don't go. Going to most classes makes it easier to study later, increases your interest in the material, helps you remember important information, and commits you to being a student.

Hideki studies a little bit more than Elana, but Elana goes to class more frequently than Hideki. Which of these two students do you think will make the better grade in the class? The answer is Elana, who goes to class

QUESTIONS TO ANSWER AS YOU READ:

- How frequently should you attend class, where should you sit, and what are the advantages of doing this?

- What should you do to be a good listener in a lecture?

- How do you get yourself to focus?

more. Of course, if Elana barely studies, she won't do well. But when everything else is equal, research shows that going to class is the most important thing a student can do to make good grades.[1]

This is true even if all the instructor does in class is go over the textbook, and it is particularly true if the instructor introduces new material in the lectures. Gordon Green went from being a high school underachiever and an unmotivated college student to eventually getting a Ph.D. and writing a book called *Getting Straight A's*.[2] He urges his readers to "never miss a class" and "always sit in the front row."

If you understand how people learn new knowledge, you'll see why going to class is so important. Knowledge is not simply passed from one person to another. The instructor does *not* "transmit" information to you. The instructor utters words, but you have to make sense out of them and build knowledge with your own words and thoughts. You have to *construct* the knowledge in your own mind. You do the construction with whatever elements you have in your mental makeup.

This is why some courses build on others. For example, you don't take advanced Spanish until you've done beginning and intermediate, and you don't do advanced algebra first either. You simply don't have the mental materials to construct knowledge in the one course until you've had the other.

Hearing how the instructor explains concepts helps you know how to do the construction. If you listen, what the instructor says will open up for you a larger number of mental elements from which to build your own knowledge. While listening to the lecture, you are thinking, and that helps you gain understanding. If all you see are someone else's notes, you aren't thinking, you are just reading, and you may not fully understand or remember what you read.

The more you work on the construction, the stronger it will be. If you construct knowledge one time while in class, and then another time while studying by yourself, your memory of it will be stronger and more complete than if you just construct it once. So, there are advantages to going to class.

But of course there are disadvantages, too. Time in class is time you cannot be doing something else. Class can be boring. Class can be frustrating, particularly if you don't easily understand what the instructor is saying. To overcome the disadvantages, remind yourself of the advantages. Refer back to the idea of life goals at the end of Chapter 1. How does going to class, and therefore doing better in your classes, relate to your life goals?

You should go to at least 95 percent of your scheduled classes. In class, you should sit near the front. Sitting in the back makes it harder to be interested in and focused on the material, and exposes you to temptations to let your mind wander. Of course, some students like to sit in the back, because that way they can delude themselves that they are trying, while at the same time letting their minds wander.

SKILL BUILDER 6.1

In class: Being there

A. Write down the advantages and disadvantages of going to class 95 percent of the time, and of sitting front and center and really listening.

Under "Advantages," tie in your life goals—see Skill Builder 1.2 in Chapter 1.

Advantages		Disadvantages
_____	■	_____
_____	■	_____
_____	■	_____
_____	■	_____
_____	■	_____

B. Keep records of attendance.

Keep a record for two weeks of attending class and of where you sat in class. Place a ✓ if you met your goal.

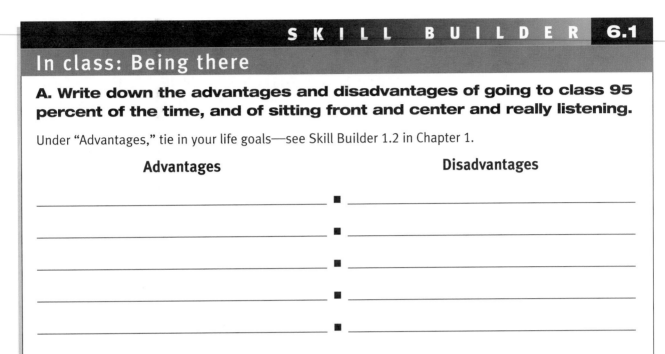

	Did I go?			Did I sit near the front?	
Class	**Week 1**	**Week 2**	■	**Week 1**	**Week 2**
_____	— —	— —		— —	— —
_____	— —	— —		— —	— —
_____	— —	— —		— —	— —
_____	— —	— —		— —	— —
_____	— —	— —		— —	— —
_____	— —	— —		— —	— —

Example:

Biology	✓ ✓ ✓	✓ ✓		✓ ✓	✓ ✓

Keeping a record like this all term helps you stay on goal. If you notice that after the two weeks your attendance drops off, reinstate record keeping, and do it as long as it helps you meet your goals for class attendance. Many keep records for a semester or more, some for their whole college career. Sometimes all it takes is a record to remind us to do what we want to do, like the runner who keeps herself jogging by keeping a record of her jogging.

Some people find it easy to go to nearly every class. This Skill Builder isn't for them. If you're one of these folks, skip ahead to ideas you do need to work on.

Some students are truly uncomfortable sitting too close to the front. If that's you, fine; don't punish yourself. But do sit as close as you comfortably can, because it really does help you stay focused on the class.

Set a goal for yourself: What percentage of the time do you want to go to class, and where do you want to sit in the class? What will you get out of it? Keep records on your class attendance and where you sit. That helps you meet your goals.

Focusing in class

Being lectured to puts us all into a passive mode, but to get the most out of a lecture, we need to be active, thinking about what we are hearing. What can you do to "focus"?

At the beginning of the lecture, be sure you're sitting away from distractions, such as other students talking to each other. This is why sitting near the front is a good idea. Give yourself instructions to concentrate on the lecture. Set your mind like an alarm clock to notice when your attention wanders in the lecture, and snap yourself back, sitting up and taking an alert posture.

> Pedro arrives in his ethnic studies class about two minutes before the class begins. He has worked out a little drill to allow himself to get the most benefit from being in class, so he proceeds with his drill. Actually, Pedro has already performed the first step in his drill, because he is wide awake and has arrived on time. Now he gets his mind ready for the lecture by looking back over his notes from the last time. This brings his mind to bear on today's topic. Sometimes he also glances over the part of the textbook that the professor is lecturing about, to see where the lecture will probably go. He thinks for a minute about the interesting points made last week when the class discussed ethnic stereotypes. Now the professor begins the day's lecture, and Pedro says to himself, "Okay, pay attention." He leans forward in his chair and works on listening deeply to the professor's words.

Pedro's drill is worth copying.

First, he has managed his time well, so he isn't too sleepy during the day. Sleeping in class is self-destructive because (1) it keeps you from learning anything and (2) it really irritates the professor. It seems disrespectful and implies that you care nothing about learning in this class.

Arriving on time is a good idea because professors often review the important points from last lecture in the first few minutes or outline where today's lecture is going. Also, it does not make a good impression on the professor if you often come late. In the world of work, coming late is the kiss of death.

A small but important tip: Lecturers hate to be asked "I wasn't here last time. Did I miss anything important?" Think for a moment, and you'll see why this irritates professors. It implies the possibility that they were talking, talking, talking, but saying nothing important. Irritating. If you do miss a class, ask instead "Is there any way I can get the information I missed?"

Pedro's idea to warm up his mind to get more out the lecture is good. You can do this by going over the last lecture notes or looking at the topics in the text. Your job in the lecture is to construct your own knowledge from the words the lecturer utters, and if your mind is warmed up to the topic, the construction is much easier. It's always a good idea to keep a construction site warm, because things don't build as well when it's too cold. In one class the professor wants the students to read the chapter before coming to class, and Pedro tries to do that each week.

Using self-instructions to get your mind focused is a good technique. You can do this not only at the beginning, but any time you notice your mind is wandering. "No," you think to yourself. "Don't think about Saturday now; focus on this lecture now."

How to listen in a lecture

Listen for the main ideas. How to spot them? Notice if the lecturer

- Repeats certain ideas.

- Goes over material you know is in the textbook.

- Stresses material with his or her voice or movements.

- Writes items on the board or overhead.

- Says certain ideas are important.

- Summarizes concepts or information.

Material stressed in this way probably contains a main idea or other important information. You may be tested on it, and you should write it down.

> Taryn wrote, "I'd never realized the instructors gave out clues about what is important in the lecture. I wrote down the six clues [above] and kept that list posted in my notebook where I would check it before each lecture. Then I would watch in the lecture to see if the instructors gave out those clues. Sure enough, they did, and—hey!—I finally knew what to take notes about in lectures."

If you miss information during a lecture, skip spaces but continue following the lecture. Don't scramble to remember what was said while the lecturer is going on to the next topic, as this will cause you to miss the next topic as well. Ask someone later for the missing information.

Sometimes you can get confused in a lecture and not be sure what to write down. It's important then to make some kind of note, so you can figure out later what the content was. If you don't note your problem, you'll not learn that material. You might just write "Check this" or "?" to alert yourself that you didn't get good notes on that topic. Then later find out what you should have written. This is an important technique to develop, because the material you miss may be on the test and because it helps you notice when you do not yet know something, an important step in regulating your own learning.

If it's hard to get good notes from a lecture, work over your notes with other students later, to be sure you got the main ideas. If you are not sure you're getting all the important ideas, it always helps to check your notes with someone else in the class.

Try to find interesting material in the lecture. Ask yourself, How does this connect with what he or she just said? or said last week? Looking for connections like that is a good way to learn, as you will see in Chapter 7.

Don't waste time judging the lecturer's delivery. Thinking, "Man, he's boring" only distracts you. Listen for the ideas, and don't judge the person's lecture skills. After all, it's the message that counts. That's what you're going to be tested on. A few months from now people will not care if the messenger was boring, but they will care if you don't know the stuff.

Let's not be naive: Some lecturers are boring or disorganized, talk too fast, or are difficult in some other way. What to do? *Ask questions.* Ask the boring lecturer for an example from real life to make material less abstract. Ask the disorganized one to provide an overview or outline of whatever process he is talking about. Politely asking the rapid talker to slow down, or to repeat, usually works. Instructors almost always like your asking questions because it shows you're interested.

THINK PIECE 6.1   **Lecture prep checklist**

Make out your own checklist to follow before a lecture, similar to Pedro's drill: Was I awake for class? Did I arrive on time? Did I get my mind warmed up? What did I do to focus during the lecture? If you keep a checklist like this, you are more likely to perform the behaviors you want.

_____

_____

_____

_____

_____

_____

Taking notes

QUESTIONS TO ANSWER AS YOU READ:

- How do you know what to write in your notes?
- What are the outline method and the Cornell system for note taking?

Making sure notes are usable

Notes don't help if you can't use them. What can you do to make notes usable?

Don't write too much. You don't learn much from a lecture if you act like a stenographer during it. Trying to write down almost everything the lecturer says means you spend no time thinking, no time searching for the main ideas. Researchers have compared the stenographic approach in class note taking to a form of note taking that encourages students to think about the material, and the results show that using a system that encourages thinking leads to better performance on tests later.[3] It's to your advantage, then, to learn a system of note taking that encourages you to think. Two systems that have proved successful are described later in this chapter.

Write in phrases, not sentences. Take notes in your own words, because you will remember the ideas better. Use abbreviations, such as dropping all the vowels in words—*drp vwls*—and use symbols, such as "+" or "&" for *and*, so you can keep up with the speaker.

Take notes on three-ring paper. This practice gives you flexibility later, because you can move the notes around to follow different organizations of the material.

Take notes on just one side of the paper. This way your notes don't get too confusing. Also make your notes in pen so they don't smudge. You will use your notes to study for tests, and if they are messy you are less likely to study them carefully, so it pays to keep them neat.

Leave lots of blank space in your notes. For example, skip a line between main ideas. This makes it easier to read the notes and to find information later. The notes look more inviting. Books use white space in order to look readable. Notice how much white space there is on this page. It's not filled up right to the edges.

Try using different note-taking formats for different courses. What format should you use for your notes? There is no one best way, but it is important that your notes be easy to read later. For example, Angie uses one method, the outline system below, for her English class because that helps her organize the discussions they have in that class, but she uses the Cornell system, described next, for her psychology class, because there is more information to be written.

The outline method

The basic idea is simple:

> Main topic
>> Supporting detail
>> Supporting detail
> Main topic
>> Supporting detail
>> Supporting detail

Novina has been taking notes in her abnormal psychology class. The illustration "Outline Notes" shows what she wrote, with a few vowels added back and abbreviations spelled out to make the notes more readable. Notice how Novina keeps plenty of white space in her notes, and doesn't act like a stenographer.

Outline Notes

Mood disorders   probs of emotion   colors all of life   severe
    pers. depressed or elated
3 disorders: depression, bipolar, suicide

major depression
    very sad   low self-esteem   pos. insomnia, fatigue, loss of appetite.
    Ernest Hemingway   Winston Churchill
    most common disorder   10% of pop.   2/3 are women
        on rise in US
    often measured with Beck scale—scores over 12
        below that is normal sadness—continuum
pos. causes   biology & environment
    neurotransmitter deficits
    runs in families
    stresses   too much punishment, too little pleasure
    learned helplessness theory: just takes punishment
    cognitive theory: notices bad, ignores good thinking as helpless or hopeful

bipolar disorder   "manic depressive"   Gustav Mahler (!)
    mood swings over time.   wild elation or irritation then depression
        high self-esteem, racing thoughts, rapid talk, wild plans
    1% of pop.

The lecturer went on to discuss the causes of bipolar disorder just as he had for depression. Then he discussed suicide in the same way, listing the characteristics and discussing the causes.

You can see how Novina organizes her notes in an outline form, with main topics such as depression and bipolar disorder and subtopics under them.

The advantage to this system is that it highlights the main ideas, making it easy to find information when you come back later in the notes. It also helps you see connections between ideas, and it really helps organize notes if the lecturer is disorganized.

The disadvantage is that you are supposed to outline as you go, but your mind may be too busy with all the incoming information to do this. In Novina's example, the instructor has a clear outline covering the three types of disorders, but sometimes the lecturer does not follow such a clear outline.

The Cornell system

Named after the college where it was invented by Walter Pauk,[4] this system requires you to review your notes after class and make additional notes.

Divide your note-taking sheets with a vertical line into two parts, the left-hand part taking up about 2 inches on the left side of the page.

While listening to the lecture you take all your notes in the right hand side. Then you go back later and make other notes in the left hand section. The basic outline of each page is shown in the illustration "Cornell System Format."

Cornell System Format	
Headings	
Main ideas	
Key words/phrases	Notes taken in class
Summaries	
Your questions	
Your ideas	

Suppose Novina had kept her abnormal psychology notes using the Cornell system. While she was writing the notes in class, Novina would have written only the material on the right hand side of the line. She would have gone back later and written in all the notes on the left side. The same notes you read in "Outline System Notes" would look like the notes in "Cornell System Notes."

Cornell System Format

<u>Mood disorders</u>	mood disorders—probs. of emotion
	colors all of life severe pers depressed or elated
three types	3 disorders: depression, bipolar, suicide
<u>major depression</u>	major depression
	very sad low self-esteem pos. insomnia,
	fatigue, loss of appetite.
	Ernest Hemingway Winston Churchill
frequency	most common disorder 10% of pop.
	2/3 are women on rise in US
Beck	often measured with Beck scale—scores over 12
	below that is normal sadness—continuum
causes	pos. causes biology & environment
biology	neurotransmitter deficits runs in families
	stresses
environ.	too much punishment, too little pleasure
	learned helplessness theory—just takes punishment
cog. theory	cognitive theory: notices bad, ignores good
	thinking as helpless or hopeful
<u>bipolar disorder</u>	bipolar disorder "manic depressive"
	Gustav Mahler (!)
	mood swings over time. wild elation or irritation
	then depression

The left column provides a summary of the material in the right. You write in organizing information, such as "major depression" and summarizing information such as "three types." You can write in your own ideas and comments such as "Who was Mahler?" or "good subject for the term paper" or "may be on the test."

The advantages to the Cornell system are that it encourages you to review your notes and to think about them so you can organize the right-side writings. You can take notes like mad in a hurried, disorganized lecture, then go back later and organize your writing with your remarks on the left side. Another advantage is that it cues you where information lies in your notes, so when you come back to study for a test, you can go straight to what you need. "Where is that stuff on cognitive theory? Yeah, here it is." Use the material written in the left side to lead your review of the ideas in the right side.

The need for review

The main purpose of lecture notes is to store information outside your memory so you can learn it later.

Lecture notes help only if you review them. To learn well, you need to review within twenty-four hours of making the notes, to organize them and to fill in missing points. What do you do in that first review period?

- Fill in gaps in your notes, such as improving spelling or adding missing information.

- Improve the organization, for example, moving a detail from one spot to another, or adding headings.

- If you use the Cornell system, you write in all the material in the left-hand column, such as headings, questions, notes to yourself.

- Begin learning the material; for example, test yourself by covering up the notes, looking only at the heading, to see if you remember what's hidden.

Reviewing your notes only takes a few minutes a day, and it's time very well spent, as it makes learning later easier. Of course, when you are studying for a test, you study your notes just as you would study the text-book. We cover how to do that in a later chapter.

Participating in Class

QUESTION TO ANSWER
AS YOU READ:

- What can you do to make it easy to participate in class?

There are at least three reasons why it's a good idea to talk in your classes: (1) talking furthers your learning, because it encourages you to think, one of the main goals of college education, (2) professors like it when you talk, assuming this means you are interested and motivated, and they will remember you when grading time comes, and (3) talking is good practice at speaking in public, a skill you will want to have in your career.

Very large lecture classes are not designed for asking questions, so perhaps you will not talk much in them. But some students actually graduate without ever having spoken to a professor, and that's too bad, for their education has suffered. Smaller classes are designed for talking, the idea being that you develop your thinking by engaging in the class conversation, and you should expect to participate.

Some students have no difficulty speaking in class. Good questions seem to pop easily into their minds, and they can ask them in a friendly,

---

S K I L L   B U I L D E R   6.2

Note Taking

A. Practice the note-taking methods.

1. Practice each of these two methods of note taking in at least one class.

   Check here when you did each.

   Tried the outline method for a whole class: _____

   Tried the Cornell system for a whole class: _____

2. Decide which you like best, or best fits that class. Then practice that method each time the class meets for a week.

3. Keep a record of the dates you used your chosen system.

   Class

   _____   __ __ __

   _____   __ __ __

   _____   __ __ __

   _____   __ __ __

B. Review your notes.

1. To encourage yourself to review your notes within twenty-four hours of making them, keep a record of doing it.

   Class   **Week 1**   **Week 2**

   _____   __ __ __   __ __ __

   _____   __ __ __   __ __ __

   _____   __ __ __   __ __ __

   _____   __ __ __   __ __ __

   Some people find that simply keeping records will encourage them to review their notes; without the records, they don't do it. If that's your case, keep records.

---

interested way. But that's not true of all of us. Most of us can use a few hints on how to participate in class. Here's what the experts say.

Remember that instructors almost always love you to talk. After all, they love what they're teaching, and like when you show interest in the subject too. Also, in small classes the instructor dislikes periods of silence, because he or she feels a lot of pressure to keep the class moving. So if you talk, it helps the instructor teach.

Try writing down questions earlier to use in class. This eliminates the stress of having to think of a question on the spot. When the instructor asks "Any questions?" you can ask one you thought of earlier.

What kind of questions might you ask? You could

- Ask about something you are confused about, a good idea because it's a safe bet others in the class are confused, too.

- Relate some concept to your personal experience or knowledge, and ask, "Is this a correct example of the concept?"

- Disagree with a theory or statement, or offer a polite criticism of it, for example, "I've read this theory now, but it is really hard for me to believe that all little children have those ideas."

- Express an opinion about some issue.

- Mention an idea, for example, an application of some concept, such as "If this is true, then wouldn't it be a good idea to . . . ?"

- Agree or disagree politely with something someone else has said, giving your reasons for your opinion.

When you do speak in class, speak loudly enough that the person farthest away can hear you. This is good practice for later, because if you speak in too low a voice when dealing with your boss, she may think you lack self-confidence. When you're in a discussion, don't interrupt others, and don't get angry even if others say things you greatly disagree with. You are much more effective if your voice and body language are under control. Your task with people you disagree with is *not* to blow them out of the water, but to change their minds, or at least change the mind of anyone listening to your discussion.

The point of participating in class, remember, is to develop your thinking. You'll best accomplish this by listening carefully to what other

---

THINK PIECE 6.2   Goals for participating

To encourage yourself to participate in class, set a goal for how often you would like to talk; then keep a record in your notebook for each subject. Start low, and gradually increase how much you participate. Give yourself reminders to talk. Pick classes that are easy to talk in because the instructor is supportive.

Reminders to talk: _____

Classes it will be easy to talk in: _____

Record the number of times you talked in class. For each class each week, place a ✔ if you talked.

people say, and by pondering what you think about what they say. So, don't participate just to participate; talk to develop your thinking.

> Taryn, who had made a list of ways instructors might indicate the main points in their lectures, also made a list of the ways she could participate in class. She copied the list and kept it in her notebook. When she felt she should participate in a class, she would check her notebook, scribble down a statement that occurred to her, and, when the right time came, volunteer it. Once an instructor said to her "You were right on the borderline between A and B, but I remembered how you always participated in class, so I gave you the A."

Critical Thinking

PREVIEW WITH QUESTIONS TO ANSWER

Thinking critically means asking questions

- What is the difference between a memory question and a thinking question?
- What are six thinking questions you could ask in class?

Problem solving: A way of thinking

- What is the four-step process for solving problems?

In the last chapter we discussed participating in class discussions. Students shouldn't participate in class just to make a good impression on their instructors, although that, of course, is nice. They should participate because talking in class encourages people to think, and *thinking* is what college is about. Thinking means talking about ideas. One of the main things employers are looking for when they choose to hire someone with college training is the ability to think, because thinking greatly helps people do their work well.

Many students come out of high school believing that there are right and wrong answers to things, and they just want to learn the right ones. Then in college they find that the instructors often don't talk that way, but instead want to "discuss" ideas. Learning the "correct answer" is not the only point in college. Instead you are asked to analyze, evaluate, conceptualize. That is, think.

Thinking doesn't occur automatically. It's a skill, which means that, like other skills, it requires practice. You need to know what to do, and then practice doing it.

Thinking Critically Means Asking Questions

The key to thinking is asking questions. This means you take an *active* approach to the ideas you learn about in your class. If you are passive, you just write down the idea, maybe memorize it, and that's that. If you are active, you ask questions about the idea. What are its parts? How does it relate to other ideas? What do you think about it?

QUESTIONS TO ANSWER AS YOU READ:

- What is the difference between a memory question and a thinking question?
- What are six thinking questions you could ask in class?

There are real advantages to developing your skill at asking questions. Research has shown that if you ask questions, you will learn the material more easily[1] because you think about it more intensely and make connections between ideas. Asking questions doesn't just make you look good, it actually helps you learn the material in a course. But it's important to understand what kinds of questions we are talking about.

Make a distinction between memory questions and thinking questions. An example of a memory question is "What are the planets in our solar system?" An example of a thinking question would be "How is Earth similar to and different from the other planets in our solar system?" Memory questions ask only for regurgitation of information: "In what country is the play *Hamlet* set?" Thinking questions ask us to think about the information in some way. "Why did Hamlet waver so long?"

Sometimes you have to ask memory questions. The first question you should always ask yourself is "Do I understand this?" when you are trying to get the information straight. "Excuse me, what did you say were the three main points?" Or "Can you, please, explain how this process works?" These are inevitable, but don't limit yourself to memory questions. Understanding comes more easily if you ask thinking questions.

How do you ask thinking questions? It helps to have a guide. Professor Alison King, of California State University at San Marcos, has developed generic questions students can use to ask thinking questions about the material they are studying. King's research shows that asking these questions helps students learn the material better and do better in their courses.[2] Below are questions which combine King's work with that of others to produce a guide to asking thinking questions.

How to use the guide

Use the generic questions as starters, then fill in the blanks with the material from the course you are studying. For example, one of the generic questions is "What do you think causes . . . ?" In your English class you might ask, "Well, what causes Hamlet to act that way?" In a psychology class you might ask "What causes people to use stereotypes so much?"

You can either ask the question directly in class, or ask *yourself* the question to stimulate a question you can ask in class. One of the generic questions is "What is an example of . . . ?" In your class when the instructor is discussing some concept, you could ask the instructor, "What is an example of that?" Or, if you asked yourself, you would say to yourself, "What is an example of that?" Then you would think of an example, and that would give you your question: "Is . . . an example of this concept?"

Initially, Kurt was skeptical about the idea of asking himself questions that would lead to asking questions in class. "I don't see how that will work." But he promised himself he would try.

In his sociology class the topic was the statistics used in doing public opinion polls, specifically, the law of large numbers, which he was not sure he understood. He decided to use one of the generic questions and asked himself, "Why would a large sample of some group be better than a small sample? For example, would a large sample of African-Americans tell us more about African-Americans in general than a small sample?"

Immediately, he saw the truth of the law. "Yeah," he said to himself. "There is a tremendous variety in the attitudes and beliefs of African-Americans, and if you had only a small sample, you might miss some of it; you would just get a stereotype. But with a large sample, you would probably get all the varieties, so you would have a better overall picture of the group."

He raised his hand and said to the instructor, "Let me see if I have this straight. Take African-Americans: They are tremendously varied in their attitudes and beliefs. If we sampled a great many African-Americans, we would have a better chance of getting the full picture, but if we had a small sample we might not. Is that right?"

"Perfect," said the instructor.

The directions for using the guide are simple: Pick a generic question, then fill in the blanks with material from the class you are in. Either ask the resulting question directly, or ask it to yourself and let that lead to a question you ask in class.

Generic questions

Here's a list of six generic questions, with examples and some discussion, you can use to stimulate your thinking in class and out. These questions[3] encourage you to think in several different ways: to seek definitions of concepts, to analyze them, to think about cause and effect, to ask for evidence, to apply the concepts to the rest of life, and to evaluate them.

Question 1: "What is your definition of . . . ?" Whenever there is a classroom discussion, it is a good idea to be sure everyone is using a similar definition of some word. Commonly, we assume that everyone is, but this is often *not* true. Many disagreements between people occur because they are using different definitions of a word. For example, suppose you are in English class and one of the students says, "I just think Hamlet was dumb, that's all." You are confused. Dumb? Does he mean unintelligent? or self-destructive? or indecisive? or what? So you ask, "What is your definition of *dumb*?" or "What do you mean by *dumb*?" If you think *dumb* means "unintelligent" but the other person is using it to mean "self-destructive," you need to clear that up.

Question 2: "Why . . . ?" or "Explain why . . ." This kind of question encourages you to analyze something you are studying. In an astronomy course, the question might be "Why do the planets stay in their orbits?" In a psychology course, the question could be "Why do researchers need a control group to be sure of their conclusions from an experiment?" In English class the question might be "Why is this example of writing better than that one?" Asking "Why?" is a good way to get yourself to think. But note that this is a Ping-Pong kind of question, for the instructor may bounce it right back to you: "Well, why do you think?" Then you get to answer it, which may be the best way to develop your own understanding.

Question 3: "What causes . . . ?" or "How does . . . affect . . . ?" These questions ask for an analysis of cause-effect relationships. In your astronomy class you might ask "What causes moons to spin off from planets?" In psychology you could ask "What causes racial prejudice?" or, to use the other question, "How does a person's educational level affect his or her racial prejudice?" Asking yourself these questions will lead you to ask thoughtful questions in class. For example, if you asked yourself the question "How does a person's educational level affect his or her racial prejudice?" then you might ask in class "Does racial prejudice go down or up as a person's educational level goes up?"

Question 4: "What is an example of . . . ?" or "Is . . . an example?" Examples encourage us to apply a concept to the world, to find if we understand the concept well enough to see it operating in the world. Often, when you first learn an abstract concept, you won't be able to see any examples, so it helps to ask the instructor for examples. Some instructors teach the basic concepts in class, then ask for examples of them on the tests. If you ask in class "Is . . . an example of . . ." then you get to find out if you understand the concept well. If it is an example, you've got the concept, and if it isn't, you've learned an important difference. If you ask yourself if something is an example of a concept, you are testing your understanding of the concept.

Question 5: "What is the evidence for this statement?" or "How do we know this is true?" or "Why do you think that?" Is some statement true or merely an opinion? If there is evidence that supports its being true, how strong is the evidence? If someone says, for example, "You know, college students are pretty lonely," you can ask, "How do you know that? What's your evidence?" If the person says, "Well, the two guys who live near me in the dorm are lonely," that's weak evidence, because those two may not be typical. If the person says, "I read a research report that

SKILL BUILDER 7.1

Using generic questions to encourage thinking

A. Practice asking questions.

1. Make a list of the six questions to use and keep the list in a convenient place for use during class. (You may find that you tend to use one or two of the questions more than the others, which is okay, but try using a variety of questions.)

2. Set a goal for yourself: How often do you want to ask a question and therefore practice thinking?

   Goal: _____

   _____

3. The goal may be too far away to be reached immediately. Use small steps to move toward it.

   Beginning step _____ Next step _____

   Next step _____ Next step _____

   Next step _____ Next step _____

Example: "I'd like to ask one good question in each class each time it meets. Right now I almost never ask a question. So I will begin asking one question in one class per week. Then I'll go to two classes, then three, and so on, until I'm asking one question per week in each class. I won't try in Professor Brown's class, because he just lectures all the way through and doesn't seem to like it when we ask questions. If I encounter difficulty in any class, I will not try to advance in that one, but will press on in the other classes."

B. Keep a record of meeting or not meeting your goal.

Class _____ Date _____

Class _____ Date _____

Class _____ Date _____

Class _____ Date _____

Class _____ Date _____

Class _____ Date _____

Class _____ Date _____

Class _____ Date _____

Class _____ Date _____

Class _____ Date _____

Class _____ Date _____

Class _____ Date _____

Class _____ Date _____

Class _____ Date _____

Class _____ Date _____

Class _____ Date _____

Class _____ Date _____

Class _____ Date _____

Class _____ Date _____

Class _____ Date _____

Class _____ Date _____

Class _____ Date _____

Class _____ Date _____

Class _____ Date _____

Class _____ Date _____

Class _____ Date _____

Class _____ Date _____

showed 28 percent of students were lonely," that's stronger evidence because it is presumably based on a larger, more typical sample. And, as you know, there may also be conflicting evidence.

One of the biggest differences between well-educated people and others is that the well-educated often want to know what the evidence is for some belief, and they evaluate the strength of the evidence. For example, suppose a person who passionately believes in an idea offers evidence for its truth. We know we can't be quite as confident about that evidence as we could be if someone who is uninvolved with the idea finds evidence to support it.

Question 6: "Which is best?" or "What do I think about . . . ?" or "Do I agree or disagree with . . . ?" These questions call for an evaluation of something. In English class you might ask yourself, "What do I think about Hemingway's writing?" and that might lead to an evaluation you can state in class. "It seems to me that his writing . . ." In political science class you might ask yourself, "What do I think about capitalism?" and then venture a opinion to be discussed in class. When you state evaluations, keep in mind that someone may ask you for the basis of your evaluation. "You say you don't like his writing style. Why not?" If you are prepared for this question, it's easy to answer.

> Taryn, who is enthusiastic about keeping lists, wrote these six questions on a three by five card that she keeps in her notebook. She takes out the card and keeps it in front of her while in class, so she is reminded of the kinds of questions she might ask. If there is a lull and she doesn't have to take notes for a while, she reads the questions to see if she can apply them to the present class. If she can, she asks a question.

Of course you will not learn everything there is to know about critical thinking in one chapter like this. The topic comes up again and again in your college education. For example, it comes up here again in Chapter 10, in the part on the research process, when you ask questions about the information you get from the library or the Internet.

Problem Solving: A Way of Thinking

QUESTIONS TO ANSWER AS YOU READ:

■ What is the four-step process for solving problems?

Life is full of problems, and thinking about them is often the only thing you can do to solve them. For example, the boss wants a job done in three days but it seems to you the job will take five, or you have a problem in your weekly schedule and don't see how to deal with it. Some people are better at solving these kinds of problems than others are. What are the differences between people who are good at solving daily problems and others?[4]

Poor problem solvers often don't try to do anything to deal with a problem. Just ignoring problems won't always work: They don't go away. Second, poor problem solvers often do the first thing they think of, but that is often not the best solution to a problem. The best solution may take time to figure out, and it may be a combination of the first few solutions. Third, good problem solvers try to think about a problem from different points of view. They don't focus from just one angle; doing that may blind them to the solution. Talking over a problem with others is often a good solution if you're stuck, just because others may see the problem from a different point of view.

Solving problems means thinking about the obstacles you face to figure out how to overcome them. Below is a guide to solving problems, a set of steps to go through when you need to think about a problem. Research has shown that when people use this approach, they actually solve problems better,[5] so it is worthwhile learning it. If you pay attention to your own problem solving, you get better at it.

You could think these steps through by yourself or talk them over with another person. If the problem is complex, it helps to keep notes.

You don't just go from step one to two to three to four in a line. You can go back and forth. For example, while working on step two you might think of more things to list in step one, which is good. Then later on, in step four, you go back to work some more on step three.

Step 1: List the details of the problem as concretely as possible

Don't list abstract statements like "I'm not getting along with the boss." Instead, list specific statements like "When I suggested dropping the X project, the boss got mad." Listing specific events changes how you see the problem, from something huge to something manageable.

Listing the details also helps you break big problems into small ones, which are often easier to solve. This is the same idea as dividing a large goal into subgoals, steps you can take to reach the big goal.

Sometimes just dealing with the details will actually solve the problem. For example, a couple who started off thinking they "had a problem with their love life" solved the problem by simply getting a child-proof lock on their bedroom door.

Try to list as many details as you can.

Step 2: Think of as many solutions to the problem as you can

To think of solutions, use the technique called *brainstorming,* which has four rules:

- *Try for a quantity of ideas.* Quality will come if you have quantity.

- *Don't criticize your ideas at this point.* Criticize later. Criticism tends to cut off the flow of ideas. Some people tend to criticize as soon as they have an idea—"Nah, that won't work"—but that is a mistake at this point, when you are just trying for quantity.

- *Try to think of unusual ideas, wild ones.*

- *To think of new ones, try to combine ideas.* The best solution is often a combination of approaches.

During this period you may think of more details to list in step one.

Step 3: Choose one or more solutions to the problem

Think of obstacles to each solution and see if you can think of ways to overcome them. Figure out ways to get your chosen solution to work. Use brainstorming for this.

Step 4: Putting your solution into practice, and then evaluate it to see if it works

Often people think of solutions to a problem, try them out for a few days, but then drop them before they have had a chance to work. Trying to change your study behavior, for example, is going to take several days. If you think of a good solution to a study problem but then only try it out for a couple of days, you are not giving it enough time to have a beneficial effect.

If the solution does not work, repeat this process.

> Angel wrote, "I have recently returned to college after several years working. I have been trying to learn to manage my time better—I procrastinate on school work a lot—but frankly, I am coping with a divorce at the same time, and there is just too much stress in my life. School, work, divorce, trying to make new friends—they get me down. A lot of the time I am just too stressed to do my time management right. I decided I should try problem solving.
>
> "I started making a list of the details that kept me from meeting my time-management schedule:
>
> "I feel upset and have a couple of drinks, which makes me lazy and I don't work.
>
> "Sometimes I spend a long time thinking about my stupid, failed marriage, wondering what I could have done better, or what he could have done better.
>
> "I cry a lot; I just feel stressed-out a lot.
>
> "I have to work forty hours per week, which, plus commuting, takes maybe forty-five hours.

THINK PIECE 7.1   Practicing problem solving

Like all other skills, your problem solving gets better with practice. If you are a novice at four-step problem solving, realize you will need to practice several times before the four-step process becomes a habit. The research is quite clear, however; if you take the trouble to practice this, you will find that you gain much greater control over your problems.[6] Write out the four steps, and use them when you are thinking about your problems. They really work, but only if you use them.

"When it's time to do my schoolwork, I start to feel sorry for myself and think things like, 'Do I have to do this on top of everything else?'"

Angel then brainstormed a bunch of solutions:

"I could drop out of school; I could stop the divorce and try to patch it up (ha!); I could stop drinking, I could drink more; I could quit work and go on welfare; I could stop feeling sorry for myself; I could say, 'Girl, things will get better'; I could take up exercise as a way to relieve stress. I could cut back on the number of classes I'm taking."

Angel then picked several of these as the solutions to try. "First, I've got to stop feeling so sorry for myself; it wrecks me. So, I will tell myself to stop thinking that way. I'm going to use a lot of positive talk to keep myself up. Things will get better, I know. Second, I am going to start an exercise program, which will help with stress and will have the added benefit of making me look better, which I'm going to need. Third, I think I will drop one of my courses, at least for now."

Finally, Angel realized she had to really do these things in order for them to help. "I began keeping a record of my exercise in the kitchen: Each day I would check off whether I did it or not. I told myself never to feel sorry again, and each time I started, I gave myself a mental jerk and substituted some positive thought such as 'This will pass. Things get better over time.' And I told the school I was dropping that one course: no problem. Then I worked out my new time-management program, and started life again."

Part IV

Reading and Researching: Exercise for the Mind

Our bodies need exercise. Without it, we become dull and flabby. Physical exercise even lifts mild depression, and it makes us feel alive. It gets rid of the blahs. People often say, "I can't believe how much better I feel when I get some exercise."

Our minds, too, need exercise. *Reading is exercise for the mind.* It gets rid of the mental blahs. Some people think of reading as passive, but it is not. Your brain is active when you read. The squiggles on the paper have to be converted into words, and the words have to be given meaning. That is accomplished in your brain, not on the printed page.

Meaning does *not* move from the page into your mind. You have to *make meaning* from the words on the page. You have to *construct* meaning from the words. That requires mental activity, good exercise for the mind.

Chapters 8 and 9 focus on development of excellent reading skills. The exercises make you more skilled at reading. Do you need them? Here are some questions to answer to assess your need for or interest in improving your reading skills:

❶ How much do you like reading? (Place a check mark at the spot that represents your feelings.)

NOT AT ALL   LOVE IT

Reason for this question: If you work on developing your reading skills, you will like reading more. If you don't like it now, try the exercises in this chapter and see if you like it more later. You will, because you will be better at it. It's hard to dislike something you're getting better at. Liking reading means you will read more, and that is good for your grades and job prospects.

❷ Is it worth your while to put out effort to increase your reading skills?

Yes _____   Maybe _____   No _____

❸ Do you believe that if your reading skills improve, you will make better grades and will probably earn more in your career?

Yes _____   Maybe _____   No _____

Reasons for these questions: It's true that you will make better grades and earn more if your reading skills improve. If you believe that this is true, does that affect your answer to question 2? Is it worth while working on your reading skills if your grades and later job prospects will improve?

❹ Do you believe you can improve your reading skills through practice, if you just know what to practice?

Yes _____   Maybe _____   No _____

Reason for this question: The next two chapters show you how to improve your reading skills. They tell you what to work on and how to work on it.

❺ How much do you know about college libraries and the Internet? (Pick one.)

1	2	3	4	5
NOT MUCH	A LITTLE	SOME	PRETTY MUCH	A LOT

Chapter 8

Increasing Reading Skill

PREVIEW WITH QUESTIONS TO ANSWER

Beliefs and facts about reading

- What are the advantages of increasing your reading skill?
- Is speed reading a good idea for students?
- What bad reading habits should you try to stop, if you have them?

Increasing your reading

- What steps can you take to increase how much you read?
- How can you bootstrap to increase reading?
- What does it mean to adopt a skills-development attitude about reading?

Reading and TV

- What is the effect of extensive TV viewing on reading?

Beliefs and Facts about Reading

Some people think of reading as a skill they learn in elementary school, needing no more development in later years. Their assumption is that people learn to read as children and all they have to do after that is increase their vocabulary. Actually, this is wrong. People do *not* stop developing their reading skills after elementary school. These skills increase throughout our lives, *if* we continue to read.

Our bodies need exercise throughout life, and so do our minds. Recent research shows that the development of reading skills goes on throughout life. Working on your reading skill in college is not remedial.[1] You're *not* making up for some lack. Rather, you are developing your mind. College is a particularly good time to increase your reading skills, because there are heavy reading assignments in college.

QUESTIONS TO ANSWER
AS YOU READ:

- What are the advantages of increasing your reading skill?

- Is speed reading a good idea for students?

- What bad reading habits should you try to stop, if you have them?

Advantages of reading well

Being able to read well gives you power. There are real advantages to increasing your reading skills. Reading is the basic verbal skill. If you are good at reading, and do it enough, your writing, spelling, vocabulary, and critical thinking all improve. There is a strong relationship between reading skill and grades in college.[2] The better the reading, the better the grades.

Reading well gives you access to higher-level jobs. People who develop excellent verbal skills in college earn a higher level of lifetime income.[3] There is a lot of discussion about what the good jobs of the future will be like, but one thing we know: They will require much reading.

Students can significantly improve their reading skills. If you use the kinds of exercises outlined in these two chapters, your reading comprehension—your skill in understanding what you read—will increase.[4] The goal is to become a reading expert. The route to this goal is through practice. If your current skill level is high, then only a little bit of practice is required. If your current skill level is lower, you will need more practice, but you can still reach the goal.

You may not be sure what your current level of skill is, but that doesn't matter. Just try the exercises and do the practice.

The mechanics of reading

When reading, you need to be comfortable, but not so comfortable that you fall asleep. Sit upright in a good chair. Be sure to have good lighting. Pick a place with no distractions. If there are distractions, move.

Speed reading is *not* recommended. In speed reading your eyes skim down the page one line at a time. Unfortunately, this reduces your understanding of what you have read, because you miss ideas.

Some instructors tell their students to skim over the textbook material they have to read, but research shows that this is a mistake. If you are already expert at some topic, as the professors are, you can skim material and learn from it. But if you are *not* yet an expert, which describes most students, then skimming lowers your comprehension of the material.[5] With skimming, we only comprehend the most basic ideas. We miss all the important details, the complexities. About one of the most complex and detailed novels ever written, Tolstoy's *War and Peace,* the comedian Woody Allen joked, "I took a speed reading course once. We read *War and Peace* in twenty minutes. It was about Russia."

There are some things you can do to increase your reading speed without sacrificing comprehension. Number one is to read more. The more you read, the better you get at it—just as with any other skill that you practice—and this means your reading speed and comprehension will improve.[6]

THINK PIECE 8.1 Bad Habits

Subvocalization and going back over words are bad reading habits. Both can be eliminated by conscious practice on your part. The more you practice reading, the less these problems will occur. If you think you often subvocalize or go back to reread phrases, use these exercises to encourage yourself to stop.

1. When you are beginning to read, give yourself instructions *not* to subvocalize or reread unnecessary phrases.

Write your self-instructions: _____

_____

_____

> **Example:** Harry says to himself, "Okay, sometimes I say the words when I'm reading. Don't do that. Try to read in phrases, not individual words." Gail tells herself, "Break this habit of rereading phrases. When I'm reading, don't let myself go back to read stuff again."

2. While you are reading, you can't constantly be paying attention to how you are reading; you want to read, not think about reading. But you do want to notice if your bad reading habit occurs. It is possible to set our minds like an alarm clock to go off when a certain event occurs. Set your mind to notice when you do your bad habit, so you will automatically stop. Just tell yourself, "Notice when [my bad habit] occurs."

Write self-instructions to notice (take the time here to actually write out instructions to yourself):

_____

_____

3. Keep track of reminding yourself in these ways. When you begin to read, pause to give yourself the instructions and then make a check in your notebook to show yourself that you did it. If you have already started reading and then remember, pause for a moment to give yourself the instruction. After you have developed the habit of self-instructions to read well, your problems will go away.

When we read, our eyes don't move smoothly across the words. They actually jerk from phrase to phrase across the page, fixing on each phrase for a moment and then jerking to the next one. These eye jerks—called *saccades* (pronounced "sa-KADS")—should occur phrase by phrase, *not* word by word. For example, look at this sentence:

> She flushed the alligator down the toilet in San Diego,
> but it came up in L.A.

If you read that word by word, you have to make sixteen saccades across the sentence because there are sixteen words. But suppose you read it in phrases:

She flushed the alligator   down the toilet   in San Diego but it came up   in L.A.

That's only five saccades; fewer saccades means much faster reading. If you could read the sentence in four saccades, you would read even faster.

Some writers suggest trying to widen your saccades, including a larger number of words per unit, because if you can do this you will read faster. The easiest way to accomplish this, however, is *not* to consciously think about your saccades. Simply practice reading more. If you read more, you will read better, with fewer saccades. The more you practice reading, the easier it is to use good-sized saccades. Your eyes and brain automatically make the adjustment.

Bad reading habits

If you notice that when you read, you almost say the words out loud—this is called *subvocalization*—you should try to stop. That's because saying each word causes you to fixate on each word. But you need to read in phrases, not words. Subvocalization slows you down because each word gets too much attention. Try to group the words in phrases, and jerk your eyes from phrase to phrase.

Going back to reread material also slows you down. If you read "She flushed the alligator . . ." but then go back to read "the alligator" again, you're slowing yourself down. Read each phrase just one time. Then move on to the next.

There are times when you need to go back to read material over. For example, If you are reading very difficult material, you may want to go back to read sentences over. But even then, you reread sentences to get the idea, not individual words. If you are going back to reread words as a habit, even for easy material, you should try to stop.

Increasing Your Reading

In a report for her Freshman Experience course, Luz wrote, "When I was a girl I used to love to read. I could read my favorite Judy Blume or R. L. Stine books all day. I would even stay in the house to read instead of going out to play in the sunshine. Now that I'm in college, I realize I have to read more and I have to be sure I comprehend what I'm reading. You have to pay attention to the details and know the meaning of the material. Every class has tons of reading to accomplish.

"I figured I should set myself the goal of reading four hours a day. I know this won't happen right away because, as of today, the maximum I read a day is about one hour or so, and I do that only about three or four times a week. In order for me to be able to read four hours a day, I have

QUESTIONS TO ANSWER AS YOU READ:

■ What steps can you take to increase how much you read?

■ How can you bootstrap to increase reading?

■ What does it mean to adopt a skills-development attitude about reading?

to set a schedule that slowly leads me to the goal.

"The first week I will read four hours, the next five, the next six. Then I'll increase by thirty minutes each week. This is going to be a long process. It might even take a year, but I can accomplish the goal by the end of spring semester."

Luz decided that if her goal for each week was accomplished, she would buy herself small things on the weekend to make her feel good about her progress. "One weekend I bought ice cream and a movie; the next daisies; the third sushi."

She also kept a chart on which she scheduled reading for each week. "Below each scheduled time was a little box. In each empty box a sticker could be placed, but only if the reading time was accomplished. Those cute little stickers were an incentive for me to fill up all the boxes. I love them, and it really got me when I didn't get to put one in.

"My schedule worked for two weeks, but not the third. I missed three times because of my job responsibilities. I realized that once in a while, things are going to come up unexpectedly and you have to deal with them. When this happened, I told myself, 'Luz, you'll have to just get back on the path, and you'll be all good.' The important part for me was to try again the next week and not give up."

When Luz analyzed her chart, she realized that reading four hours a day five days a week was too much for her. "It was overwhelming and left me no time to enjoy myself. I'm an outgoing, nineteen-year-old college female. So I made some revisions. I scheduled more hours on Monday, Tuesday, and Thursday, and less time on Wednesday because of job meetings, and even less on Fridays. I felt that this way I wouldn't get sick and tired of reading, plus I would have time to go out with my friends.

"Looking at my six-month plan inspires me. I put it on my door so I can see it every day as a reminder. I think it's going to be a pretty successful project after all."

Taking steps to increase your reading

Followed up a year later, Luz was quite successful in college. She was taking challenging courses like chemistry and calculus, was doing well in them, and was having a good time. She was reading at her goal level. Her plan had several elements that led to her success:

- She set reading goals.

- She scheduled her reading time—didn't just wait for it to happen.

- She gradually increased her reading time.

SKILL BUILDER 8.1

Increase your reading

A. Decide on your reading goals.

Reading Goals: _____

_____

B. Schedule your reading.

Start at a level near your current level; then gradually move toward your goal. If you are not sure what your current level of weekly reading is, make an estimate. Over several weeks, gradually increase so you can move toward your final goal.

Scheduled reading times for the first week

Sunday	Monday	Tuesday	Wednesday	Thursday	Friday	Saturday
___	___	___	___	___	___	___
___	___	___	___	___	___	___
___	___	___	___	___	___	___

Example: Wendy thinks she reads about 2 hours a week, but would like to do much more. Her first goal is to read 4 hours per week. Her schedule:

Sunday	Monday	Tuesday	Wednesday	Thursday	Friday	Saturday
5:00–6:00	5:00–5:45	(Work)	4:30–5:45	5:00–6:00	5:00–6:00	___

C. Reward yourself for sticking to the schedule.

Your rewards: _____

_____

Example: Wendy wrote, "If I stick to my schedule, I can watch any TV program I want all week. If I don't stick to my schedule, I will first do some reading and only then let myself watch TV."

D. Problem-solve

If you are able to meet your schedule, gradually increase in later weeks. At the end of the first week, Wendy met her goal, so she increased her goal to 4 ½ hours for the following week. If you do *not* meet your schedule, revise your goals and your schedule.

What interferes with meeting your goal? How can you deal with that little problem? Write down the details of the problem and possible solutions:

_____

SKILL BUILDER 8.1

Increase your reading

_____

_____

_____

Examples: "I scheduled too many hours. I will lower my requirements." "I scheduled hours right after three hours of class and was too tired to read seriously. Take a break, then read." "I just was not in the mood. I asked myself, 'When will I be in the mood?' and scheduled reading for then."

E. Revise your reading goals.

Revised goals: _____

_____

F. Revise your reading schedules.

Revised schedule

Sunday	Monday	Tuesday	Wednesday	Thursday	Friday	Saturday
_____	_____	_____	_____	_____	_____	_____
_____	_____	_____	_____	_____	_____	_____
_____	_____	_____	_____	_____	_____	_____

If you meet your schedule, repeat it each week, with any increases you want.

G. Keep a record of your practice.

Keeping a record will encourage you to read. Are you moving closer to your goal?

Total time spent reading:

Week 1: _____   Week 2: _____   Week 3: _____

Week 4: _____   Week 5: _____   Week 6: _____

Week 7: _____   Week 8: _____   Week 9: _____

Week 10: _____   Week 11: _____   Week 12: _____

Week 13: _____   Week 14: _____   Week 15: _____

SKILL BUILDER 8.2

Bootstrapping reading

Should you try bootstrapping to increase your reading? Do you feel you are reading enough, or nearly enough? If your answer to the second question is "Yes," then you don't need to bootstrap. If—in all honesty—your answer is "No" or "Probably not," then give bootstrapping a try. Remember, if you want something you have never had, you need to do something you have never done.

A. Follow the bootstrapping procedure.

1. Decide on the material to bootstrap.

2. Decide on the unit of time you will read.

3. Schedule the reading.

4. After each unit, decide to continue or to stop.

5. If you decide to stop, do one more unit and then stop.

Reading material to bootstrap: _____

Size of the (small) time unit: _____ Scheduled times to begin: _____

Example: "I'm going to bootstrap reading my sociology text. The time unit will be 15 minutes. I will begin at 8:00 P.M. this Monday. Then I'll start again at 8:00 on Wednesday."

B. Schedule times to repeat

Schedule enough times to get yourself reading. If you don't want to schedule too many times now, schedule just a few. See if you have scheduled enough to get you reading regularly. If so, great. If not, schedule more, and continue until you're reading regularly.

_____   _____   _____

- She rewarded herself for sticking to her schedule with goodies and stickers.

- She expected failures and was not thrown by them.

- She revised her plan when necessary and never gave up.

To increase your reading, set goals for yourself: "I will read for thirty minutes" or "I will read ten pages." Whatever your ultimate goal is, start where you are now and take small steps to reach the goal. Expect some failures, and make adjustments when failures happen.

Keep a record of your total time spent reading each week. If you value reading, keeping a record of your reading will encourage you. The record

SKILL BUILDER 8.2

Bootstrapping reading

_____   _____   _____

_____   _____   _____

_____   _____   _____

_____   _____   _____

C. Keep records of your practice.

1. Make a ✓ each time you begin as scheduled. (If you don't have many successful beginnings, use a smaller time unit—so small you can't not do the reading—and then reschedule.)

2. If you decide to stop after the first unit but correctly do one more unit before stopping, place a second ✓. That will mean you did two units.

3. If you decide to continue, place a ✓ for each time you decide to continue. The number of checks will equal the number of units you did.

Example: "I'm bootstrapping reading my astronomy text: Ten-minute units."

Your schedule might look like this:

| Mon. 1:30–1:40 | ✓ [began on time] | ✓✓ [did two more units] |

encourages you to read up to your goal level and allows you to see how you are progressing.

Skill Builder 8.1 will help you schedule and keep track of your reading.

Bootstrapping reading

In Chapter 4 you met the idea of bootstrapping to deal with procrastination. You can use this idea to get yourself started reading, if you do not start up on your own. If you are already reading several hours per week, you don't need this, but if you are not, you should give this a try.

To bootstrap reading, decide on a small unit of time that you are willing to read. You might pick fifteen minutes. Pick a unit so low that you know you can do it. Then, schedule that time. For example, "Monday night, 7:30—read for fifteen minutes." At the appointed time, do the reading.

When the fifteen minutes are past, you decide whether you will stop or not. If you want to stop, you do one more unit and then stop. If you want to continue, do another unit. Repeat this, unit by unit, until you stop. There is no rule about how many units you have to do.

Many students have used bootstrapping to get themselves started reading challenging material. Picking a time unit small enough that you know you can succeed gets you started. Yet you can stop after any unit without guilt as long as you do one more.

Use Skill Builder 8.2 to help you with bootstrapping reading.

Bootstrapping will work—it will get you reading more—but only if you

- Follow the rules for bootstrapping.

- Keep records of doing the bootstrapping.

- Repeat the process several times.

> "I had been dreading starting reading my Spanish because it seemed hard, but by bootstrapping I got myself into it. It turned out reading Spanish wasn't as hard as I had feared. And I didn't have time to get too frustrated, because I could always quit after one more unit."

You feel as though the process is under your control, so if you begin to be frustrated or bored, you do just one more unit and then quit.

Adopting a skills-development attitude and focusing your motivation

Just work on increasing the amount you read. Compare yourself to yourself, not to others. You are *not* competing with other people, only with yourself. "Let's see. Last week I read for three and a half hours, but this week I did four. That's good."

Don't worry about grades for now. Just work on doing the practice.

Realize that sometimes you will make a mistake. "Uh, last week I read three and a half hours, but this week I only read three. Better work on my schedule."

THINK PIECE 8.2   Self-reminders

When you find your motivation lagging, use self-reminders about

- The advantages of improving your reading skills.
- How you need to put out more effort to do better.

Write here some self-reminders to use:

_____

_____

_____

Realize, also, that you will need to put out effort. Practicing a skill requires effort.

Some people avoid reading because they think it requires too much effort or is boring. Reading seems like jogging: They may know it is good for them, but it seems like too much work. Reading isn't really that hard, and learning new ideas is not boring. Like jogging, you can start at a very low level and increase only as the activity gets easier for you. You wouldn't try to jog three miles until you could comfortably jog one, and the same idea holds for reading. The more you read, also, the easier it gets.

Reading and TV

QUESTION TO ANSWER AS YOU READ:

- What is the effect of extensive TV viewing on reading?

The more you watch TV, the less you read.[7] There are only so many hours in the day, and if you spend many of them watching TV, that's several hours you aren't doing anything else. Watching TV is definitely *not* exercise for the mind. In fact, while most people feel better after physical exercise, many people feel *worse* after watching TV for a long period. TV requires only our gaze, but reading engages our minds.

Some TV, of course, is relaxing and entertaining, and TV can be informative. It's too much TV that is the problem. TV is like food: Some is beneficial, too much creates problems. If you kept track of how you spend your time in Chapter 2, you already have a good idea how much you view TV.

In your own view, are you watching too much? If you are, TV viewing is cutting down on your reading, and on your education. Ask yourself, "Does watching TV a lot fit with my life goals?"

If you feel you are watching too much, there are a few actions you can take. First, don't watch just anything. Look through the *TV Guide* to see what's on, and then turn on the TV only to watch specific programs. Make a list of your favorite programs, and watch only them. Schedule some reading time when you might watch TV. For example, "Tuesday night, 7:00 to 8:00—don't watch TV; read instead."

Schedule something else *instead* of TV. If you don't do this, the empty time created when you try to cut down TV will fill up—"Nature abhors a vacuum" the philosopher Spinoza said—and it might fill up with more TV. Your new schedule might be as follows:

Mon. 8:00 P.M. [when you used to watch] Exercise—walk or bike
Tues. 9:00 P.M. [when you used to watch] Read
Wed. 7:00 P.M. [when you used to watch] Call friends or go out with them

The hours when you used to watch TV, but now want to do something else, are scheduled with some other activity that you value more highly.

SKILL BUILDER 8.3

Life goals and TV viewing

A. If you haven't already done so in Chapter 2, keep track of your TV viewing for several days.

1. Be careful to get an accurate count.

Total Hours Watched Each Day

Sunday	Monday	Tuesday	Wednesday	Thursday	Friday	Saturday
_____	_____	_____	_____	_____	_____	_____

2. How does that amount of viewing fit with your life goals? Write your answer here:

_____

_____

_____

B. If you want to cut down your TV viewing, try these techniques.

1. Set a limit on the number of hours to view each day.

Allowable Amount of TV Viewing Each Day

Sunday	Monday	Tuesday	Wednesday	Thursday	Friday	Saturday
_____	_____	_____	_____	_____	_____	_____

Place a ✓ each time you stay within your goal.

2. Write self-instructions to get yourself to stay within your goal:

_____

_____

Example "No, I'm going to turn the TV off now. I scheduled two hours allowable TV viewing today, and that's the two hours. I have to cut it off now to gain control."

3. Gradually lower the number of viewing hours each day.

New Goal: Allowable Amount of TV Viewing Each Day

Sunday	Monday	Tuesday	Wednesday	Thursday	Friday	Saturday
_____	_____	_____	_____	_____	_____	_____

Place a ✓ each time you stay within your goal.

4. Write self-instructions to get yourself to stay within your new goal:

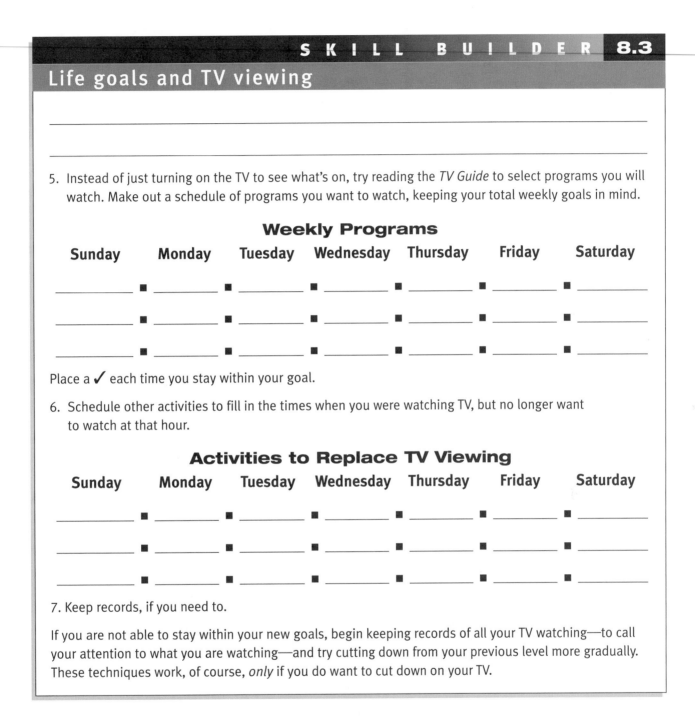

SKILL BUILDER 8.3

Life goals and TV viewing

_____

_____

5. Instead of just turning on the TV to see what's on, try reading the *TV Guide* to select programs you will
    watch. Make out a schedule of programs you want to watch, keeping your total weekly goals in mind.

Weekly Programs

Sunday	Monday	Tuesday	Wednesday	Thursday	Friday	Saturday
___ ▪ ___	___ ▪ ___	___ ▪ ___	___ ▪ ___	___ ▪ ___	___ ▪ ___	___
___ ▪ ___	___ ▪ ___	___ ▪ ___	___ ▪ ___	___ ▪ ___	___ ▪ ___	___
___ ▪ ___	___ ▪ ___	___ ▪ ___	___ ▪ ___	___ ▪ ___	___ ▪ ___	___

Place a ✔ each time you stay within your goal.

6. Schedule other activities to fill in the times when you were watching TV, but no longer want
    to watch at that hour.

Activities to Replace TV Viewing

Sunday	Monday	Tuesday	Wednesday	Thursday	Friday	Saturday
___ ▪ ___	___ ▪ ___	___ ▪ ___	___ ▪ ___	___ ▪ ___	___ ▪ ___	___
___ ▪ ___	___ ▪ ___	___ ▪ ___	___ ▪ ___	___ ▪ ___	___ ▪ ___	___
___ ▪ ___	___ ▪ ___	___ ▪ ___	___ ▪ ___	___ ▪ ___	___ ▪ ___	___

7. Keep records, if you need to.

If you are not able to stay within your new goals, begin keeping records of all your TV watching—to call
your attention to what you are watching—and try cutting down from your previous level more gradually.
These techniques work, of course, *only* if you do want to cut down on your TV.

Valerie reported, "I resisted the idea of keeping a record of
how many hours a week I watch TV, until I realized I was
resisting because I really didn't want to admit to myself how
much TV I was watching. I was fooling myself, thinking I
would keep it a secret from my professor if I didn't have
records, but I was really keeping it a secret from myself. So
I kept a record for one week. I was upset to see I watched
TV more than eighteen hours that week. That really seemed
like too much. That's more relaxing than I need.

"By looking at my record I could see that there are eight programs that are favorites: a weekly basketball game, *Antiques Roadshow, Law and Order, Baywatch,* and some others. So I scheduled those eight hours. I didn't want to try to cut down just to eight, however; so I also allowed myself three free viewing hours each week. That gave me some flexibility, and the total was only eleven hours, quite a cut from eighteen. I felt good about that.

"The first week, however, a problem came up. I would watch one of my eight favorites and then just keep on sitting there after it was over, and watch something else. I realized

---

B O X 8.1

Encouraging Your Kids to Read

If you don't have kids, read this anyway, because the chances are you will someday. Hodding Carter, a great Southern journalist, once said, "There are only two lasting bequests we can hope to give our children. One of these is roots; the other is wings." Encouraging your child to be a reader does both.

The best thing you can do to help your kids become readers is to read to them. Jed Gaines, the founder of Read Aloud America, has these suggestions:[8]

- Pick a reading time when you and the kids are relaxed, for example, bedtime or snack time. Get comfortable.

- Don't make reading time a chore. It's not class time. Have fun.

- You don't have to be a great reader yourself. Read from the heart.

- Keep it short.

- Make connections between the story and other things. For example, talk about the story—perhaps relate it to something on TV, at school, or at home.

- Let the kids have books of their own, to take them to bed, to be encouraged by.

- Have your own little library of favorite books at home.

- Take your kids to the library, and get each one a library card.

I had to schedule something instead of TV for those hours. I made up a new schedule. It had my eight scheduled hours to view TV, and allowed three freebies, but four other new hours were scheduled for reading, which I need to do anyway, and one for exercise.

"I taped my schedule to the TV, with instructions to myself to get control of my TV watching. If I went over the limit, I made a frowning face on the sheet. That only happened a few times, because mostly now I am only watching what I schedule, plus those freebies. And I actually do feel better about myself."

You can even use TV to reward reading. First do the reading; then follow that with a favorite program that you don't get to watch unless you have done the reading: "I don't allow myself to watch TV until I have done the scheduled reading for the day. I do the reading, then I watch."

Strategies for Reading Well

Reading Like an Expert

The goal is to practice reading so that you are reading more effectively. But what does "reading more effectively" mean? What would you be doing? Educational psychologists have studied reading experts, people who do a lot of reading, such as professors. They find that these experts actually do some things that others may not do.

First, they have a set of reading strategies they employ, and they use these in different situations. For example, they tend to look for answers to questions they have when they read something and they adjust the speed of their reading to the kind of material they are reading.

QUESTION TO ANSWER AS YOU READ:

- What characteristics do reading experts exhibit?

Second, reading experts pay close attention to their own understanding as they read, so they are very aware of how well they are getting whatever they are reading.

Third, the experts do a lot of thinking while they are reading—relating what they read to what they already know and making evaluations of what they are reading.

Those characteristics of expert readers give us a plan of study: Practice what the experts do. We will cover

- Using reading strategies
- Monitoring understanding while reading
- Thinking while reading

First, you learn what they are, then you can practice them.

Using Reading Strategies

Adjust your speed and the depth of your reading to the material

QUESTIONS TO ANSWER AS YOU READ:

- When should you skim and when read actively?
- What can you do to warm up your mind for reading?

Solana is reading the newspaper over her morning coffee. Her eyes skim over the headlines, looking for an article she might want to read. She finds one, reads the first two paragraphs, gets the idea, doesn't need any more details, abandons that article, and looks for more headlines. She finds another, reads the first paragraph, decides she isn't interested in this, abandons it. She finds another; it's interesting, related to her main love, travel. She reads every word; she goes back and reads parts over again; she stops and thinks about the content for a minute, relating the topic to a recent trip she took. Interesting. Then, her eyes skim on.

All reading is not the same. It's not necessary to read everything at the same speed or with the same amount of concentration. Adjust your reading speed, and degree of concentration, according to what you are reading. Solana would not read her textbooks the way she reads the newspaper. She has different purposes for reading the newspaper and her textbooks, and the materials differ in their ease of reading. She adjusts her reading depending on what and why she is reading.

Later in the morning Solana is studying her chemistry textbook. She selects a four-page section to work on. First, she skim-reads only the headings, subheadings and **bold-faced** material in the four pages. Then she reads a summary at the end. She then goes back to the beginning of the section and reads every phrase, carefully, trying to understand the material as she goes. She has changed her reading considerably since she was reading the newspaper.

Skimming. Skimming is the fastest way to read, but it gains us the least depth of understanding. When should you use skimming?

First, as Solana does while reading the paper, skim when you are looking for something specific. She was looking for articles of interest to her. You might just want to get the general idea of some article or a textbook assignment, not read the details, so you would skim it. For example, Solana runs into an article on the cost of travel in France. She skims it to get a general idea of whether France is cheap or expensive, but skips information about details such as museum hours and locations.

Second, skimming is good for getting an overview of the material you will then read more carefully. That is what Solana did when she first read the headings and subheadings of her chemistry text. She was trying to get a general idea of the material to come. Having an outline of the material in mind as you read makes it easier to learn the material.

Third, skimming is good when you have already learned the material and are going back to review, as before a test. When Solana reviews for her tests, she does not want to have to read all the material over again. She skims material she has read before, searching for the main ideas to remember on the test.

Reading for understanding. Most of the time your goal in reading something is to understand it. For example, you want to understand some ideas in your textbook because you will be tested on them.

If your goal is to understand the material, then normal reading—your usual pace in which you read each phrase—is the best choice. You are probably using your active, normal pace as you read this text. Be sure that your eyes don't just skim over the material. Try to understand it as you read it.

If you can read the material at your normal pace and understand it the first time, that's great. If you have difficulty getting the material, try slowing down a bit. Also, go back and reread critical sentences, a phrase at a time, looking for the *meaning* of the sentence, not the particular words.

Have your goals in mind

It is helpful to have in mind what your goals are when you begin to read something. Why are you reading this material? When Solana scans the newspaper, for example, she is looking for interesting stuff. When she reads her chemistry text, she is preparing for a class. Clarifying the purpose of your reading helps you adjust your reading speed and depth, and tells you what you should be doing while reading.[1]

Skip around, if that helps

Some people think that when they are reading they *must* go from the start to the ending just as the material is written. This is *not* necessary. There is no law that you have to start reading at A and go on through to Z without any detours.

> Solana's eyes, for example, when skimming the newspaper, don't go in any particular order. She might skim three or four headlines on page 1, then turn to page 2, see it is mainly ads, skip on ahead to the editorials on page 9, and then go back to page 3.

Expert readers do *not* start at A and read right through to Z. They skip around in the material, looking for answers to questions that come up in their minds, looking for the big picture and checking on facts.

In fact, reading straight through from A to Z can make understanding the material harder. A group of college students were given an article on the medieval Battle of Hastings in England.[2] The article started off with a mass of detail about the people who were in the battle. After three pages readers were mired down in too much detail, too many knights and shires and debts and allegiances, too many marches and detours. On page three was a summary, which if read first, would have set everything straight. But most students did not read the summary. They just started at the beginning and plodded on, growing more confused with each paragraph. (In Chapter 13 you'll get a full-fledged plan for previewing material to avoid this kind of problem.) Not skipping ahead to read the summary, to get your bearings, can make it much harder to understand the material.

If you are bogged down in whatever you are reading, look around for signposts that will help you understand the material. These might be summaries, or the headings. Or you might reread some material. If you are confused, do not just slog on. As a student who had a tendency to blindly plough on ahead once jokingly remarked, "Having lost sight of my goals, I redoubled my efforts." Not a good plan.

Get your mind warmed up for reading

No sensible runner would start out at a fast pace without warming up first. You're not likely to sprain your brain if you don't warm up before reading, but you won't get nearly as much out of the material if you don't warm up before reading. You need to get your mind in gear. The purpose of these activities is to make your brain active, so you process the incoming information well and learn it more easily, and to organize your mind so you can construct knowledge from what you read.

Previewing. One of the best ways to warm up your brain for reading is to look ahead at what you are going to read. If you are reading a textbook, you can look ahead and read the headings to come, to begin to develop a sense of what you will be reading. For example, if you had looked ahead in this section you are now reading, you would have seen these headings:

Using Reading Strategies

> Adjust your speed and the depth of your reading to the material

> Skimming

Reading for understanding

Have your goals in mind

Skip around, if that helps

Get your mind warmed up for reading

> Previewing

with other heads yet to come.

If, as you began to read this section, you had looked ahead to read just those headings, you would have found out what you were going to read. Previewing the material in this way warms up your brain. Once you know what to expect, your brain can more easily construct the knowledge you need to get from your reading.

Asking questions. One good trick for warming up your brain before reading is to ask questions about what you're going to read. An experiment at a museum in Amsterdam shows the advantage of this technique.[3] The museum houses one of Rembrandt's famous paintings, *The Night Watch*, depicting a group of men who patrolled and protected the city. It's a huge painting, taking up a whole room. In the experiment people who were going in to see the painting could pause to ask any sort of question about the painting before they saw it. They might ask "Who are the people in the painting?" or "Why is it so large?" or "Why is it so famous?" or "How much was Rembrandt paid for it?" or "When did Rembrandt live?" or "What was the night watch?" People who asked questions like this found the painting *more interesting* than people who did *not* ask questions.

Questions bring our brains alive. They create interest, and they give us something to look for—the answer to the question.

Talented sports announcers, for example, create interest by raising questions. At the beginning of an important game, the announcer asks, "Can the university remain undefeated?" "Will the coach's notorious problems affect how the team plays?" "Will Wallace's bad leg be a problem? Can she play at all?" "And what about the opposition? Will they cave in, or stand tall in the face of this great offense?" The audience is now primed to watch to get answers to those questions. Questions make things interesting.

The questions you ask don't have to be particularly deep. For example, when you previewed this section you saw the heading "Skimming." You might have asked, "Is the author going to recommend skimming, or not?"—a good question. Then you could read looking for an answer to your question.

Making predictions. A related strategy to warm up your mind is to make predictions about what you will read. Someone just going in to see *The Night Watch,* for example, might say to himself, "Gee, Rembrandt was paid by these men to paint them. They wouldn't like it if he made them look ugly. I wonder if he flattered them. I bet he did. They will all look just perfect." That's a prediction. Now the viewer can see if his prediction is true or not. Did Rembrandt flatter all of them?

> When Solana notices the article on the costs of traveling in France, she thinks to herself, "I bet it's expensive." That's a prediction about what the article will say. Then she reads the article, but with her brain engaged by the prediction. She is looking for information to support or refute it.

Experts often make predictions about what they are going to read.

If you know very little about the material, how can you predict anything? A good source of predictions comes from previewing the material. If you look over the headings before you start detailed reading, ideas will occur to you. Suppose you had previewed this section and seen the heading "Skimming." You might have predicted to yourself "I bet he doesn't recommend skimming."

Suppose you are reading a section in your psychology textbook on hypnosis. The heading is "Are Hypnotic Effects Genuine?" In other words, are they real or fake? You don't know, but you can make a prediction to yourself: "I bet they're real." Then you read looking to see if you are right.

As you read, relate what you are reading to what you already know

While Solana is reading an article about travel to France, she is relating the material to what she knows about travel, and about France. If she reads, for example, that a typical hotel room in France costs about $80 a day, she may think, "Gee, a hotel room costs only about $60 in Spain." Experts often relate what they are reading to what they already know.

You may not know the subject matter you are reading—this might be your first course in psychology or chemistry—but you can still relate the material to what you know. Suppose you're reading in your chemistry book that gasses can be compressed. You might think "Oh, yeah, that's like putting oxygen into a scuba tank under pressure." Or suppose you're reading about a principle in your psychology text. You might think to yourself, "I remember the time my mother did something like that." By thinking of these examples, you have related the material to what you already know.

Use questions like these to relate what you already know to new material you're reading:

- Do I know an example of this?

- Do I know about anything in life that is like this?

- Is this useful somehow?

Summary: Strategies for expert reading

Adjust the kind of reading you do to (1) your goals and (2) the kind of material you are reading. Skim sometimes, read actively sometimes, skip around sometimes.

Get your mind warmed up for reading. Ask questions. Make predictions. Relate what you are reading to what you already know.

Practice these ideas extensively. If you do only a little practice at this, you will not get much effect.[4] unless you are already a very expert reader. If you practice these skills a lot, you can expect a strong improvement. Remember, the measure of your success now is *not* immediately better grades. The important question is, How much do you practice using the strategies? If you do the practice, the grades will follow.

Skill Builder 9.1 will help you practice strategies for expert readings.

Getting the Main Ideas

QUESTION TO ANSWER AS YOU READ:

- Where are the main ideas in a text likely to be found?

Expert readers of nonfiction don't read for the words; they read for the ideas. In poetry and fiction, the words are all important, but for textbooks or articles in magazines and newspapers, it is the ideas that are important. It is of the greatest importance that those ideas be expressed clearly. Your task while reading is to search for the ideas.

Look at the first sentence in a paragraph

Where can you find the main ideas? Chapters and articles are constructed by paragraphs. The main building block for a writer trying to explain something is the paragraph. Each paragraph contains one unit of thought. In clear writing each paragraph contains one main idea, along with details that support that main idea in some way.

The main idea in a paragraph often comes as the first sentence. For example, where is the main idea in the paragraph you are currently reading? It's the first sentence.

SKILL BUILDER 9.1

Practicing expert reading strategies

A. Prepare to practice reading strategies.

1. Make copies of this form to use several times.

2. Select some material to use while you practice these exercises. You can use one of your textbooks, a novel, a magazine, or a newspaper. However, it is important to repeat this practice several times using different reading materials, because that allows you to practice varying your strategies as the material varies.

3. If this is all new to you, practice the techniques one at a time, but be sure at the end to practice all techniques together.

B. Warm up for reading.

Preview the material you have chosen. Then ask questions and make predictions about what you are going to read. Write instructions to yourself to warm up:

_____

_____

_____

_____

Example: Lindsay begins to read her textbook, saying to herself, "Okay, I should warm up first. Let's see. Look over the headings . . . [pause] Okay, got the headings. Now, what questions occur to me? Oh, yeah . . ."

Write questions to ask about your practice reading:

_____

_____

_____

_____

_____

Write predictions about this material:

_____

_____

_____

_____

_____

C. Adjust your reading depending on your goals and the type of material.

Write instructions to yourself to make this adjustment as you do the reading:

_____

_____

_____

_____

Example: Luis begins to work on his College Success textbook. The page has outlined questions, and some paragraphs. He thinks to himself, "I'll just skim this. It isn't too hard, and I don't have anything written to do on it." Later Luis is working on his English composition text. "I better read this slowly," he thinks. "It's hard, and the instructor will want me to know it."

S K I L L   B U I L D E R   9.1

Practicing expert reading strategies

D. Relate what you read to what you already know.

Write instructions to yourself to relate what you read to what you already know:

_____

_____

_____

_____

Example: Before beginning to read his English composition text, Luis reminds himself, "When I'm reading this, I'm going to think about papers I've written before, or need to write now, so I can relate this stuff to what I know."

E. Reflect on what you have done.

1. For this reading, did you . . .
   Use warm-up questions?_____
   Use predictions? _____

2. While reading, did you . . .
   Skim? _____ Read thoroughly? _____
   Both? _____ Skip around? _____

3. How could you do this whole procedure better next time?

   _____

   _____

   _____

   _____

   _____

   _____

F. Keep a record of doing this practice.

Occasion and date:_____

Practiced which strategies? (warming up, adjusting reading speed, relating material to what you already know)

_____

_____

Occasion and date:_____

Practiced which strategies? _____

_____

_____

Occasion and date:_____

Practiced which strategies? _____

_____

_____

Occasion and date:_____

Practiced which strategies? _____

_____

_____

G. For the remaining practice sessions, focus on your textbooks, but use different ones on different occasions.

Occasion and date:_____

Practiced which strategies? _____

_____

SKILL BUILDER 9.1

Practicing expert reading strategies

Occasion and date:_____

Practiced which strategies? _____

_____

_____

Occasion and date:_____

Practiced which strategies? _____

_____

_____

Occasion and date:_____

Practiced which strategies? _____

_____

_____

Occasion and date:_____

Practiced which strategies? _____

_____

_____

Occasion and date:_____

Practiced which strategies? _____

_____

_____

Occasion and date:_____

Practiced which strategies? _____

_____

_____

Occasion and date:_____

Practiced which strategies? _____

_____

_____

Occasion and date:_____

Practiced which strategies? _____

_____

_____

Here is another example of the main idea coming first. The author has been discussing categories of drugs—depressants such as alcohol or stimulants such as caffeine.

Marijuana does not fit neatly into one specific category of drugs. In some ways it acts as a depressant, but in other ways it does not. In very high doses it can produce hallucinations: seeing or hearing things that are not there.[5]

Some authors write almost all their main ideas as the first sentence in each paragraph. You could read just the first sentences and get most of the ideas in the material. For example, look at the first sentences of the first three paragraphs in this section:

1. "Expert readers of nonfiction don't read for the words, they read for the ideas."
2. "Where can you find the main ideas?"
3. "The main idea in a paragraph often comes as the first sentence."

Those three first sentences tell all.

Look at the last sentence in a paragraph

Not all main ideas come in the first sentence. Look again at the first paragraph of this section, which begins "Expert readers . . ." Although the first sentence has an important idea in it, the most important idea in the paragraph is the *last* sentence, "Your task while reading is to search for the ideas." The statement about expert readers ties this material to the earlier material about what experts do when reading. The next few sentences lead up to the conclusion, the final sentence.

If you don't find the main idea in the first sentence, look at the last.

If the paragraph begins with a question, the main idea will be the sentence in the paragraph that answers the question. For example:

> Is marijuana smoking harmful? Marijuana smoke is harsh, and users typically hold it in their lungs as long as possible, so it is not surprising to learn that it damages lung tissue.[6]

The second sentence answers the question raised in the first.

Check for unfocused paragraphs

Unfortunately, authors do not always put the main idea in an easy spot to find. Sometimes the most important idea in a paragraph is buried, neither the first nor the last sentence. Here's an example:

Pavlov showed that salivation could be conditioned. Watson showed that fear could be conditioned. What else could be? The immune system—the set of systems within the body that seeks out and eliminates foreign objects such as tiny pieces of dirt, germs or cancer cells—can be conditioned.[7] . . . . There are then six more sentences in this paragraph, so the main idea—"The immune system can . . . be conditioned"—is buried in a mass of words. That can make getting the main idea much harder for the reader. The first three sentences in this example lead up to the main idea. If the author had a chance to write this again, the sentence about the immune system would start a new paragraph, and its definition would not interrupt the main idea. No writer is perfect, so sometimes you have to search for the main idea in a paragraph.

Sometimes the main idea is not stated at all. This is particularly true in literature. In good literature the writer's job is to "show, not tell." You don't write, "Tom was mad"; you write, "Tom slammed his fist into the door." The reader has to use her brain to figure out that Tom was mad. That makes fiction more engaging. In textbooks, however, the author usually is clear enough to state a main idea, but not always.

You can practice finding main ideas with Skill Builder 9.2.

Keeping Track of Your Understanding

QUESTIONS TO ANSWER AS YOU READ:

■ What is comprehension monitoring?

■ What techniques can you use to get meaning from your reading?

When experts read, they pay attention to their understanding. They ask themselves, "Am I getting this?" That is constantly on their minds. When they don't get something, they notice right away, and do something about it. This is called *comprehension monitoring.*

Cassie is reading her general science textbook, impatient that it is taking so long. She looks ahead to the end of the chapter, asking herself, "How much longer is this going to take?"

Not the right question. Cassie should be asking herself, "Do I understand this?"

If you want to avoid wasting your time, then you should *want* to understand what you are reading. Just skimming your eyes over a text is a waste of time if you are not building your understanding. Even if you will eventually be tested on some textbook material, your first goal is *not* memorization; it is understanding. Understanding makes memorization easier. (We will get back to this in Part V.)

When you are reading, your task is to construct meaning from the words on the printed page. If your eyes are moving over the words but you are *not* building meaning from them, then you should notice this, and do something about it. There is little point in just moving your eyes around.

One of the most important skills you can learn in college is to notice when you do *not* understand something. Remember that one mark of an educated person is knowing when you don't know. You need to engage in *metacognition,* which means thinking about your own thinking, noticing what you are thinking.[8] You need to pay attention to your level of understanding, asking as you read, "Am I getting this?"

> Reid is reading a paragraph in a magazine article about philosophy. It's explaining postmodernism. As his eyes move over the material, Reid thinks to himself, "I don't understand this." He slows down his reading, trying to take in the ideas. At the end of another paragraph Reid thinks, "I still don't understand this." He goes back and reads the two paragraphs over again. He still does not think he is getting it.
>
> Reid skips ahead to look at some later paragraphs to see if perhaps they will help him understand. Maybe if he understands the later material, the earlier paragraphs will be decipherable. However, it doesn't help.

SKILL BUILDER 9.2

Finding main ideas

How good are you at finding the main idea in a paragraph? If you feel you're pretty good, skip this exercise. If you feel you could use some practice, do A, B, and C below. If you feel you're "average," do the exercise so you'll get better than average. If you think you know how to do this but usually do not do it, do B and C.

A. Over a period of a few days, pick three different paragraphs from at least three different books.

Find the main idea in each paragraph. Spread out this practice; don't do it all at once.

To check on your understanding, do this exercise with another person. Each of you separately finds the main idea, then you check with each other to see if you both agree. If you don't agree, talk about why not.

1. Text: _____ Page: _____

   Main idea in the selected paragraph: _____

   _____

   _____

2. Text: _____ Page: _____

   Main idea in the selected paragraph: _____

   _____

   _____

3. Text: _____ Page: _____

   Main idea in the selected paragraph: _____

   _____

   _____

C. Look for main ideas.

Do you look for main ideas when reading? You will increase the chances that you will if you have self-instructions to use. Write self-reminders to look for the main ideas:

_____

_____

_____

_____

Keep a record of consciously looking for main ideas while reading.

Occasion and date: _____
Looked for main ideas (✔):____

Occasion and date: _____
Looked for main ideas (✔):____

Occasion and date: _____
Looked for main ideas (✔):____

Occasion and date: _____
Looked for main ideas (✔):____

Occasion and date: _____
Looked for main ideas (✔):____

Occasion and date: _____
Looked for main ideas (✔):____

Occasion and date: _____
Looked for main ideas (✔):____

Occasion and date: _____
Looked for main ideas (✔):____

Occasion and date: _____
Looked for main ideas (✔):____

Occasion and date: _____
Looked for main ideas (✔):____

Occasion and date: _____
Looked for main ideas (✔):____

"Man," he says to himself, "this is terrible writing. It's way too abstract. The author needs to give an example or something."

Reid asks himself, "Do I really need to know this?" Since he is not going to be tested on this subject and will probably have chances later to understand postmodernism, he drops the material. Bad writers get dumped.

Reid was engaging in metacognition, thinking about his thinking. He monitored his understanding of what he was reading and made adjustments when he concluded he was not understanding. This is a reading skill often employed by reading experts. It would be inefficient to read without understanding.

Problems with understanding what you are reading

There are a variety of reasons why you might not understand something as you read it. It could be badly written like the material Reid was reading. You cannot assume that just because something has appeared in print, it is well written. A lot of material in newspapers, for example, is written hurriedly and then edited accommodate to space limitations, and it can become garbled. A lot of material in textbooks is too abstract, without clarifying examples. Some writers fail to appreciate their duty to explain things clearly.

A second reason you might not understand something is that you do not have the background necessary for understanding. That could have been Reid's problem. He didn't know enough about philosophy to understand an abstract description of postmodernism.

A third reason for not understanding is *not relating* the material to what you already know. If you think of an example, or explain the material to yourself, or tie the ideas to things you already know, it is much easier to understand what you are reading.

A fourth reason, of course, is simply not trying hard enough to understand, not moving slowly enough or paying close attention. If all Cassie is doing is dragging her eyes over the material until she gets to the end, she is not likely to fully understand what she reads.

Strategies to use when you don't understand what you are reading

Here let's list some basic things to do. You probably do some of these already.

- Read the material over again.

- Read more slowly.

- Read it aloud to yourself.

- Find the parts you don't understand, and see if there are words there you don't know the meaning of. Look them up.

- Rephrase the material in your own words.

- Try to think of an example.

- Relate the material to what you already know.

- Look ahead to see if there are clues there that will help.

Research shows that many adults do not efficiently pay attention to their understanding as they read.[9] This means that many of us would benefit from practicing this skill. Other research shows that the more readers monitor their comprehension while reading, the more they get out of the material.[10] Paying attention pays off.

Practice monitoring your reading comprehension with Skill Builder 9.3.

Evaluating and Thinking about the Material

QUESTION TO ANSWER AS YOU READ:

- What questions should you ask as you read something?

When you are reading, think about what is written. Is it true? Is it accurate? When experts read, they evaluate the material as they read. They do *not* simply accept what is written as true. As you read, ask yourself, "Do I agree or disagree with what I am reading?"

We all know to do this at some level. For example, most adults know that tabloid headlines are fiction.

"Woman Gives Birth to Frog!"

"Aliens Take Over Stock Market!"

It's easy to tell that headlines like these are not true. But a lot of what is written is not so outlandish. Much material is written in shades of gray. Is it true? Is it false? Both true *and* false? There may be no obvious clue one way or the other. We have to think.

Experts think while they are reading. They question what they are reading. Even if you are new to a subject, you can think about it, ask questions about it. Not everything we read is true, but we have to think to realize this.

The best way to think while you are reading is to ask questions as you read. Various authors have written long lists of the kinds of questions you could ask yourself while reading. A long list won't help, however, because it is too much to remember. So, here's a short list.

Question One: What are the author's biases, or the point of view?

A lot of what is written has a viewpoint, some bias that the author follows. If the bias is very obvious, it is easy to notice. For example, if you

Practicing comprehension monitoring

If you think you already keep track of your understanding well, you don't need this. But don't fool yourself. If you are making less than very good grades, this is a skill you should work on.

A. Select some textbook material to use while you practice paying attention to your understanding.

Write instructions to yourself to pay attention to your understanding as you read:

_____

_____

_____

_____

Example: "Without thinking about it, sort of automatically, I will ask myself if I am understanding what I am reading, and if I am not, I'll go over the material again."

B. Practice daily.

Stop at the end of every paragraph or page, whichever fits the reading better, and ask yourself if you understand the material. Do this consciously, deliberately, for at least ten units of reading—paragraphs or larger—every time you read for ten or more days.

Example: Ronnie is working on his astronomy text. After each large paragraph, or two small ones, he stops and says out loud, "Did I understand that?" He does this for ten paragraphs. Then he tries to remember to do it for the rest of the reading.

The next day he is working on his philosophy text and repeats the exact procedure.

C. Record your practice.

Keep a record of your practice (✓) with the date:

Day 1:_____   Day 2:_____   Day 3:_____   Day 4:_____

Day 5:_____   Day 6:_____   Day 7:_____   Day 8:_____

Day 9:_____   Day 10:_____

If you find that you pay attention to your understanding without this conscious practice and record keeping, that's great. If you do _not,_ however, continue to practice deliberately and keep records of your practice. When you realize you are, automatically, keeping track of your understanding, you can stop the deliberate practice.

read "This truly evil man . . . ," you know the author doesn't like him. But biases can be more subtle.

A bias can be a slant in favor of some position or other. An article by an official of the National Rifle Association (NRA), for example, is likely to be against gun control. An article by a National Football League (NFL) coach is probably going to be in favor of football. A person trained in psychoanalysis is going to like psychoanalysis, and a philosopher is going to like philosophy.

Question Two: Is what you are reading fact or opinion?

A fact is some piece of information that has a basis in reality. It's a fact, for example, that a particular person has two eyes and that they are dark brown. An opinion is a judgment we make, a favorable or unfavorable evaluation. It is an opinion that the particular person's two dark brown eyes are beautiful.

Suppose you read in the newspaper, "Today the state House of Representatives passed House Bill No. 129. This is going to have dire consequences for our state." Which part is fact and which part is opinion?

Facts and opinions are often mixed this way, so that as you read, you have to think to disentangle them. If you just accepted everything as fact, then, in this example, you would think it was a fact that there were going to be dire consequences. But that's not yet a fact; it's only an opinion.

Question Three: What is the evidence to back up what the writer is saying?

If a statement is true, then there should be evidence to show it is true. Writers often make statements that have no evidence to back them up. "Astrology works!" For any statement you read, you can ask, Does the evidence back that up? If someone says "Travel in Costa Rica is really cheap," you might respond, "Really? How much does a hotel room cost?" You're asking for evidence to support the idea that travel there is cheap.

If a writer offers no evidence, we need to notice that, take it into account. You can write anything, after all—for example "My uncle has no belly button"—but the crucial question is, Is there evidence?

THINK PIECE 9.1   Thinking while reading

The point of this exercise is to practice thinking—asking questions—while you read.

1. Pick some reading material, like an editorial in a newspaper or a textbook to practice with. Don't use a news article or a science text because these may contain only facts. You want some opinions to deal with.

2. Write self-instructions to ask questions while you are reading.

_____

_____

Sometimes it helps to say your questions out loud, so you notice them.

Example: Rochel is set to read her history text. She says to herself, "Okay, remember. While I'm reading this first page, ask things like 'Is this fact or opinion?' or 'What is the evidence for that?'"

3. Keep a record of your practice.
   Record your practice (✓) with the date:

   Day 1: _____ Day 2: _____ Day 3: _____ Day 4: _____ Day 5: _____

   Day 6: _____ Day 7: _____ Day 8: _____ Day 9: _____ Day 10: _____

SKILL BUILDER 9.4

Practicing what expert readers do

You've just read about the techniques of expert readers. Maybe you already do all these things, or maybe you don't do very many of them. If you don't do them, you should practice them. But practicing all of them at once can be too much. So, make choices.

A. Below is a summary of the techniques of expert readers: Read them, and think about them.

Which do you *most* need to practice? Which are you already pretty good at, so you need less practice?

Expert readers:

1. Adjust their speed of reading to their goals and the material. They skim, they read thoroughly; they skip around.

2. Warm up their minds before reading. They ask questions and make predictions about what they are going to read.

3. Relate what they are reading to what they already know.

4. Look for the main ideas, and tie these together.

5. Continuously keep track of their comprehension. When they don't understand, they immediately take steps to correct this.

6. Evaluate what they are reading. They think critically about the material. They ask questions like, What is the bias here? or Is this fact or opinion? or What is the evidence?

B Prioritize the reading techniques for yourself.

Which should you practice first, which second, and so on? If you have not yet done them, go back and repeat the Skill Builders for the activities you most need to develop. Later do the ones you postpone.

Assign practice priorities to the techniques—which to practice most, which next most, and so on:

1: _____ 2: _____ 3: _____

4: _____ 5: _____ 6: _____

C. Keep a record of your practices.

Record what you practice, with the date.

Occasion: _____

Technique used: _____

Occasion: _____

Technique used: _____

Occasion: _____

Technique used: _____

Occasion: _____

Technique used: _____

Occasion: _____

Technique used: _____

Occasion: _____

Technique used: _____

Occasion: _____

Technique used: _____

Occasion: _____

Technique used: _____

Occasion: _____

Technique used: _____

Also, how good is the evidence? If a person says, "I went to Costa Rica for three weeks," we feel that person's evidence is stronger than the evidence of someone who says, "Oh, I just heard travel there was cheap." A small amount of evidence is not as convincing as a large amount. Suppose a person says, "My aunt smoked all her life, but she lived to be eighty-nine." We have to balance that statement against statistical evidence based on millions of people that smoking shortens lives.

There are two traps we can fall into here. One is the failure to notice that you are only getting *some* evidence, that something is left out. An astrologer writes, "Here's a case of someone who benefited by listening to my predictions." Is this a case of selective evidence, where we only hear evidence that supports the idea, and don't get the evidence that doesn't? We might think, "How many people didn't benefit?" Often writers present the evidence that supports their idea, but neglect the evidence that does not.

The other trap is failing to see that the writer is substituting *an appeal to some authority for evidence.* An authority is someone who is an expert in the subject, or someone who is in command. Often it is reasonable to take the word of an authority. If Eugene Fodor, the career travel writer, says Costa Rica is cheap, there is good reason to believe him. But sometimes people use appeals to authority to support their opinions. "The president believes the same thing I do." We're supposed to believe the statement because of that, but is this evidence good enough?

Summary: Questions to ask while reading

1. What are the author's biases or the point of view?
2. Is what you are reading fact or opinion?
3. What is the evidence to back up what the writer is saying, and how good is it as evidence?

If you find that you ask questions without this conscious practice and record keeping, that's great. If you do *not,* however, continue to practice deliberately and keep records of your practice. When you realize you are asking questions automatically, you can stop the deliberate practice.

Chapter 10

Using Libraries and Computers for Research

Malia G. Watson
Online Computer Library Center[1]

PREVIEW WITH QUESTIONS TO ANSWER

Know your library, love your library

- What are the different kinds of information you might need from the library?

The Research Process

- How can you organize the process of doing research?

Searching by computer

- What are Boolean operators, and how do they help in a library search?
- How do you use Boolean operators on the Internet?

Return to the research process

- What are the final steps?
- What are important questions to ask to evaluate material you find?

Jorge Luis Borges, the great Argentinean novelist, once wrote "I have always imagined that Paradise will be a kind of library." What is your perception of the library? Are you . . .

- Positive? "It's awesome. Everything known in the world is in there."

- Negative? "Librarians are only interested in shushing me!"

- Neutral? "It's a good place to study, but it's so big, I can never find anything!"

An important skill in becoming well educated is learning to use a library and computers to your advantage. Your college or university library can be your gateway to knowledge and the world of ideas. The books, articles, and other resources made available by your library will help further your education and enhance your life.

Librarians, who select and organize the library's resources, are your guides through this maze of information. Together, your college library and librarians can be your salvation during your college career, providing the information, and the tools to use that information, that you will need to succeed.

Know Your Library, Love Your Library

Becoming familiar with your library's resources

QUESTION TO ANSWER
AS YOU READ:

■ What are the different kinds of information you might need from the library?

To get the most out of your college library, first become familiar with its layout and resources. Many libraries offer tours or a short course on using the library. Take one. The tour will show you how the collection is organized, where the current and previous issues of magazines and journals are, where the copier machines are, and how to use the online library catalog. The tour may also cover the available services, such as interlibrary loan, or access to a special computer room where you can type your papers or search the Internet. If you see something that arouses your curiosity, ask about it. Library staff are there to help you.

THINK PIECE 10.1   Getting to know your library

For each of the exercises below, place a check mark next to the number of the exercise once it has been completed.

1. List all the campus libraries. Circle each library that offers tours.

   _____   _____

   _____   _____

2. Schedule a tour for the main student library. After the tour, write a brief description of the library below. Include the number of floors it has and what can be found on each floor.

   _____

   _____

   _____

3. Gather as many handouts as you can about the library and put them in a folder with a label indicating the name of the library.
   Don't forget to ✓ when you've done each step.

Your college may have more than one library, in which case you will need to know where each library is and what resources each library offers. Become familiar with your college libraries early in your college career. This will save you time and energy when you have an assignment to do.

Defining your need for information

Before going to the library, try to develop a general idea of what you want to find. What you want to find depends on what you want to do with the information you find. Are you writing a research paper? preparing a speech or participating in a debate? What type of information do you want to find?

Introductory. Broad overview of a given topic written for the general public. Example: An article titled "What everyone needs to know about nutrition."

Exploratory or analytical. In-depth information on a topic, often written by experts in the field for an audience with some prior knowledge of the topic. Example: An article titled "Does Vitamin C Help Ward Off the Common Cold?"

Current. Information about a recent event or idea. Example: An article from this year titled "Recent Research on the Effects of Vitamin C."

Contemporary. Information about a particular topic in the past written during the same time period. An article from 1930 titled "What Scientists Think Is the Role of Vitamins in Health."

THINK PIECE 10.2 Which type of information do you need?

1. Take a look at the syllabus for a course in which you need to do library work. Which of the types of information listed above do you think you may need to find to complete each assignment?

Course: _____

Information needed: _____

2. Discuss your conclusions with other students. Do you agree or disagree on the type of information you may need for each assignment? Why?

_____

_____

3. Bring your syllabus, or a description of your assignment, with you when you go to the library to help you focus your search and determine how much information you need, what type of information you need, and where to find it.

Biographical. Information about someone written by another person. Example: A book about Linus Pauling, the Nobel prize–winning scientist.

Autobiographical. Information about someone written by that person. Example: The book *Me,* by Katherine Hepburn.

The Research Process

QUESTION TO ANSWER AS YOU READ:

■ How can you organize the process of doing research?

With your assignment in hand, and a clear picture of the library's layout in your mind, you are ready to tackle the library and begin your research. But where to start? With an article? a book? The steps that follow will help you with the research process.

Step 1: Focus on what you are searching for

There is a tremendous amount of information out there, and in order to avoid being buried in it, you have to really focus your ideas. For example, Eva has a five-minute presentation due for her women's studies class. The purpose of the presentation is to describe an influential female politician or leader. Throughout history there have been many influential women in politics and world affairs. There is enough information to write many books, let alone prepare for a five-minute presentation. What country should she focus on? What time period? Which politician or leader?

Before preparing a presentation, or writing a paper, you need to narrow the focus of the presentation or paper to a topic you can adequately research. Eva needs to pick a time period (for example, the twentieth century) a place (for example, the United States) and decide on what general kind of leader (a politician or a scientist or an educator or an activist or what?).

Ask yourself "What aspect of this topic do I want to write about?" to help narrow the focus of your paper. Spend some time thinking about this. As you search for material, you may realize several times that your search is still too wide, and you may need to narrow it again. You may need to ask this question several times to come up with an appropriate topic. Eva, for example, picks "politicians" but later realizes she has to distinguish between people who actually ran for office, such as Hillary Clinton, and people who tried to influence the political process but did not run for office, such as Eleanor Roosevelt.

Step 2: Be prepared for work

Being prepared for your sojourn in the library will save you a lot of frustration and time. Before you leave your dorm room or apartment to trek to the library, be sure that you have:

■ Your library card

■ Ample change for the copier

■ Your assignment

■ Plenty of paper for writing down notes and citations

■ Several pens and pencils

Step 3: Start with what you don't know

If the topic of your assignment is new to you, consult an encyclopedia to learn the basic facts related to the topic. There will be several encyclopedias in the reference section of the library. General encyclopedias, such as the *Encyclopaedia Britannica,* provide short articles offering an overview of each topic. In an encyclopedia the articles are arranged alphabetically by subject and are usually indexed in the last volume of the set. The index is probably the best place to begin your search.

For longer, more detailed articles, consult a specialized, or subject, encyclopedia. There are many encyclopedias that are entirely devoted to a specific subject, such as psychology or music. The articles contained in these encyclopedias often include a bibliography of the books and journal articles relevant to the topic. Write these down because this list will help jump-start your research.

If there are words that are unfamiliar to you in the encyclopedia article, look them up in a dictionary. Your library will probably have several dictionaries. The most helpful dictionary may be among the subject dictionaries, which, like specialized encyclopedias, are devoted entirely to a specific subject. These dictionaries provide more detailed definitions of the terms related to a specific subject.

Step 4: Expand your search

After you have consulted the basic encyclopedia about your subject, search your library catalog for the books cited in the encyclopedia article. A library's catalog is a list of all the materials held by the library, with a short description of each item and where it is located.

Books. Most college libraries have their catalog online, that is, accessible from a computer. The computer will also indicate whether the item is checked out, or available for check out. The library tour that you took earlier in the semester probably showed you how to use the library's catalog. If you are not sure what to do, ask a librarian.

When you find a book that was cited by the encyclopedia article that you read, take note of the book's *subject headings,* if there are any. These are the words and phrases librarians have used to describe the book. You can use these subject headings to search for other books related to your topic. Also note the book's *call number*, which will tell you where the book is located (See box 10.1).

When you go to the stacks to retrieve the books you've found in the library catalog, take a look at the other titles on the shelf. Do they seem relevant? interesting? You may stumble upon a book that will open new and exciting doors for you.

About Call Numbers

Call numbers in any library are generally assigned according to the rules of one of two library classification systems: the Library of Congress system, or the Dewey decimal system. Most college libraries follow the Library of Congress classification system, but many city and state libraries use the Dewey system.

Library of Congress System

In the Library of Congress system, each book is given a particular set of letters and numbers, with the letters preceding the numbers. Each letter in the Library of Congress system stands for a general subject area, or category. The nineteen categories of the Library of Congress system are as follows:

A	General works
B	Philosophy, psychology, and religion
C–D	History and topography (except North and South America)
E–F	History: North and South America
G	Geography and anthropology
H	Social sciences
J	Political science
K	Law
L	Education
M	Music
N	Fine arts
P	Language and literature
Q	Science
R	Medicine
S	Agriculture
T	Technology and engineering
U	Military science
V	Naval science
Z	Bibliography and library science

B
O
X
10.1

Dewey decimal system

The Dewey decimal system uses numbers instead of letters to identify a general subject area. The ten categories of the Dewey decimal system are as follows:

000–099	General works, including bibliography
100–199	Philosophy and psychology
200–299	Religion
300–399	Social sciences
400–499	Language
500–599	Pure science
600–699	Technology, medicine, and business
700–799	The arts
800–899	Literature
900–999	History and geography

You don't need to memorize this information, but you might want to keep this box handy to help you remember some important information.

Periodicals. After locating the books relevant to your subject, search for journal or magazine articles about your subject. These may contain more current information than the books that you've found. Your library may have a periodical room, or section, which will have the most recent issue of many of the periodicals it subscribes to. The articles in these issues, as well as those in previous issues, can be found by consulting a *periodical index.*

Most periodical indexes are organized alphabetically by subject. The type of periodical index to consult depends on the type of information you are looking for. If you are looking for articles written by experts in a particular field, and that may be reviewed by other experts, consult a specialized periodical index. These are indexes that provide citations to articles in periodicals pertaining to a specific subject. The *Social Sciences Index,* which contains references to articles in periodicals about sociology, psychology, and other subjects in the social sciences, is a specialized periodical index. Other examples include the: *Business Periodicals Index,* and the *Humanities Index.*

If you are looking more for general articles written by journalists, consult a general periodical index, such as the *Readers' Guide to Periodical Literature.* A list of the magazines and journals indexed by each index is usually found in the first few pages of each volume.

Searching by Computer

QUESTIONS TO ANSWER AS YOU READ:

- What are Boolean operators, and how do they help in a library search?
- How do you use Boolean operators on the Internet?

Your library may also have several periodical indexes "online" or accessible by computer, which makes searching the indexes both easier and more complicated.

Searching a periodical index by computer is easier because the computer-based index is usually more flexible than its paper counterpart. Instead of searching for articles by subject, as in the paper version, you can usually search for articles by subject, title, author, or keyword. However, this flexibility also makes your searching more complex, as it requires you to figure out what words to use and how to combine these words to search the index effectively.

How to search

To construct a sound search strategy for the index on computer, begin by stating your topic in a phrase or sentence: "I am writing a paper about the sociology of women's sports organizations."

Look at the sentence you have just written, and underline the main concept of the sentence. This will probably be the words after the word *about*. In the example above, "the sociology of women's sports organizations" is the main concept.

The words that you've underlined are some of the words to use in your search. You may also want to use the synonyms for each underlined word. For example, you might want to use *athletic* as well as *sports* in your search.

The ideas of the mathematician George Boole (1815–1864) are very helpful in wording your search. Boole assigned very specific meanings to three basic words—"and," "or," and "not." These words are called *operators* because they operate on the meaning of a phrase or sentence. They change the meaning in important ways. These days they are called *Boolean operators*, after Dr. Boole.

How do these Boolean operators change the meaning of a sentence? "She wants to marry George *or* Billy," for example, has a very different meaning from "She wants to marry George, *not* Billy." Just the one little operator makes a big difference. And "She wants to marry George *and* Billy" would really be a different situation!

To combine the words you underlined in your sentence in an effective search strategy, use one or more Boolean operators, like this:

1. Use "and" between two or more search terms in order to specify that the articles returned should have *both* search terms. "Women and Soccer" calls up information on women who are involved with soccer.

2. Use "or" between two or more search terms in order to search for articles that contain *either* term. "Teenagers or children" calls up more than just "children."

3. To exclude a term, type "not" before it. "Women not teenagers" calls up only adult information.

Example: To turn the concept "the sociology of women's sports organizations" into a search strategy, use the Boolean operators like this:

Women's and (sports or athletics) and organizations

The parentheses signal to the system that the search for "sports or athletics" should be completed first. You want that before you get into organizations.

There may be other search strategies that the particular periodical index at your library allows you to do that will further focus your search and retrieve more relevant records. Use the online Help screens that can pop up on the computer screen for more information about the index you are using, or ask a librarian to help you.

When you have your search strategy, your next question is where should you search? Most periodical indexes on the computer allow you to search by title, author, subject, or keyword.

Once you have searched the periodical index, you will probably have to go back to your library's catalog to check if the library holds the journal or magazine in which the articles are found.

The Internet

A lot of information can now be found on the Internet, a large network of computers around the world. Useful Internet resources include electronic mail (e-mail) and the World Wide Web.

The Web allows computer users to "explore" its content using Web browsers like Netscape or Microsoft's Internet Explorer. Most universities and colleges provide Internet access for students in a special room in the dorms, classroom buildings, or libraries. No one knows for certain how many Web pages there are on the Web, but there are a lot!

There are several types of resources you may expect to find on the Web:

- Pathfinders or gateways: A list of Web sites organized by subject, discipline, or other meaningful categories. Pathfinders are often built by librarians to provide students and faculty with a list of Web sites they think may be helpful.

- Commercial and public databases

- Agencies and offices of the federal and state governments

- Professional associations

- Recreational associations and clubs

- Student groups and organizations

Ask your professor and classmates if they know of any useful Web sites in your field.

To help you search the Web to find relevant pages and sites for your research, you will want to use one of the many Web *search engines* that are available. Yahoo!, AltaVista, and Northern Light are three such search engines. Internet search engines use the Boolean operators "and," "or," and "not."

To make searching the Web even easier, many search engines also allow you to use the symbols "+" (plus) and "-" (hyphen) to focus your search. These are substitutes for the Boolean operators "and" and "not." These symbols must be used *in front of* a search term, just as "and" and "not" would be. The "+" symbol acts like the Boolean operator "and." The symbol "-" (hyphen) acts like the Boolean operator "not."

Use Skill Builder 10.1 to build your Web-searching skills.

Return to the Research Process

Now that you've done your computer search, we can finish the research process.

Step 5: Evaluate your sources

Would you use statistics from 1980 in your paper on recent population trends in the United States? Is a study on nicotine addiction done by the tobacco industry entirely objective? These are the types of questions you may need to ask when you evaluate the resources you've found during your research. This is the process of critical thinking discussed in Chapter 7, one of the basic processes you should learn in college.

Evaluating your sources will ensure that the facts presented in your paper or presentation or project will be accurate and reliable.

Any information that you draw upon to write your paper or prepare your presentation should be evaluated according to the following criteria:

Authority. Who wrote the article or created the Web page? What credentials do they have? Are they experts? Is there any reason to think they might not be objective? You have to ask yourself if they are objective, because they are not going to tell you if they are not.

Accuracy. Are the facts presented by the author accurate? Ask the librarian to help you check with several sources to corroborate the facts presented in the resource.

Currency. How current is the information presented by the author? Is currency important for your purposes? Recent studies may shed light on past mysteries—or may refute them entirely.

QUESTIONS TO ANSWER AS YOU READ:

- What are the final steps?
- What are important questions to ask to evaluate material you find?

Searching the Web

A. Doing a Web search.

1. Find a computer with access to the World Wide Web.

2. Get on the Web. Open a Web browser such as Netscape or Internet Explorer.

3. Choose a topic to search (anything you are interested in):

   _____

   _____

4. Now find a search engine. Go to the Web site for Yahoo! at http://www.yahoo.com, and perform a *keyword* search on your chosen topic. List the first five items returned:

   _____

   _____

   _____

   _____

   _____

5. Now use the "+" sign in front of the keywords you used in number 4 to focus your search. List the first five items returned:

   _____

   _____

   _____

   _____

   _____

6. Instead of using the "+" sign in front of one of your search terms, use the "−" sign. List the first five items returned:

_____

_____

_____

_____

_____

B. Compare search results.

1. Are the results of your searches different depending on the type of search that you performed? How?

   _____

   _____

   _____

   _____

2. Do the same searches using AltaVista, Northern Light, or another search engine. Are the search results different? How?

   _____

   _____

   _____

   _____

3. Is there a situation in which you would use one search engine over another?

   _____

   _____

   _____

   _____

Completeness. Is the source that you've found complete? For example, if you've found a Web site you would like to use in your assignment, are there many "Under Construction" signs?

Step 6: When in doubt, consult a librarian.

Librarians are trained guides of the world of information. They are there to help you. Talking with a librarian about your paper, speech, or interview will save you time and energy.

When you do discuss your paper with a librarian, there are some tips to keep in mind that will help you make the most of your conversation.

First, let the librarian know what the purpose of your library visit is. If it's for a research paper, let him or her know what the topic is and how long the paper needs to be. If you have the assignment on paper, show it to the librarian. Just like doctors, librarians are bound by their professional values to keep the reason for your visit confidential. Second, let the librarian know what you've done so far to research your topic. Include what reference books, periodicals, books, and Web pages you've referred to, and what words you've used to search for material about your topic.

Step 7: Putting it all together with word processing

Once you've done your research, you are ready to complete your assignment. For many students, this means using a program on a computer, like a word processing program. Your university or college probably provides access to computers where students can do their homework. What computer resources are available at your university or college?

There may be a specific program your professor wants you to use. For example, a statistics program might be required for a sociology or psychology class, or a graphics program might be required for an art class. What computer programs does your professor suggest?

Learning how to use a computer will be immensely helpful to you during your college career, and beyond. Computers can save you time and energy. You can also explore new and exciting areas *via* a computer. Here are some basic suggestions for making your computer experience productive:

- Learn how to start and stop the computer. This includes learning how to restart the computer.

- Make backups of all your work. You might want to make multiple backups of your work, in case you want to keep different drafts of your paper or project.

- When in doubt, ask for help. There is usually a computer room monitor, either in person or *via* phone or e-mail, who is available to answer your computer questions.

■ Explore and have fun. The computer will be an immense help to you. Exploring the ins and outs of a computer can open up new vistas.

Part V

Studying:
Work smarter, not harder

If you ask five-year-olds to memorize something—for example, a list of cities—they don't follow any clear strategy. Furrowing their brow, they just try to think real hard. They don't know how to memorize. If you ask ten-year-olds, on the other hand, they have a definite strategy to follow. They say the list over and over; their strategy is repetition.[1] They have learned a memory strategy. That's good improvement in five years.

We need to keep on improving. The strategies you used when you were ten may not be enough when you are twenty. The kind of learning ten-year-olds do in school is different from, less complex, than the kind you do in college. Ten-year-olds are learning things like "the capital of France is Paris" or "*community* is spelled with two m's." A basic study strategy like repetition works for their needs. In college more sophisticated learning strategies will help. Have your study strategies improved in the last few years?

A lot of college time is devoted to studying. Do you use a variety of strategies to deal with different kinds of study situations, or do you tend to use the same kind of strategies you developed in elementary school and high school?

Improving your studying will help you tremendously in college. Students who make better grades tend to use a wide variety of study strategies.[2] If you improve your study strategies you won't feel as though you are wasting your time when you are "studying," because each hour you put in using strong strategies will have direct, positive benefits. Preparing for tests will also be easier because stronger strategies make you more strongly prepared. There are immediate benefits of working on your studying.

There are also long-term benefits. When we study, we are learning on our own. No one is there to guide us, to make suggestions about how to do it. This is similar to the kind of learning you will do after college, on your own. Remember that college graduates are more likely to continue learning after school. Gaining greater control over and sophistication about your studying now will make it easier for you to learn throughout your life, with positive effects.

Here are a few questions you can ask yourself about your studying. Answer each honestly; no one will know but you. Your answers will help you decide which chapters in this part you might profitably concentrate on.

❶ How well do you concentrate while you are studying? (Chapter 11)

1	2	3	4
NOT WELL	SO-SO	PRETTY WELL	VERY WELL

Reason for this question: To learn well, you have to concentrate well on the material. If you paid a lot of money for a course in improving your memory, the first thing you would be taught is to pay close attention to what you want to learn. If your concentration is less than very good, you will benefit from working on it in Chapter 11.

❷ When you want to memorize something, do you primarily use repetition—just saying it over and over—or do you use other strategies? (Chapter 12)

1	2	3	4
USE NO STRATEGY	ENTIRELY REPETITION	MOSTLY REPETITION	USE SEVERAL STRATEGIES

Reason for this question: There are actually several techniques you can use to memorize something. In fact, repetition is *not* one of the best, even for a fact like "the capital of France is Paris." If you mainly use repetition to memorize, you will benefit considerably from learning the stronger strategies laid out in Chapter 12.

❸ When you are studying a textbook, how systematic is your approach to studying? For example, do you use techniques to get the big picture, to interest yourself in the material, to be sure you are learning the material? Or do you mostly just plod through the text reading and underlining over and over? (Chapter 13)

1	2	3
I MOSTLY READ AND UNDERLINE OVER AND OVER	I HAVE A LITTLE VARIETY OF TECHNIQUE	I HAVE PRETTY GOOD VARIETY OF TECHNIQUE

Reason for this question: Studying involves several different tasks—getting the big picture, getting yourself involved, reading, finding and learning the main points, seeing the relevance of ideas, and being sure you remember what you are learning. If you just read and underline, it's hard to get all of that done. If you follow a system such as the one taught in Chapter 13, you will do much better in your studying.

❹ Sometimes we have to memorize material that is basically meaningless. Do you know techniques for that task? (Chapter 14)

1	2	3
I DON'T KNOW WHAT MNEMONICS ARE	I SOMETIMES USE MNEMONICS	I OFTEN USE MNEMONICS

And how effective are you when you need to study subjects like math, science or literature?

1	2	3
NOT EFFECTIVE	SLIGHTLY EFFECTIVE	PRETTY EFFECTIVE

Reasons for these two questions: Studying math and science can require special attention and special techniques because the information is really packed into texts. Chapter 14 will show you how to deal with this.

Chapter 11

Concentrating on Your Work

PREVIEW WITH QUESTIONS TO ANSWER

Dealing with distractions

■ What are your major distractions, and how can you cope with them?

Focusing your concentration

■ When you are studying, how can you increase the percentage of time you are focused on the task?

In his report for class, Tyrell wrote, "As soon as we had to deal with this issue of distractions while studying, I knew I was in trouble. But I started keeping records, just as the assignment said. My first major mistake was trying to study with my girlfriend in my room. That was a lot of fun, but it did not lead to any studying. Since we both need to get our grades up, we agreed to study apart for a while. She left and I turned on the radio, but that distracted me too much, also. Plus all the noises outside.

"I estimate I studied about 50 percent of the time. The rest of the time I was listening to the DJ talk, or listening to the lyrics, or daydreaming. Since I was 'studying' for two hours, this fifty percent time off track meant I wasted approximately one of the two hours. And the trouble is, that one hour wasn't 'quality time.' I wasn't doing something I really wanted to do. I was just not being very efficient."

Tyrell decided he needed to study in a place that was free of distractions like the radio and the sound of mopeds outside, and that he should also try to eliminate thinking about other things when he was studying.

"I tried studying with a group of buddies and girlfriends at the library. We all sat at one of those big, round tables. This may sound studious, but in all honesty I don't think I studied much more than I did alone in my room with the radio on. Someone was always whispering something funny, or passing notes, or horsing around, and the girls were so pleasant to look at. I didn't get much studying done. Man, the world is full of distractions.

"I finally had to face reality: if I'm going to improve my studying, I need to concentrate more, not waste so much time, and if I'm going to do that, I'm going to have to study alone, in a quiet place. Yes, it's going to be lonely (not really), but hopefully it won't take too much time, and it should lead to an improvement in the old GPA."

Dealing with Distractions

> **QUESTION TO ANSWER AS YOU READ:**
>
> ■ What are your major distractions, and how can you cope with them?

Tyrell is right: the world is full of distractions. Students have to cope with the TV, the radio, CDs, friends, roommates, parents, the telephone, doors slamming, shouts and screams, mopeds, auto backfires, thruways, loud birds, girlfriends, boyfriends, brothers, sisters, hunger, boredom, loneliness, worry, a beautiful day, storms, being in love, getting dumped, gossip, the evening news, and anything else in the world that is more involving than studying.

Identifying distractions

Sometimes it is easier to be distracted than other times.[1] If you try to study when you are tired, for example, your mind wanders more easily. If you are cramming, as the hours go by it is easier and easier to be distracted. If you use passive study techniques—just reading and underlining, reading and underlining—you are more likely to be distracted. (Later, in Chapters 12 and 13 you will learn about active study techniques.) If what you are studying is boring or badly organized or difficult to understand, it is easier to be distracted from it. This means it is a good idea to take steps (also described later) to make things interesting.

Here's the most interesting finding: the better your study skills, the less easily you are distracted while studying.[2] Learning the ideas in later chapters will help you concentrate.

Your first step is to find out what distracts you. "I start out studying okay, but the phone always rings—some friend of mine—and I end up talking to him instead of studying." Keep track of your study times and what distracts you from studying. You could make a list:

Time and topic	Distractions
Monday night, studying English	Tom came in for a chat
Tuesday, working on term paper	Janie called
Wednesday, math homework	Tried to listen to CDs

Minimizing distractions

Look for patterns. Then use problem solving. Think about the details of the problem, and think of several solutions to the problem. Put the best one into operation, and keep track to see if it works.

> "I realized I don't have to answer the phone. I can let the answering machine do it. So I tried that, but I found I would stop concentrating to listen to the message on the machine. Then I realized I could cut down the volume so I couldn't hear the message, and I could cut down the phone volume so I could barely hear it ring. Also, I would tell myself, 'Don't answer the phone. You can call back. It is more important to keep studying.' Now I can keep on concentrating even when someone calls."

Set up a situation where you think you will be able to concentrate on studying, a place without major distractions. Then keep track to see if you actually can concentrate there. Tyrell, remember, thought he could concentrate at the library with his friends, but learned he could not. That is a common experience. Keep making adjustments until you have eliminated all major sources of distraction.

What kind of situation encourages concentration? It should be pretty quiet, though it need not be totally so. Some people like to have soft music on in the background, others don't. Experiment to find what's best for you. Loud or exciting music, or music with lyrics you listen to, however, won't work. The TV should be off. Eliminate distractions in the area, such as bills you should pay, letters you should write, photos you can study instead of the text. Sit upright, because trying to study while lying down is the beginning of a nap.

Some people find it works best to have one place where you do your studying, and nothing else, so that your mind grows used to concentrating there. You come to associate concentrated studying with that place, and it becomes easier to concentrate when you work there. The trick is to do just the one thing in that setting—studying and nothing else. Many writers use this kind of arrangement to get their minds focused. They have a desk at which they write, and they do everything else somewhere else. You might use one particular table in the library, or a desk at home you don't use for anything else.

Minimize interruptions of all sorts because they are distracting and frustrating. If your kid brother keeps popping in, get him to stop. If you're at home, turn the phone off, or use the answering machine and cut its sound off so you can't hear who it is. For some, the phone is always too tempting, and for them it is best to study where there is no phone.

Certain times will be best for you. Pick a time when you're wide awake. Don't try to study for long periods: an hour at a time is best. If you want to study longer, take a break at the end of each hour, and be sure you return refreshed. As you learned in Chapter 3, it helps to set a starting and stopping time.

Sometimes your own thoughts are the distraction. "Every time I start studying math, I start worrying that I don't understand it and am going to fail. I think I spend more time worrying than I do studying."

If recurring worries distract you, give yourself instructions to worry about them later. "Argh, I'm thinking about being on probation again, instead of concentrating. Well, I'm doing the right thing to get off probation; I'm studying. So stop thinking about it, and focus on the material." You may have to repeat this several times, but usually self-instructions to worry later and to concentrate now work well. If something occurs to you that you need to cope with later, you can just make a note and then resume studying: "Don't forget to pick up Mom."

Examining your ambivalence

Sometimes we welcome distractions. This usually happens if we are ambivalent about doing the studying. We would really rather be doing something else, and so we allow ourselves to be distracted. "I don't know why, but every time I try to do my history homework (which I hate), I try to do it with the TV on. But that never seems to work. I end up just watching." If you don't like any of your studying, you might perform self-sabotage like this all the time.

Some people try to kill two birds with one stone. Their plan seems to be "I'll study with my friends, and we can talk a lot, and every now and then I'll study." Or "I'll study in the cafeteria and hope I get interrupted enough that it isn't boring." Often this does not work, however, because your concentration is so broken up.

Some students fool themselves; they say they are "studying," but what they are really doing is socializing or daydreaming. "I told myself I had studied enough; and I expected to get a B on the test. But I was shocked when I only got a D. I had to admit to myself that I really had not been studying; I'd been goofing off most of the time. Now it's time to force myself to be realistic."

The cure for this kind of problem is to get your own goals straight in your mind. Maybe you really do *not* want to be in college at this time, or just want to be with your friends now, in which case studying can be pointless. If you do want to be in college, how does studying fit with that goal?

Make a list of the advantages and disadvantages of concentrating while you are studying. Then see if the advantages outweigh the disadvantages enough to get you to eliminate the distractions.

Massoud wrote just such a list:

Advantages of concentrating	**Disadvantages of concentrating**
More efficient	I'll have to think about it
Less frustrating	

He then wrote, "Well, graduating from college does fit with my life goals. Since I do want to be in college, therefore I should study. If I am going to do any studying at all, it might as well be efficient. Otherwise, I am frustrating myself. This means I should turn off the TV when studying."

Of course you have more goals in life than just to be in college. You do want to have friends, and you do want to be entertained. Instead of trying to reach those goals while studying, use the trick of arranging things so they come *after* you have concentrated on your studies, so that they reinforce your studying. First, you concentrate on studying for a certain amount of time; then you get to call your friend or watch TV. Use whatever distracts your concentration to reinforce *concentration*. "First, I will work on my history for twenty minutes without interruption; then I will call Jill."

Focusing your Concentration

QUESTIONS TO ANSWER AS YOU READ:

■ When you are studying, how can you increase the percentage of time you are focused on the task?

The total time you spend studying was covered in Part II, on time management. Here we're going to deal with *how well you concentrate while you are studying*. Concentrating means focusing your attention. It doesn't do you much good if you schedule an hour to study but actually spend only half the time studying and spend the rest of the time spent daydreaming, tidying up, or talking on the phone.

Focusing your concentration is like anything else you do: if you pay attention to it and practice, you get better at it. Research has shown that students who carry out exercises like the one in Skill Builder 11.1 improve their grades because they improve the quality of their study time.[3]

First, establish a good setting. Be sure you aren't bored or tired, and get rid of interruptions. Be sure you are in a place without distractions. Then you are ready to focus your attention on your studies.

If you don't want to do this, you may be showing signs of ambivalence. Remind yourself of your goals. Go back and make a list of the advantages and disadvantages of studying well, outlined in the section above.

Your ability to fully concentrate will develop in small steps. At first you should ask yourself to concentrate for only a short time, say, ten minutes. Then gradually increase the time period until you can work for longer periods concentrating well all along. When you first begin each study period, you will experience a period of warming up, so your first few minutes of studying will not be as concentrated as later in a given study period. Take breaks if you become tired, bored, or frustrated.

Guide your concentration with self-instructions. "I'm going to study for thirty-five minutes now, and I'm really going to concentrate while I do it. If I begin to think about other things, I'll switch back to the studying."

Focusing your concentration while studying

There are two steps to take: Make a record of your time concentrating while studying, and make plans to increase your concentration while studying.

A. Phase One: Make a record of your time concentrating while studying.

1. In the first column, write the name of the subject you are studying, such as "English."

2. In column 2 write down your starting and stopping times.

3. In column 3, "Time off target," write down any periods of time you know you were *not* studying.

   Example: If you got up to make a cup of coffee and this took eight minutes, you'd write "8 min." there. You may have to estimate. For example, if a friend calls, you might estimate you talked for five minutes.

   If possible, don't estimate, keep an accurate record, for the danger in estimation is that you will fool yourself.

4. In column 4, make a check mark (✓) each time your attention wanders for a short period. If you suddenly realize you've been thinking about an upcoming football game for a few seconds, make a ✓. Don't count thoughts that just flash through your mind, but if you spend several seconds on it, count it.

5. In column 5, list the reasons for distractions, such as "Worrying about the test" or "Thinking about Margaret."

6. In column 6 estimate your total time lost by counting each ✓ *as one minute,* and adding this to the other time off target.

6. It is important to keep this record *during* your study periods. If you wait to make entries later, you will miss important information and can easily fool yourself.

7. Keep this record for at least eight separate study periods.

Records of time concentrating while studying

Subject being studied	Time period	Time off target	Number of inattentions	Reasons for distraction	Total time lost
_____ ■	_____ ■	_____ ■	_____ ■	_____ ■	_____
_____ ■	_____ ■	_____ ■	_____ ■	_____ ■	_____
_____ ■	_____ ■	_____ ■	_____ ■	_____ ■	_____
_____ ■	_____ ■	_____ ■	_____ ■	_____ ■	_____
_____ ■	_____ ■	_____ ■	_____ ■	_____ ■	_____
_____ ■	_____ ■	_____ ■	_____ ■	_____ ■	_____
_____ ■	_____ ■	_____ ■	_____ ■	_____ ■	_____
_____ ■	_____ ■	_____ ■	_____ ■	_____ ■	_____

S K I L L   B U I L D E R   **11.1**

Focusing your concentration while studying

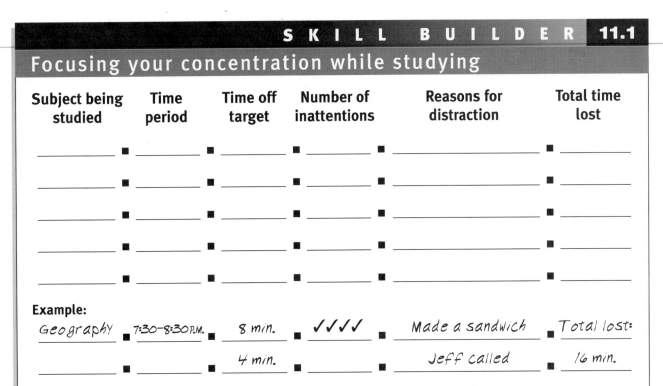

Subject being studied	Time period	Time off target	Number of inattentions	Reasons for distraction	Total time lost
_____ ■	_____ ■	_____ ■	_____ ■	_____ ■	_____
_____ ■	_____ ■	_____ ■	_____ ■	_____ ■	_____
_____ ■	_____ ■	_____ ■	_____ ■	_____ ■	_____
_____ ■	_____ ■	_____ ■	_____ ■	_____ ■	_____
_____ ■	_____ ■	_____ ■	_____ ■	_____ ■	_____

Example:

Geography ■	7:30–8:30 P.M. ■	8 min. ■	✓✓✓✓ ■	Made a sandwich ■	Total lost:
_____ ■	■	4 min. ■	■	Jeff called ■	16 min.

Don't be upset if your total time wasted is high. This is a common experience. That's why we have phase two.

B. Phase Two: Now work out a plan to increase your concentration while studying.

1. Set your mind like an alarm clock to notice whenever your attention wanders while studying.

    Write self-instructions to do this:

    _____

    _____

    _____

    _____

    Example: "I want to notice when I'm not concentrating, so each time my mind wanders, I'll snap myself out of it and return to my studying."

2. At the beginning of a study period, give yourself instructions to focus well during that period.

    _____

    _____

    _____

    _____

    Examples: "I'm really going to focus on this." "I'll resist any distractions." "I'm going to work well on this."

3. During study periods, give yourself short-term instructions also, such as "For the next ten minutes I'm really going to focus on this material." Write your ideas:

    _____

    _____

    _____

    _____

4. Develop short periods in which you deliberately practice concentrating. The more you practice the better your concentration will become. Schedule twenty-minute periods for concentration practice. (If twenty is too much, use ten or five. Begin where you cannot fail to do it.)

S K I L L   B U I L D E R   11.1

Focusing your concentration while studying

Write your schedule:

_____   _____   _____   _____   _____

_____   _____   _____   _____   _____

Example:

Mon 7:30   Tues 4:00   Wed-Thurs 7:30   Fri 9:00 A.M.   Sat 1:00
_____   _____   _____   _____   _____

5. Cope with sources of distraction. If you think of Margaret too often, make plans to use a call to her to reward concentrating. First, concentrate; then call Margaret. If you are worrying about a text, learn to relax using the ideas in Chapter 16.

    Write your problems and your plans to deal with them:

    _____

    _____

    _____

    _____

6. Once your plans for improvement are in place, keep records as you did in phase one to see that you are making progress. If you don't keep records, you are less likely to carry out your plans.

Be prepared to practice several times. Remind yourself that you are in a period of skill development. Expect to make mistakes. Your performance—measured, for example, by your grades on a test—is *not* important now. What is important is the practice. If you do the practice, the grades will come.

Chapter 12

Making Material Meaningful

Self-explanation

■ What is the effect on understanding and memory if you explain material to yourself as you study?

Elaboration: Tying new material into what you know

■ What is elaboration?

■ What study techniques involve elaboration?

Some people study as though they were memorizing telephone numbers. They memorize material as if it has no meaning. If you want to see how hard that is, memorize the following list of telephone numbers: 395-3769; 876-4964; 618-9034; 489-6615. It's difficult to do this because all the numbers are meaningless. We do remember familiar telephone numbers, of course, but they are the ones we use over and over.

Suppose, on the other hand, that one of the numbers was 348-1979, and that 1979 was the year you were born. Then it would be much easier to remember that number, because the year you were born is meaningful to you. All you have to remember is "348-the year I was born."

Here's a second demonstration of how it is difficult to remember material that is not meaningful, but easy if the material is meaningful. Read this story, and as soon as you finish, write down without looking as many of the sentences as you can remember.[1]

A newspaper is better than a magazine. A seashore is a better place than the street. At first it is better to run than to walk. You may have to try several times. It takes some skill but is easy to learn. Even young children can enjoy it. Once successful, complications are minimal. Birds seldom get too close. Rain, however, soaks in very fast. Too many people doing the same thing can cause problems. One needs a lot of room. If there are no complications it can be very peaceful. A rock will serve as an anchor. If things break loose from it, however, you will not get a second chance.

It's hard to remember much of the material, isn't it? That's because there is no overall meaning.

If you know what the paragraph is about, all the sentences have meaning, and the paragraph is much easier to remember. Try reading the passage over again, and again at the end write down as many sentences as you can remember. But this time, know that the paragraph is about . . . flying a kite. Flying a kite. Before reading on in this chapter, try the story again.

Did you find the paragraph was much easier to remember when the overall material had meaning? Whenever you are studying, try to make the material *meaningful* to you, because you will remember the material much, much more easily if it is meaningful.

The purpose of this chapter is to show you techniques for making material meaningful so you can remember it more easily. There are several techniques to use. The goal is understanding the material, because that makes it easier to remember.

Self-explanation

QUESTION TO ANSWER
AS YOU READ:

■ What is the effect on understanding and memory if you explain material to yourself as you study?

The best method for remembering material is to explain it to yourself as you are reading. Learning involves integrating new material into your existing knowledge. Explaining material to yourself is the best way to accomplish that. You have to construct knowledge in your mind in order to remember it, and you have to do the construction with whatever elements you already have handy. Self-explanation means thinking with what you already know in order to understand something new.

What are the advantages of self-explanation?

The improvement using this technique is considerable. In one study a group of students who used self-explanations when studying for a difficult biology test scored on the average 32 percent higher than people who did not use self-explanation.[2] Those who did *not* use self-explanation in their studying averaged grades of low C or high D. The ones who used self-explanation averaged high B to low A. In another study it was found that students who do well in science classes use self-explanation in their studying a lot, but the students who do not do well in the classes do not use it.[3]

An advantage of self-explanation is that it tells you what to do when studying. Many students want to "work harder" at their studying, but are not sure what to do. This idea tells you specifically what to do. It's different from just putting in more time. (Remember our motto: "Work smarter, not harder.")

Explaining ideas from textbooks also helps you overcome weaknesses in the text. Authors sometimes give incomplete examples of a concept, or fail to explain it adequately. They know it so well they forget how to explain it well to the rest of us. If you explain the concept to yourself, you will fill in the missing ideas and gain a better understanding.

How does self-explanation work?

We need to distinguish between giving explanations and receiving them. Receiving them means that someone else explains something to you. This does *not* improve your understanding or memory.[4] Unfortunately, some teachers don't understand this. They keep on explaining to us, but don't give us a chance to explain back. You've got to do the explaining to get the benefit. If you think for a moment, you'll remember from your own experience that this is true. Countless lectures or TV programs have explained many scientific principles to us, but we don't remember them very well because we were receiving, not giving, the explanation. To aid understanding and memory, it is better to give than to receive.

For example, let's say you read the following sentences in your psychology text: "There seem to be levels of consciousness, illustrated by the cocktail party phenomenon. Suppose you are at a party and are talking to someone while all around you others are also talking. You focus your attention on the conversation with the person you face, and all the other conversations are just background noise. Suddenly you hear your name spoken by someone behind you, and you switch your attention to listen to that conversation. Think what this implies about how your mind works."

You stop reading and explain the paragraph to yourself: "It wasn't really just background noise behind you, because when your name was spoken, you recognized it. It's as if you had been screening the background noise to listen for anything important. When something important did pop up, you switched your attention to listen to it. Your name probably wasn't spoken any more loudly. What made it stand out was activity in your mind. Your mind decided the name was important and switched attention to hear what was being said there." This example shows how self-explanation works. You use what you know to explain something to yourself.

You can encourage yourself to explain things by asking, Why? Why are you able to pick up your name when you hear it amidst a bunch of background noise? In answering the question Why?, you have to give yourself an explanation, and that helps your memory.

This is a very good technique to use when you are studying science. As you read some new fact or concept in the science text, ask yourself, Why is that true? By answering your own question, you will have to explain the concept to yourself, and that will greatly help you remember it.[5]

How often should you stop to explain material to yourself?

The amount of self-explanation you do depends on the kind of material you are reading. If you are studying physics, chemistry, or math, where the textbooks are very dense, you might need to stop to explain almost every sentence. If you are studying biology, psychology, or history, you might need to stop after every paragraph. Try different units and see which works for each textbook you have to study. One good rule: Never turn a page until you have explained to yourself what's on that page. If you go longer than that, you will miss something that you might need to know.

Be careful not to delude yourself. If the material is dense, like material in a physics textbook, but you only self-explain once a page, you're going to miss a lot you will need to know later. Start by self-explaining once per paragraph, and then adjust up or down depending on what the textbook seems to require.

It is also important not to delude yourself about the adequacy of your self-explanation. Really explain the material to yourself. Saying "Uh, it's about, you know" doesn't do it. You should explain it clearly enough that anyone hearing your explanation would understand the idea in question. Remember, the whole point of doing self-explanations is that this leads to better understanding, and that leads to better memory of the material. Ultimately self-explanation leads to better grades.

How much time does self-explanation take?

By now you have probably realized the disadvantage of self-explanation as an aid to remembering. It takes longer. On the average it takes about twice as long as just reading the textbook. Sometimes we don't get the benefit if we don't put in the time. If you are lifting weights, for example, and lift 40 pounds three times, you won't get nearly the benefit you would get if you lifted 40 pounds six or eight times, but that does take longer. Strength comes from putting in the time.

On the other hand, using self-explanation when you first study something cuts down on the amount of time you have to put in when, later on, you review the material before a test. Since you learned it the first time, all you have to do in review is refresh your memory, instead of learning some of the material for the first time.

Do you want to use self-explanation?

Some students want to get studying over as quickly as possible. They want to minimize the effort. If you "hate" studying, that's a reasonable thing to do. But if you need to study, you have to ask yourself, "Is it best for me to hurry through my studying?" Research has shown that students who have this minimizing attitude about studying only gain superficial learning and do not do as well in school.[6] Students who perform poorly in college typically *underestimate* how much time is required to make good grades. If you want to do well, you have to ask yourself, "Am I willing to put in the time on a technique that will help me do well?"

What are the advantages and disadvantages of using this technique of self-explanation? What can be done to minimize the disadvantages?

> Ricky lived in a remote village in Alaska and was taking a course over the television station. He wanted to do well in the course and realized it was entirely up to him, as there were no classes, no meetings with instructors, just the TV on Tuesday and Thursday. Here is his list of the advantages of using self-explanation as a study technique:

Advantages	Disadvantages
Better grades	Takes longer (at first)
If I don't explain it, no one else will	I'll get frustrated
Makes reviewing for the tests easier	Means I'll really get into it

> He then asked himself, "How does doing well in the course fit in with my life goals? Since I want to get a college degree, it fits pretty well. Therefore, I should feel good that I've got a technique that will help me do well. I guess really getting into it may be good for those goals."

If you do not want to put in the time, then of course don't do self-evaluation. If you are not sure, try it; then evaluate it.

Use the bootstrapping technique, first explained in Chapter 3. Set a goal, such as, "I will use self-explanation on the first four paragraphs I read." After meeting that goal, ask yourself if you want to quit self-explaining or continue. If you want to stop, do one more unit of four paragraphs, then stop. If you want to continue, do one more unit and then ask again if you want to go on or stop. Continue this way until you stop.

Keep in mind that your focus now should be on practicing this new idea, not on immediately getting better grades. Your success is measured by how much you practice, not by grades, not yet. Use Skill Builder 12.1 to help you with self-explanation.

Keeping track of your understanding

One of the biggest advantages of using self-explanation as a learning strategy is that it tells you what you know and what you don't know. One of the most interesting characteristics of well-educated people is that they know what they don't know. At the other end, students who end up doing poorly on tests are often overconfident about how much they know, and are rudely surprised when they find out the truth.[7]

Using self-explanations

A. List advantages and disadvantages.

If you are not sure you are willing to put in the time to use self-explanations, list here the advantages and disadvantages of trying it. How can you overcome the disadvantages? How important is this technique to your life goals?

Advantages		Disadvantages
_____	■	_____
_____	■	_____
_____	■	_____
_____	■	_____

After thinking about this, what is your goal?

_____

_____

If it involves practicing the procedure, read on.

B. Practice the procedure.

1. Schedule times to practice. Make a schedule for using the technique when you are studying. Start low and increase gradually. Place a ✓ when you do it at the required level.

Day	Time	Number of times to use self-explanation	Material to be studied:
Sunday	_____	_____	_____
Monday	_____	_____	_____
Tuesday	_____	_____	_____
Wednesday	_____	_____	_____
Thursday	_____	_____	_____
Friday	_____	_____	_____
Saturday	_____	_____	_____
Example:			
Tuesday	*6:00*	*5 times, by paragraphs*	*Economics*

Using self-explanations

Or "I'm going to try to use self-explanation for every sentence in my science book, working on it two or three pages at a time. When I study my education text, I will do self-explanation once at the bottom of each page for the whole section I'm reading."

2. Keep a record of your practice. Make a copy of the schedule above to use for several weeks.

3. Write self-instructions to remind yourself to do the practice:

_____

_____

4. Solve problems that come up. List the details of any problem and think of several solutions.

_____

_____

_____

_____

C. Bootstrapping to try studying with self-explanation.

To bootstrap, decide on the (small) unit you will use, such as a paragraph or a page, and decide how many times in one study hour you will use the technique. Then schedule the work. After each unit, decide to continue or to stop. If you say "stop," do one more unit. then stop.

Task to bootstrap: _____ Size of the unit:_____

Number of times you will use the technique in one study hour: _____

Scheduled time to begin:_____

Example "I'm going to bootstrap using self-explanation on my geology textbook. I will self-explain after every paragraph. I will do this in units of five. After each five times, I can continue or quit. If I decide to quit, I'll do one more unit of five, then quit."

Keep records of your bootstrapping

1. Place a ✓ if you began as scheduled. _____

2. If you decided to stop after the first unit but did one more unit before stopping, place a ✓: _____

3. If you decided to continue, place a ✓ for each time you decided to continue:

_____ _____ _____ _____ _____

4. Once you decided to stop, but did one more unit, place a ✓: _____

S K I L L   B U I L D E R   **12.1**

Using self-explanations

5. Repeat this procedure as necessary.

If you don't have all ✓s, use a smaller unit, and reschedule. Begin again. You should be able to start this practice at least 90 percent of the time. If you don't start, that means your unit is too large. Make it so small you cannot fail to start: "I'll self-explain one sentence." Keep a record of the times you successfully start. It doesn't matter if you do one or several units. Keep practicing.

Monitor your comprehension as you are studying: "Do I know this?" If you do, then you should be able to explain it to yourself. If you can't, you need to work on it more. Some students make a check mark at the end of each paragraph when they have explained it to themselves, if they are confident they know it.

There are a couple of problems to watch for. First, don't simply ask yourself, "Do I understand this?" You might think you know it well, but be wrong, and you don't want to find that out on the test. It is very easy to think we know something that we really don't. Make yourself explain the material. If you can explain it to yourself, you'll know you understand it.

Second, when you review material, beware of paying most of your attention to the material you already understand and ignoring the irritating material that you don't. This is very common, and when test time comes, it's a problem. Even very good students tend to spend too much review time on the material they already know and not enough on the stuff they don't yet know well. It is comforting to review concepts and be able to think, "Oh, yeah, I know this," but at review time you need to work on the material that you don't yet know well. That's what is going to mess you up on the test, not the stuff you know. You have to be honest with yourself and know what you don't know, so you can spend time learning it.

Make a list of all the concepts you are studying, and check them off when you fully understand each. Students who make lists like this end up doing considerably better on tests, because they don't fool themselves about what they know or don't know.[8]

Solly is taking psychology and makes this list of topics from part of the chapter he is studying:

Chapter: Developmental Psychology

Children's mental development

Piaget's theory

Evaluation of Piaget's theory

Other approaches; alternatives to Piaget

Personality and social development

Lifelong development

Now he can ask himself, "Can I explain the ideas in each section? Can I explain Piaget's theory?" If he has done so, then he is confident he knows the topic and he checks it off. If not, he re-reads the material and explains it to himself until he is sure he knows it.

Your list should include every concept in a chapter. Textbooks usually have many subheads, often set in boldface or some other distinguishable type font, and you should make a list of all these subheads, as each will cover a different concept. Solly's example, above, is abbreviated. There were actually twenty-three heads and subheads in the chapter he was studying, and he made a list of all of them to be checked when he was sure he understood the concepts covered under each.

Elaboration: Tying New Material into What You Know

QUESTIONS TO ANSWER AS YOU READ:

- What is elaboration?
- What study techniques involve elaboration?

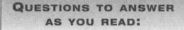

Kim is reading in her geology textbook about the way fast rivers tend to deposit sand bars at the end of a run of rapids, and about how very slow rivers tend to meander over the countryside, weaving from side to side. She stops to remember her own experience with rivers. Once she rafted down the Rogue River in Oregon, and true enough, there were sand bars at the end of each set of rapids, and once she canoed through a very flat area in Wyoming, and sure enough, the river did meander from one side to another. Later she finds that it is easy to remember the textbook's explanation for why these two effects—sand bars and meandering—occur.

Why would Kim find it easy to remember a textbook's explanation of the physics of rivers? Because she tied the explanation to her own experience. Instead of just reading the explanation and trying to remember the bare-bones physics, she paused to think about her own experience with rivers and tied that to what she was reading. This kind of study process is called *elaboration*. Kim *elaborated* on the bare-bones explanation in the textbook.

Elaboration means going beyond the material presented in the text, relating the new information to what you already know. Kim was elaborating the textbook explanation by thinking of examples from her own life. She knew about the examples; now she ties them to the text. Elaboration builds bridges between what you already know and what you are trying to learn. You connect new ideas to ideas you already know about, and in that way construct knowledge in your mind that is easier to remember later.

Students who use elaboration as a study technique do much better on tests than students who just try to memorize the bare-bones material.[9] Memorization of barely understood ideas is a very shallow form of learning, easily forgotten, but elaboration deepens and enriches understanding, making the material easier to remember. It ties the new knowledge to your old knowledge.

Elaborating material also makes it easier to concentrate while you are reading. Your mind is engaged with the material, and that makes the material more interesting, because you are putting part of yourself into reading it.

Students who make good grades use elaboration quite a bit. Really good students spend up to 50 percent of their study time *not* reading the text, but doing other study things such as elaborating it.[10] You might think such students just read the material more, or underline more, or memorize more, but that's not true. They often pause as they are reading and elaborate the material, integrating it into what they already know so they will understand it, so they will remember it.

There are a number of things you can do to elaborate as you study.

1. Think of examples from your own life that fit what you are reading

Kim did that when she was reading about the physics of rivers. Later, reading in a sociology text that the example girls see of how their mothers act influences how the girls act, Kim pauses to think about her own mother and the kinds of examples she set when Kim was growing up.

This technique works better for some courses than others. It is relatively easy to think of personal examples in a social science course, because the course is about people. In a course like astronomy, it would be impossible, unless you were a shooting star. However, you can use other techniques.

2. Think of examples from daily life of what you are reading

Ask yourself, *What is an example of this idea?* Enrique reads in his oceanography text about the action of wind on waves and stops to think about how he has noticed that even a light breeze will start ripples on a lake. At another time he is reading about asteroids—shooting stars—in his science text and stops to think about the night he saw a meteor shower. Later he reads in his communication text about differences between men and women in the way they talk about problems, and he stops to remember how his father usually acted when discussing some problem with his mother.

3. Restate an idea in your own words

Restating an idea greatly helps you understand and remember it. You ask yourself, *What does this mean?* Suppose you read in your chemistry text, "A chemical formula . . . is a notation that uses atomic symbols with numerical subscripts to convey the relative proportions of atoms of the different elements in the substance."[11] Because it is so abstract, that sentence is hard to understand and remember. But if you restate it to yourself in your own words, it is much easier to understand and remember. "Let's see. Each of the symbols, like O for oxygen, stands for one element. Hydrogen is H. Putting little numbers under them shows how much of each element is in the stuff you are looking at. Okay. Water is H_2O. This means that there are two hydrogen atoms but only one oxygen. Every formula is like that, then, with the symbol for the element and the little number below to show how many atoms of that element are present. Yeah. Now I understand."

Some students like to summarize material for themselves. This technique works much better if you use your own words instead of those in the textbook. If you use the author's words, you are less likely to understand and remember because you haven't connected the ideas to things you already know. More on this later.

4. Relate two ideas together, looking for their similarities and their differences

You read something and then ask yourself, *What are the differences between [another idea] and this one?* When Kim reads about the physics of fast rivers and slow rivers, she stops to think about the ways the two work in the same way, and the ways in which they are different. Both are flowing water, but their speed affects them differently. This allows her to see important points about each type of river.

5. As you study, look for connections between ideas

Ask yourself, *How does this tie in with what I already know?* Suppose you are studying chemistry and run into the phrase *sulfur dioxide*. Thinking of the idea of chemical formulas you read about earlier, you say to yourself, "Sulfur is S. Oxygen is O. SO would be sulfur oxide. Dioxide might mean there are two oxygen atoms because '*di*' can mean 'two,' as in *dichotomy*. So, would the formula for this be SO_2?" You look it up. Yes! You have connected this to the idea you read earlier about H_2O. Now you

SKILL BUILDER 12.2

Studying with elaborations

Your goal is practice using the elaboration techniques while studying. At present you may not be using them at all. Therefore, you should start at a low level and build up gradually.

A. Advantages and disadvantages.

If you are not sure you are willing to put in the time to use self-elaboration, list here the advantages of trying it. How can you overcome the disadvantages? How important is this to your life goals?

Advantages		Disadvantages
_____	▪	_____
_____	▪	_____
_____	▪	_____
_____	▪	_____

After thinking about this, what is your goal?

_____

_____

If your goal involves practicing the procedure, read on.

B. Practice the procedure.

1. Set gradually increasing goals for using elaboration when you study. Later you may want to set goals in terms of the percentage of time you use elaboration. Really good students spend up to 50 percent of their study time elaborating.

    Write the number of times you intend to use elaboration over your next dozen study periods:

    _____ _____ _____ _____ _____ _____

    _____ _____ _____ _____ _____ _____

2. Write self-instructions to remind yourself to use the techniques. Be very specific.

    Example: "Sunday when I study I'm going to stop at least four times and give myself examples of the stuff I'm reading."

    _____

    _____

3. Schedule times to practice. Check (✓) each time you practice, so that you keep a record of meeting your goals for practice. Make a copy of this to use for several weeks.

SKILL BUILDER 12.2

Studying with elaborations

Day	Time	Number of times to use elaboration	Which elaboration techniques used?
Sunday	_____	_____	_____ ∎ _____
			_____ ∎ _____
Monday	_____	_____	_____ ∎ _____
			_____ ∎ _____
Tuesday	_____	_____	_____ ∎ _____
			_____ ∎ _____
Wednesday	_____	_____	_____ ∎ _____
			_____ ∎ _____
Thursday	_____	_____	_____ ∎ _____
			_____ ∎ _____
Friday	_____	_____	_____ ∎ _____
			_____ ∎ _____
Saturday	_____	_____	_____ ∎ _____
			_____ ∎ _____

Example:

Monday	9/28	5✓✓✓✓	personal example ∎ goes with other idea?
			personal examples ∎ What does this mean?

3. Solve any problems. If you did *not* meet your goal for any given day, as the person in the example above, how will you solve the problem in the future? (Look at the details of the problem. Think of several solutions. Be sure you are supporting practice with self-instructions, record keeping, shaping, and other practices.)

_____

_____

_____

SKILL BUILDER 12.2

Studying with elaborations

C. Use bootstrapping.

Do you need to use bootstrapping to get yourself started? To bootstrap, decide on the unit you will use, such as a page, and decide how many times in one study hour you will use the technique. Then schedule the work. After each unit, decide to continue or to stop. If you say "stop," do one more unit, then stop.

Example:

"I'm going to bootstrap using elaboration on my history textbook. I will think of one way the ideas relate to earlier material or think of one example once each page, After three pages, I can continue elaborating or quit. If I quit, I'll do one more unit of three pages, then quit."

Task to bootstrap: _____ Size of the unit: _____

Number of times to use the technique in one study hour: _____

Scheduled time to begin: _____

Keep records of your bootstrapping.

1. Place a ✔ if you began as scheduled. _____

2. If you decided to stop after the first unit but did one more unit before stopping, place a ✔: _____

3. If you decided to continue, place a ✔ for each time you decided to continue:

   _____ _____ _____ _____ _____

4. Once you decided to stop, but did one more unit, place a ✔: _____

5. Repeat this procedure as necessary.

   If you don't have all ✔s, use a smaller unit, and reschedule. Begin again. You should be able to start this practice at least 90 percent of the time. If you don't start, that means your unit is too large. Make it so small you cannot fail to start. "I'll elaborate on one paragraph." Keep a record of the times you successfully start. It doesn't matter if you do one or several units. Keep practicing.

will remember this well, and the idea of how chemical formulas work, too. This kind of seeing connections, in fact, is one of the marks of the well-educated person.

The time it takes to use the elaboration

It *does* take longer to use elaboration than it does just to read and underline, read and underline. The payoff is tremendous, however: much better understanding and memory, and therefore much better grades.[12] Does doing well in college fit with your life goals? If not, then don't bother with elaboration. If yes, think about using this technique.

Summary

To use elaboration, ask yourself these questions as you study

1. *What is an example of this idea?* Give examples from your own life or from everyday life.
2. *What does this mean?* Explain the idea to yourself in your own words.
3. *What are the differences between [another idea] and this one?* Compare one idea with another.
4. *How does this tie in with what I already know?* You've already learned material in the text. How does what you are now learning fit with that?

Use Skill Builder 12.2 to help you with studying with elaborations.

Chapter 13

Organizing for Better Memory

PREVIEW WITH QUESTIONS TO ANSWER

Organizing the material

- What are the advantages of summarizing the material to be learned?
- How should you summarize?
- How can you create visual forms to aid your memory?

Organizing your study time

- What is P–Q–R–S–R? What do porcupines have to do with it?
- What is the best procedure for marking your textbook?

Organizing the Material

One of the best ways to remember material is to have it well organized in your mind. This is true whether you are going to take an essay test or a multiple-choice test. Students who do well in college typically spend a considerable percentage of their study time organizing the material so they can remember it.[1] They read material but then spend time writing or drawing to get the ideas well organized in their thinking.

Textbooks are organized around main ideas, along with all their details, examples, and other material. You can't remember all the material, but you can remember the main ideas if you organize them in your mind. It is much easier to remember organized material than it is to remember a disorganized set of facts.

Two good ways to organize material are:

- Write summaries of what you have read.

- Make visual representations of what you have read.

QUESTIONS TO ANSWER
AS YOU READ:

■ What are the advantages of summarizing the material to be learned?

■ How should you summarize?

■ How can you create visual forms to aid your memory?

Write summaries of what you have read

Summaries help you remember material because they organize it in your mind, encourage you to focus on the main ideas, and help you use what you already know to construct the knowledge you are acquiring.

Essay tests call upon your ability to summarize material, so writing summaries beforehand is very helpful. Summaries are helpful for getting the big picture in any subject, and that helps a lot, whatever kind of test you will take.

The point of a summary is to boil down the material to a small, highly focused statement of the main ideas. In your final review just before a test, you might not read the textbook at all, but instead review your summaries of the text.

Your summary can be in paragraphs or in outline form, whichever you prefer.

For dense material, as in a science course, you might need to summarize every paragraph. For less dense material, as in a social science course, you might write a summary of each topic, which could have several paragraphs devoted to it. For example, in the chapter on developmental psychology in your education text there might be a segment labeled, "Development of moral thinking in children," with six paragraphs devoted to it. You could write one summary paragraph of that whole segment.

The main trick to writing good summaries is to find the main ideas in the text. (See Chapter 9 for ideas on how to do this.) Write down the main idea in your own words. Get rid of all unnecessary detail. Don't summarize examples, lists, or anything that seems like filler. Summaries are like telegrams. If you're summarizing several paragraphs, collapse the paragraphs into one.

If there are several main ideas to summarize, list them in order. Under each, put important details.

Suki is studying her social psychology text. In the chapter "Prejudice and Discrimination," there is one section labeled "Combating Prejudice and Discrimination," with five pages devoted to it. Within those five pages are six subheads:

"Desegregation," with six paragraphs

"Contact between Groups," with three paragraphs

"Cooperative Classrooms," four paragraphs

"Changing Stereotypes," one paragraph

"Learning about Prejudice," three paragraphs

"Reducing In-Group–Out-Group Biases," three paragraphs

Suki has to decide what size unit to use for her summarizing. After reading the first section, "Desegregation," she is able to write a one-sentence summary of it: "It was hoped that school desegregation would greatly reduce prejudice, but it has not, because although schools are desegregated, there is still not much interaction between children of different races." She notices that she has left out the information in the text about the effects of social class on racial prejudice, and decides she'll just try to remember that, because her summary sentence is long already.

She then reads the next section and writes one summary sentence for it. She decides to try for one sentence for each of the sections. She ends up with seven sentences because one of the sections requires two sentences—one to explain the topic and one to note its effect. Those seven sentences summarize the entire section of five pages for her. It's much easier to remember the seven sentences than it would be to try to remember the whole five pages.

Suki has to take an essay test on this material. To be sure she remembers her summary sentences, she writes down the list of subheads and briefly tries to memorize them, as a reminder of what topics are covered under the overall topic, "Combating Prejudice and Discrimination." Then if she runs into a question on the test such as, "What are the ways we can combat prejudice in the United States?" she can jot down the six topic heads and thus remember the important information on each.

Notice that Suki wrote a summary of her summary, that is, a list of the topics she had summarized. She did this so she could remember better. Whenever you have to remember a set of summaries of material, such as when you are going to take an essay test, it's a good idea to write an overall summary, to help you organize your summaries and therefore remember better.

Later Suki had to give a book report in her history class. She chose a book on the history of World War II in Greece, because the previous summer she had visited Greece and loved it. To outline her book report, she wrote a summary of each chapter in the book, such as "The invading Germans occupied the lowlands because the German army was mechanized, but the mountains, where there were no paved roads, were partially under the control of the Greek guerrillas" and "The Germans took reprisals against the guerrilla raids. During one winter of the war, the Germans cut off the food supply to Athens, and thousands of people starved to death." After she had a summary sentence for each chapter, she outlined them, and that gave her the outline for her book report in class.

S K I L L   B U I L D E R   13.1

Practicing summarizing

A. If you have not been used to summarizing, try it.

You will want to set a low goal at first: "I'll summarize the first two topics that come up." Then gradually increase.

1. Keep records here of how often you summarize. That will show you if you're meeting your goals.

2. Write the date and the number of times to summarize for each study session. Set goals just a little higher than where you begin. Put a ✓ if you do it.

_____   _____

_____   _____

_____   _____

_____   _____

_____   _____

_____   _____

_____   _____

3. Remind yourself when you begin to study that you want to use summarizing.

   Example: Leave a note in your textbook.

4. Write self-instructions to use for summarizing:

   _____

   _____

   _____

   _____

   _____

5. Reward yourself for summarizing: "I'll summarize four topics, then I'll take a break and call Xavier." Write your reward for summarizing:

   _____

   _____

   _____

   _____

B. You can also use the *bootstrapping* technique.

Set a goal for how many topics or paragraphs you will summarize. Do that, then ask yourself if you want to continue summarizing or not. If not, do one more unit and then stop summarizing. If yes, do one more unit and repeat the question and the process. Keep records of your bootstrapping, so you will see your progress.

_____   _____

_____   _____

_____   _____

_____   _____

_____   _____

_____   _____

_____   _____

Remember to keep a skills-development attitude about this. You will not see an immediate, dramatic improvement in your grade just because you summarize a couple of paragraphs. But check later to see whether you remember better the material you summarized. Summarizing really does help us remember.

Compare summaries you write with someone else's. Particularly do this if (1) the textbook is a difficult one, so you are not always sure what the main ideas are, or (2) you are a beginner at summarizing and are not confident you will get all the main ideas. If you disagree on the main ideas or supporting information, discuss your points of view.

Skill Builder 13.1 can help you practice summarizing.

Make visual representations of what you have read

Sometimes the best way to remember something is to make a drawing of the idea. For example, you could draw a summary of the material in Chapter 12, "*Making Material Meaningful*," like the one in the illustration, "Sample Circle Map."

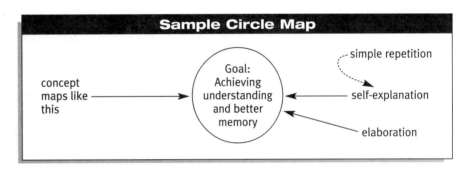

The illustration shows a circle map. The broken line between "simple repetition" and the goal shows that it doesn't lead to the goal.

You could also represent the same ideas as a branching tree, such as the one in the illustration "Sample Tree Diagram."

When in doubt, draw it out.

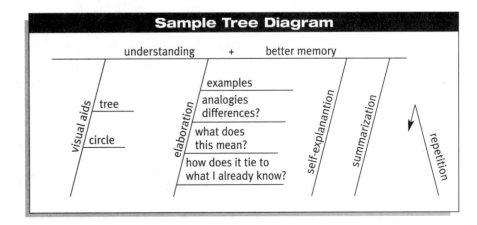

Visuals like flowcharts are very helpful for outlining processes that spread over time, or go through stages. If the text uses words to describe a process that goes through stages, it often helps to make a diagram of the process so you can study it visually. For example:

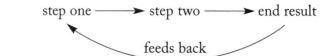

Or, for a less abstract example:

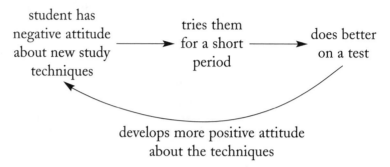

Sometimes it helps to diagram or list material in a text, so it's easier to comprehend. For example, a textbook might mention four aspects of a main idea you need to learn. Typically, the textbook author would write them like this: "There are four major aspects of this that you should consider: (1) blah, blah, blah, blah, blah, blah, blah, (2) blah, blah, blah, blah, blah, blah, (3) blah, blah, blah, blah, blah, and (4) blah, blah, blah." Because of the way the sentence is set up, it's hard to get all that into your memory. If you list them in a different way it is easier to remember them:

1. blah, blah, blah, blah, blah, blah, blah
2. blah, blah, blah, blah, blah, blah
3. blah, blah, blah, blah, blah
4. blah, blah, blah

Some students really like to use visual representations, and they fill their study time with drawings and charts, while others use it rarely. It's a question of different learning styles. Do whatever feels best for you. If you have not tried visual representations, try one or two when you study. Instead of making a written note, make a visual one. You might find that visual representations work well for you, making remembering the material much easier.

**QUESTIONS TO ANSWER
AS YOU READ:**

■ What is P–Q–R–S–R? What do porcupines have to do with it?

■ What is the best procedure for marking your textbook?

Organizing Your Study Time

Reading textbooks is very different from reading other material such as newspapers or a novel. Textbooks are more difficult to read. They have more details, are usually much more abstract, and have to be learned and remembered. Even worse, textbooks have faults. They are often too abstract, without detail or examples that make them interesting or understandable.[2] Textbook authors are sometimes forced to write this way because they are trying to cover a great deal of material in a reasonable space, but it creates problems for the student.

To deal with this problem, the best approach is to follow a system for studying, a plan that outlines for you what to do and how to do it. The original work in this area was done by Francis Robinson.[3] Robinson invented the SQ3R system, which stands for **S**urvey–**Q**uestion–**R**ead–**R**ecite–**R**eview. Research has shown that if students learn and use this system, their studying efficiency improves. Since Robinson's invention of his system in the 1940s, there have been some advances in our understanding of what is the best study system, so the system offered here is slightly different from his original one.

The advantage to following a system for studying is that it focuses your attention on where you should be in your studying. It tells you what to do at each step. It also leads to active learning by you, so you don't just read and underline. Students who do well on tests often follow a system for studying, while those who do not do so well do *not* follow a system, but just blindly keep on reading and underlining, reading and underlining.

When you are studying material that you need to learn, there are several things you need to do:

- Develop an overview of what is to be learned
- Get your mind deeply involved with the material
- Read the material, looking for the main ideas
- Use learning strategies to learn the material
- Be sure you retain the material in your memory

This suggests a *five-step process* to follow when studying, represented by the letters P–Q–R–S–R, which stand for

- **P**review
- **Q**uestion
- **R**ead
- Use **S**trategies
- **R**eview

To help remember the letters, create a personal memory aid, a mnemonic. If you think of one that's unusual or silly, it will be easier to remember. For example, PQRSR equals "**P** or **Q** pines **R** Se**R**ious." Or PQRSR equals "**P**orcupine **Q**uills **R**arely **S**tab **R**abbits."

Preview the material

Robinson called this first step "surveying" the material. Look it over before beginning to read. The idea is to "look at the forest before inspecting the trees."[4] If you get an idea of the forest in your mind, it's much easier to remember what the trees are like. This is why each chapter in this book starts with the boxed "Preview with Questions to Answer" in which you are given the outline of the chapter. If a text has previews, read the preview before you begin the chapter, to get an idea of the structure of the material you're going to read.

Next, spend a couple of minutes surveying each ten-page segment of text. This means read the heads and subheads, don't just skim them. Don't rush it, for it's time well spent.

What should you survey? Look at the headings within the section you are going to study. Read overviews and summaries, or material that is highlighted. If you were going to read a ten-page section of your biology text, for example, you would flip through the pages, spending a couple of minutes looking at the topics to be covered.

Next, ask *Questions* about the material

"What's this going to be?" "How does this relate to what I already know?" "What does . . . mean?" Questions make material more interesting and put you into an active frame of mind for reading. Questions help to focus your concentration, giving you something to look for as you read. Questions can be very simple—"What is this?"—or more complex. It doesn't matter, as long as you ask them.

In the "Preview with Questions to Answer" box at the beginning of each chapter in this book, there are one or more questions under each heading. Under the heading for this section, "Organizing your study time," is, "What is P–Q–R–S–R? What do porcupines have to do with it?" If you read this section looking for an answer to those questions, you will have an easier time learning the main ideas in this section.

Is Previewing and Questioning a waste of time? Before they have tried it, some students begrudge time spent doing it. They want to "get right to it," that is, begin reading and underlining right away, perhaps because they want to get studying over with. If you really want to learn the material, that's not an efficient way to begin. First, see the forest, and wonder what is in the forest. Only then, look at the trees.

Next, *Read* the material

But of course you cannot read the material as you would read the newspaper, because you have to find the main ideas and learn them. So, you read looking for the main ideas. (Review Chapter 9 on finding main ideas.)

When you find main ideas, mark them, or make notes about them, either in the margin of the text or in your notebook. (Review Chapter 6 for ideas on good note taking.) The purpose of marking is to highlight the main ideas so that you can go straight to them when you review the material.

Don't mark too much. Some students substitute marking for learning. Their eyes skim over the text, while their pens are marking like crazy. But unfortunately their minds are not learning much. You don't learn something just because you have underlined it. Texts should not be heavily marked.

Don't underline while reading. Underline *after* you read. First read a paragraph; then decide what is the main idea; then mark that. Your procedure should be:

- *Read*
- *Think*
- *Mark the main idea*

Emphasize the main ideas, sometimes with a bit of supporting detail.

Compare how you have marked a text with someone else who is studying the same material. That way, you will see if you agree about the main ideas, or if one of you is marking too much or sometimes missing the target.

As you find main ideas, use Strategies to learn them

This chapter and Chapter 12 are full of learning strategies you can use to help learn and remember the material:

- Self-explanation
- Elaboration
- Summarizing
- Visual aids

It's important to use them; you won't remember something just because you have read and marked it. Try varying them, so you don't use the same one all the time. You need to cement the ideas into your mind.

Remember: Learning strategies are very important. Use a lot of learning strategies, and you will learn a lot.

Review what you have learned

John is studying Spanish. He reads in his text that the Spanish word for "inexpensive" is *barrato*. A few minutes later he wants to write down that word in a sentence, but he can't remember it. He has to look it up again. That is absolutely typical. When we first learn something, it is very easy to forget it. Forgetting starts occurring almost as soon as we learn something, and there is considerable forgetting in the first twenty-four hours after learning. The only way to avoid this is to review our learning so it resists forgetting.

SKILL BUILDER 13.2

Making PQRSR a habit

A. Advantages and disadvantages.

If you are not sure you are willing to put in the time to use PQRSR, list here the advantages of just trying it. How can you overcome the disadvantages? How important is this technique to your life goals?

Advantages		Disadvantages
_____	■	_____
_____	■	_____
_____	■	_____
_____	■	_____

After thinking about this, what is your goal?

_____

_____

If it involves practicing the procedure, read on.

B. Practice the procedure.

1. **Practice P and Q.** Develop the system in small steps. For example, start by doing just step P for each study topic. To be sure you do it, keep a record. Give yourself reminders to do it, with self-instructions or a note stuck in your study workbook. Then add step Q, still keeping records and using reminders.

Record using P and Q steps when studying

Place a ✓ each time you use P and Q. Study session dates:

Date			Date			Date		
_____	P? ____	Q? ____	_____	P? ____	Q? ____	_____	P? ____	Q? ____
_____	P? ____	Q? ____	_____	P? ____	Q? ____	_____	P? ____	Q? ____
_____	P? ____	Q? ____	_____	P? ____	Q? ____	_____	P? ____	Q? ____
_____	P? ____	Q? ____	_____	P? ____	Q? ____	_____	P? ____	Q? ____
_____	P? ____	Q? ____	_____	P? ____	Q? ____	_____	P? ____	Q? ____

Write self-instructions or reminders to use P and Q:

_____

_____

Making PQRSR a habit

2. **Practice R.** Then Read as you usually do, following the ideas for marking noted here. Remember, your procedure should be: Read, Think, Mark the main idea.

3. **Practice S.** Now use the learning strategies you've been reading about: self-explanation, elaboration, summarizing, and visual aids. You've worked on these in the Skill Builders 12.1, 12.2, and 13.1. All you have to do is integrate those techniques into the PQRSR process.

   Keep a record of using one or more of the strategies as you study: Combine this with your records for using P and Q.

Your record of using learning strategies

Study session Date	Time	P?	Q?	Strategies used and number of times used
_____	_____	__	__	_____
				_____
_____	_____	__	__	_____
				_____
_____	_____	__	__	_____
				_____
_____	_____	__	__	_____
				_____
_____	_____	__	__	_____
				_____
_____	_____	__	__	_____
				_____
_____	_____	__	__	_____
				_____

SKILL BUILDER 13.2

Making PQRSR a habit

Study session Date Time	P?	Q?	Strategies used and number of times used
_____ _____	__	__	_____
			_____
_____ _____	__	__	_____
			_____

Example:

Study session Date Time	P?	Q?	Strategies used and number of times used
Oct. 3 7:00 P.M.	✓	✓	self-ex ✓✓✓✓✓ elab. ✓✓✓✓✓✓
			sum ✓✓✓✓ vis ✓✓

This student used P and Q, plus five self-explanations, six elaborations. four summaries and two visual aids.

Is it too much trouble to keep this record? If you don't keep the records, after a period you will stop practicing the habit. Record keeping encourages us to practice. Keep the record until it has truly become a habit.

4. **Practice R.** Finally, it's time to review. You should review at three different times: (a) at the end of each study period; (b) twenty-four hours later, and (c) other times before a test.

Write self-reminders to review:

_____

List your rewards for reviewing:

_____

Example: "If I do the whole three-step review—just after, twenty-four hours after, and a couple of times before the test—then I'll take off the whole weekend and do no studying at all."

Record of reviewing

Material studied	Reviewed at end of study?	Reviewed 24 hours later?	Reviewed several times before a test?
_____	_____	_____	_____
_____	_____	_____	_____

Making PQRSR a habit

Material studied	Reviewed at end of study?	Reviewed 24 hours later?	Reviewed several times before a test?

Example:

Communication test, ch. 4	✓	✓	✓✓✓

Remember to keep a skills-development attitude about PQRSR. You will not see an immediate, dramatic improvement in your grade just because you begin to use PQRSR. But once you establish it as a study habit, there will be big improvements.

Particularly when we have just learned something, it is easy to forget. This is why we have the embarrassing experience of forgetting the name of someone we just met. It's the same with studying. If you have just learned some new material, you can expect that it will fade out of memory easily.

This is why reviewing what you have learned is so important. After you have gone over a passage of text, and used the stages of P, Q, R, and S, you need to review the material to strengthen its hold in your memory. You can review just after you have completed studying a passage, and then review again within twenty-four hours.

In reviewing, don't read all the material over. Instead, read what you have marked or the notes you have made, plus any summaries available. If you have studied for fifty minutes, you might spend five more reviewing before stopping for the day.

Don't settle for one short review. After you have read through a segment of text, you will need to review it and your notes about it more than once before you can take a test on it. The most important circumstance affecting your long-term memory of something is how well you learn it in the first place.[5] And how well you learn it, is directly affected by how well you master it. What affects that? How much you practice the material.

This means you will want to *overlearn* material you are going to be tested on. Suppose John learns a list of ten new vocabulary words for his Spanish test tomorrow. If he stops practicing them as soon as he can say them correctly one time, he will forget several of them before the test tomorrow. In order to be sure he will remember them tomorrow, he needs to practice over and over *after* he can correctly say them, strengthening their connection in his mind, increasing the chance he will remember them. Your first goal should be very thorough learning, because you cannot thoroughly remember what you have not thoroughly learned.

Review, then, can occur more than once. You should review right at the end of a study period, and then again briefly the next day. You will also want to spend time learning material over and over, at a deeper level, while you are using learning strategies, to be sure you get the material well connected in your memory. Review again for any test you have to take. Each time you review you decrease the chances that you will forget important material.

Summary

Remember: PQRSR ("**P**or**Q** pines **R** Se**R**ious") means

- **P**review
- **Q**uestion
- **R**ead
- **S**trategies
- **R**eview

If your goal in studying is to get it over with quickly, then this information about reviewing is distasteful to you. Try resolving your ambivalence. We're not talking about working harder, after all, because reviewing what you have already learned is easier than learning it in the first place. Does it fit with your values to spend some time learning material, but then not put in the extra time needed to cement that material into your memory?

Using the PQRSR system may be completely new to your way of studying. Try it before you evaluate it. You can try one part at a time, or try the whole system for just one part of the material you need to study. If you don't try it, you may never learn its secret beauty: it helps you do well in school.

To help make the PQRSR system a habit, do Skill Builder 13.2.

Chapter 14

Studying in Special Situations: Mnemonics, Math, Science, and Literature

PREVIEW WITH QUESTIONS TO ANSWER

Mnemonics

- What are mnemonics, and how do they help?
- What are examples of using the method of locations and the method of first letters?

Studying math, science, and literature

- What are the best procedures in math and science?
- What is the best procedure in literature?

Mnemonics

When you learned the PQRSR system in Chapter 13 you were encouraged to develop a memory aid to remember the letters, something like "Por Q pines R SeRious." Another word for *memory aid* is *mnemonic* (pronounced "nay-MON-ik," derived from an ancient Greek word related to *memory*).

Mnemonics are useful when the material you have to learn is basically meaningless. PQRSR, for example, makes no sense by itself. Mnemonics give meaning or make things very simple, so we can remember them. For example, in what months is it safe to eat oysters? It's hard to remember, "January through April is okay, and September through December, but avoid May through August." An easy mnemonic for remembering this important information is "Any month with an R in it."

Or what months have only thirty days in them? Remember this verse?

> Thirty days hath September,
> April, June, and November,
> All the rest have thirty-one, et cetera.

The rhyme of the first and second line helps us remember. Remembering just the September part gets you started, and the need to rhyme finishes the idea.

QUESTIONS TO ANSWER AS YOU READ:

- What are mnemonics, and how do they help?
- What are examples of using the method of locations and the method of first letters?

Method of locations

Suppose you want to remember the letter series PQRSR, from Chapter 13. Think of a place very familiar to you, such as your room. As you look around the room, you see, in order: your bed, the closet, your chair, the desk, the large poster on the wall, and other objects. You picture a large purple letter *P* standing on your bed. The letter *Q* is peeking out of the closet. *R* stands very red on your chair. *S* sits on your desk, bleeding over the side. And another *R* is on the poster, boldly bright green in the middle of it.

That's the method of locations. Picture a very familiar spot, one you cannot possibly forget because you've seen it a thousand times, one you can easily picture in your mind. Use that spot as your Peg-Board. Associate any new set of items that you want to remember with that old, familiar scene. One item goes in each spot. If you make the association unusual or dramatic, it's even better, which is why you think of that second *R* hanging bright green in the poster, or *Q* peeking shyly from the closet.

Once you select the old, familiar scene to use as your Peg-Board, you can attach new memories to it any time you need to. If you're going to the office supply stores and need to remember what to buy, peg those items into your familiar spot so you will remember them later. There are broken pencils lying on the bed, there is an almost-empty bag of paper clips in the closet, and so on.

This is a great method. It always works if you firmly nail each thing to be remembered into its place on the Peg-Board, and if you make an unusual association (*S* isn't just sitting there, *S* is bleeding).

Method of first letters

PQRSR equals "Porcupine Quills Rarely Stab Rabbits." Making up a sentence like that, particularly if it is a little unusual, makes it much easier to remember some basically meaningless set of names or words. Suppose for your American history class you need to remember the names of the Great Lakes: Huron, Ontario, Michigan, Erie, and Superior. These are hard to remember because nothing ties them together. But if you learn the word *HOMES*, you have a much easier time remembering them. Use the first letter of each word to make up a word or sentence.

Medical students, who have to memorize many lists, like a list of all the bones in the hand, often use this technique to help them remember. If you can make up a rhyme, that works even better.

THINK PIECE 14.1 Locations, locations, locations

Like all other skills, you get better at using locations if you practice. Look for chances to practice. For example, instead of writing down your grocery list, peg each item into place in your memory location, then see if you don't remember them all when you get to the store. "Let's see, what's on the bed? Oh, yeah, a bottle of milk spilling out."

The most important idea here is to learn to use mnemonic strategies.[1] They don't do you any good if you don't use them. There are lots of opportunities to use them in the world. For example, suppose you want to remember three steps in a chemistry process. Or you want to remember the names of four rivers in Africa. Or you want to remember several new words in Spanish. Look for chances to use mnemonics, because they really help your memory a great deal.[2]

Studying Math, Science, and Literature

Cooking up good grades in math and science

QUESTIONS TO ANSWER AS YOU READ:

■ What are the best procedures in math and science?

■ What is the best procedure in literature?

Shantel is taking a first year course, Mathematics for Business, and sits down to study for it. She took the course because she believes that the more math she can do, the better the job she will get.

Shantel solves the first two problems, but can't figure out what to do on the third. She starts to get nervous. "Oh, no!" she says. But immediately another part of her mind steps in and takes over. "No," she says to herself. "Don't get nervous. You can probably figure it out." She calms herself with some deep breathing. "And suppose I can't figure it out," she says to herself. "So, what? I'm still learning this stuff. I'll ask Ms. Jones-Blackburn how to do it."

Shantel talks to her math instructor, Ms. Jones-Blackburn, often. She is always careful to go to class and be totally prepared by doing whatever the reading was. She has noticed that Ms. Jones-Blackburn sticks very close to the reading, pretty much covering the same material in class. Shantel never misses a class, though sometimes she is tempted. When that happens, she reminds herself that a major goal of hers is to get a good job and that this course will help her reach that goal, so she should go to class. In class Shantel tries to follow what Ms. Jones-Blackburn is talking about, but sometimes she is confused. When that happens her hand shoots up and she asks a question.

Now Shantel is trying to solve the fourth problem in the homework assignment. First, she translates the problem into

---

THINK PIECE 14.2   Practicing mnemonics

If you don't remind yourself to use learning strategies, you won't use them. Keep a record of using mnemonic strategies. Set a goal, such as, "I'm going to use one memory aid strategy each week;" then keep a record of actually using it.

English, from math, and she asks herself, "What is this problem about?" She tries to understand it. She makes a sketch of the problem to see if that helps her understand it. It does, so now she asks herself, "Well, how should I proceed to solve this? Where am I trying to end up?" She forms an estimate in her mind of what the solution might look like. She tries a couple of different ways of solving the problem. They don't work, but she doesn't give up. "I'll give it eight more minutes," she thinks. She tells herself, "Try one of those solution strategies Jones-Blackburn was talking about in class today." Finally she hits on the path to the solution. "Be careful, now," she tells herself. "Don't make any dumb errors." The rest of the day is easy.

You can be as good a student as Shantel if you just do what she does. Let's analyze that.

First, Shantel is right. If you can come out of college with some math skills—not great ones, just some—you will greatly improve your job prospects. Many students are stuck in math bozohood, so if you can become motivated, you will do very well. Math is a tool that helps you get good jobs. Even a little bit of skill helps.

Deal with anxiety and doubt. Shantel copes with the anxiety that math sometimes causes. Many of us feel this anxiety, because in the past we've found math frustrating—perhaps because it was taught badly—and we feel threatened by it. Now as soon as we encounter difficulty, we begin to get nervous, and we often avoid math altogether to avoid that dread feeling.

If you begin to get nervous, take some time to relax yourself. Try meditation and deep muscle relaxation from Chapter 16. Watch what you say to yourself. If you have thoughts like, "I can't do this; I can't do math," you're setting yourself up for a bad experience. Get rid of self-defeating thoughts, and substitute ones that tell you how to get rid of the anxiety. "I will relax. I am just beginning at this, so I won't be great. All I have to do is stay relaxed and practice developing my skills." Take a break, get calm, and then resume the math. Take a skills-development attitude. When Shantel couldn't solve a problem, for example, she thought, "So, what? I'm still learning this stuff."

You may believe that you do *not* have much math ability. Where will that self-defeating thought lead you? First, you could be wrong. Maybe you just haven't developed your ability yet. Second, and more importantly, *it doesn't matter*. We are *not* talking about becoming a math major; we are talking about learning enough math skills to get a nice job. The trick to getting to that level is not talent, it is persistence. (Your author started graduate school making the lowest grade in the class in a math course, but ended tying for the top grade simply because he never, never gave up. The people he was tied with probably had lots more talent, but who cares?)

You *can* get to a medium level of math skill—which will be a great help on a job—if you are simply very persistent.

Be persistent. Being persistent makes up for a great deal of low self-confidence. Notice how Shantel does not give up easily. When she gets frustrated because she can't understand the problem, she gives herself a time limit: "I'll give it eight more minutes." Setting a time limit is a good method for reducing frustration. That way, you don't feel as if you are trapped in some awful math problem and will never get out, and you don't have to keep working until you have tears in your eyes.

(Try this method when you make a phone call and are placed on hold. Tell yourself, "Okay, I'll wait two minutes." If someone comes on, great. If not, hang up and call back later. It reduces frustration.)

Attend classes. Go to all the classes, and concentrate in class. Keep records of class attendance, use self-reminders and rewards, but be sure to go to all classes. Math and science are very dense subjects, so you cannot afford to miss even one class period. Arrive in class having already done any reading you were supposed to do, even if it won't be tested that day. Math and science classes usually follow the outline of the text closely, so your learning benefits if you come to class prepared.

Sit near the front where you will be sure to focus. Listen carefully as the instructor explains things. Try to follow his or her logic. Ask questions whenever you are confused. Most instructors welcome questions. It shows you are interested, which they like.

Take a problem-solving approach. When you are studying on your own, read very slowly. Explain each sentence to yourself. Translate problems into English. For example, if the algebra problem is $a \times 6 = 12$, say to yourself, "Okay, a times 6 equals 12, so what is a?"

Take a problem-solving approach to any math or science problem. This gives you a way to think about problems. First, be sure you understand what you need to do. Then, work out a plan and carry it out. Talk yourself through solving problems. This gives you a model, your own speech, to follow, so you're not struggling blind.[3]

Here's an example of a schoolboy solving the following math problem:

$$\frac{176}{4} = ?$$

(You already know how to do this kind of math problem without talking to yourself, but this is a good example of someone coping with a problem that is at the limit of his skill. It's the kind of situation you will be facing, but at a higher level.)

So, 176 over 4 equals what? To find out, I've got to divide 4 into 176. I start on the left of 176 and move over until I've got a number big enough to divide 4 into. Let's see. 1 is too small. So, 17. Right. Now, 4 goes into 16 four times, and it goes into 20 five times. My number is 17, too small for five times, so the first number is 4. Gives me 16. Subtract the 16 from 17, that leaves 1 to carry down. Now bring down the next digit. Oh, it gives me 16 again, and I can divide 4 into that four times, and nothing is left over. So the answer is 44.

First, the boy tells himself what he needs to do: "I've got to divide 4 into 176." Then he tells himself how to do that, and keeps talking himself through the problem as he goes. Talking your way through math or science problems can be a big help.

Use learning strategies for studying and test taking. Turn word or symbol problems into visual scenes. This can be particularly helpful if you favor a visual learning style. For example, suppose the problem is, "A man wants to build a fence 180 feet long with supporting wooden 4 x 4's set in cement every 10 feet. How many 4 x 4's will he need?" You might be tempted just to divide 180 by 10, but if you visualize the fence you will see that this leads to the wrong answer.

When studying for tests, make lists of concepts you will need to know. For example, someone studying geology and earthquakes might make this list:

Tectonic movement

Plates

Fault zones

Tremors

Richter scale

Then ask yourself if you fully understand each concept. Beware the temptation only to review the material you know and skip the scary stuff you don't yet know well. Check off each concept only after you fully understand it.

Beware of holding the *wrong* understanding of a concept. Common sense gives us explanations that can make it harder to understand the real science, that is, holding the wrong idea makes it difficult to understand the right idea.[4] For example, many people believe that objects float on water because they are light and sink if they are heavy. (If you think for a moment, you'll realize this can't be true, because heavy metal ships float.) People can find it difficult to understand the scientific explanation, which emphasizes the relative density of the particles that make up the object and the weight of the water displaced.

Always check your answers, particularly on tests. Careless mistakes are common in math and science, and they rob you of the credit you deserve.

Remind yourself to use strategies like these: "Hey, remember to translate into English" or "Talk myself through this one step at a time." People who remind themselves to use these strategies are more likely to continue to use the strategies after their first practice sessions, and that helps them, because these strategies really do help.

You can use Skill Builder 14.1 to practice study strategies for math and science.

Studying Literature

Some students think that since all they have to do is read a story, there's nothing special to studying literature. But in a literature class you will be asked to talk about what you have read and will be asked test questions about it, too. Yet there's nothing to memorize, so how do you study?

First, do the reading. If you're taking a course in literature, make sure you read the literature. Don't go to class unprepared.

Second, be prepared to talk about the reading in class. That's where important points can come out. For example, what are the moral implications of what happened in the story? Or, could this kind of situation really happen?

Third, keep the following questions in mind as you read. If you can answer these, you will go a long way toward being ready to talk about the material you've read:[5]

- Who is the main character?

- Where and when does the story take place?

- What did the main character do?

- How did the story end?

- How did the main character feel?

You can then add to this your own reactions.

- How do you feel about the story?

- What questions does it raise in your mind?

THINK PIECE 14.3   Practicing literary skills

If you wanted to develop these skills for a literature course, what would you do? You could set goals for yourself, such as "I will always do the reading before class" or "I will say at least one comment in each lit class." You could keep records of how well you achieve your goals. You could give yourself instructions, such as "Learn the answers to those questions so I can talk about them in class." You could keep records of going to class, and participating in class. Try setting up your own habit-forming skill builder.

Study strategies for math and science

Are these skills for you? Do you believe your job prospects will improve if you develop some skill at math and science? Is it worth putting in the time, and coping with your possible negative feelings? Does developing these skills fit in with your life goals?

A. Think through and write down the advantages and disadvantages of developing study strategies for these subjects.

Advantages	Disadvantages
_____	■ _____
_____	■ _____
_____	■ _____
_____	■ _____

Example:

Might get a better job.	■ *Might get nervous.*

B. Practice the skills.

1. **Practice anxiety and boredom control.** Control negative self-talk, such as "I can't do this," "I'll never understand this," or "I hate this." Write what you will do to control these thoughts (stop them when you notice them; substitute self-talk that leads to a skills-development approach):

   _____

   _____

   Write which relaxation techniques (meditation, exercise, or muscle relaxation) you will use.

   _____

   _____

2. **Plan your class time.** Write what you will do to get the most you can out of class time (always going to class, sitting in the front, being prepared, or asking questions):

   _____

   _____

3. **Plan your study time.** Write what you will do to make study time productive (translating all problems into English, talking your way through problems, making a visual representation of the problem, or limiting your frustration time when working on a problem):

   _____

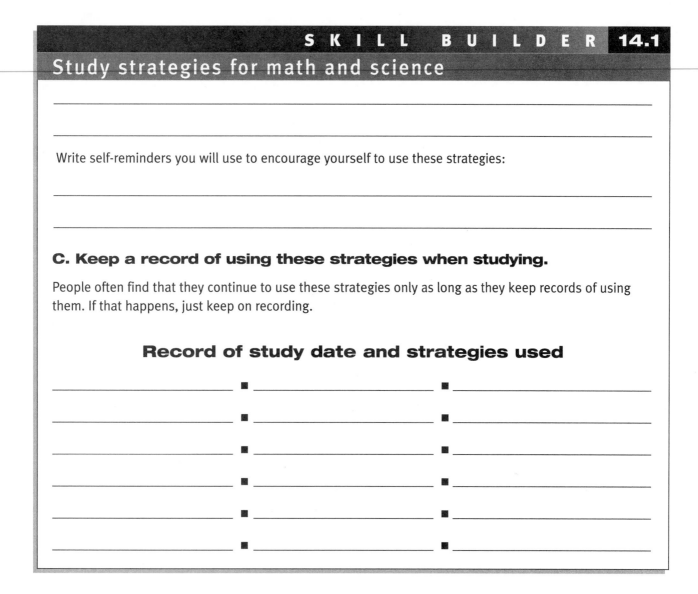

SKILL BUILDER 14.1

Study strategies for math and science

_____

_____

Write self-reminders you will use to encourage yourself to use these strategies:

_____

_____

C. Keep a record of using these strategies when studying.

People often find that they continue to use these strategies only as long as they keep records of using them. If that happens, just keep on recording.

Record of study date and strategies used

_____ ■ _____ ■ _____

_____ ■ _____ ■ _____

_____ ■ _____ ■ _____

_____ ■ _____ ■ _____

_____ ■ _____ ■ _____

_____ ■ _____ ■ _____

Part VI

Taking Tests:
The Good, the Bad, and the Ugly

Which would you rather do, take a test or have an injection? When a large psychology class was asked that question, 84 percent said they would rather have an injection. One guy shouted, "Give me the shot!" Suppose you could substitute a series of injections for all the tests you have to take during a semester. Would you rather have all those shots or take all those tests? Seventy-four percent of the class said they would rather have all those shots.

Tests are stressful.

What's the difference between the people who take tests in their stride and the ones who find tests nerve wracking? It is *not* their personal characteristics that make the difference. The calm ones are *not* necessarily smarter or calmer in general. It's what they do to *prepare for* and *take* tests that keeps them calmer and helps them do well. In this part of the book, you'll learn their secrets.

The advantages of learning this material are less stress and better grades. You can reach those goals if you practice the skills taught here.

Students show on average a twenty-five percent improvement in their GPA after practicing these ideas for only one semester.[1] That would mean moving, for example, from a GPA of 2.4 to a GPA of 3.0, a big jump. If you get anxious while taking tests, and don't do as well as a result, you can expect *even more* improvement. People who get anxious on tests have been shown to benefit *most* from the practices you will learn.[2]

You may already have developed some of the skills outlined here. What is here that might help you, and what is here that you don't need?

Here is a series of questions covering the test-taking skills taught. Your answers will tell you what skills you might work on.

❶ Are you usually well prepared for a test?
Do you put in enough effort studying?   Yes___ No___
Do you manage your study time?   Yes___ No___
Do you cram too much?   Yes___ No___

❷ Do you try to predict test questions?   Yes___   No___
How well do the ones you predict fit the actual questions?
Well_____   Not well_____

❸ When you take a test, are you at your best, physically and mentally, or do you sometimes do things that keep you from being at your best?
Usually at my best_____
Sometimes do things that keep me from being at my best_____

❹ Do you think of tests as a test of how you look socially, or you do think of them more as a test of your current level of skill development?
More like a test of how I look_____
More like a test of skill level_____

❺ Are you nervous while taking a test?   Yes___   No___

❻ Do you calm yourself before a test?   Yes___   No___

❼ During the test, do you keep your mind focused on doing the work, and not let yourself worry?
Yes___   No___

❽ Do you have a system to follow to answer multiple-choice tests?
Yes___   No___

❾ Do you have a system to follow to answer essay tests?
Yes___   No___

What do you learn from these questions? What skills should you work on? Pick the skills you definitely need to improve, but also pick one you are good at but would enjoy getting even better at. Make a list here of the skills you think you will work on while reading these chapters.

_____

_____

_____

Chapter 15

Preparing for Tests

PREVIEW WITH QUESTIONS TO ANSWER

Be well prepared

■ How should you prepare for an upcoming test or a distant test?

■ What is your academic two-minute drill?

■ What are the rules for cramming?

Predict test questions

■ Where can you get ideas to predict test questions?

■ How can you develop this skill?

Be Well Prepared

One of the main reasons students get nervous or frustrated on tests is because they have *not* prepared adequately. The more you prepare for a test, the better you will do on it.

Time management

When you have a test coming, you should schedule study times to prepare for it.

> Joanne had two midterms coming, one in communication and one in psychology. She scheduled study times in the days before the midterms:
>
> | | | |
> |---|---|---|
> | Monday, | 8:00 – 10:00 A.M. | Study Communication |
> | Tuesday, | 7:00 – 8:00 A.M. | Study Psychology |
> | | 6:30 – 7:30 P.M. | Study Psychology |
> | Wednesday, | 8:00 – 10:00 A.M. | Study Communication |

A schedule like this reduces cramming—and therefore reduces stress. It also allows you to learn more—and therefore do better on the test.

Skill Builder 15.1 can help you practice planning for an upcoming test.
Some courses have a quiz nearly every week. All you have to do to
keep up is follow a weekly schedule of studying. For courses that have
only a midterm and final, however, there is a temptation not to study until
just before the test, which leads to stressful cramming.

Set aside time every week to work on that material, even if you won't
be tested for weeks. When the time for the midterm or final comes, your
study work can be focused on reviewing, instead of trying to learn all the
material for the first time.

Jennifer was a single, working mother who had come back
to school after years away. "In one of my courses we only had
a final exam, plus a paper, and I worried about being ready
for that final. I set aside one hour each week for the whole
semester to study for it. Every Friday at 3:00 I would work
on that course for one hour. This worked out great. When
finals time came, all I had to do was review because I had
already been over the material."

SKILL BUILDER 15.1

Planning for an upcoming test

**A. Pick a test that is coming in a week. Decide how many hours you
need to study for it.**

Estimate of necessary hours: _____

This estimate may change as you get into the material and find that you need more or less time.

**B. Work out a schedule from now to test time to put in the necessary
hours. Spread out the study hours.**

Schedule only as many hours as you will actually do. If you need eight hours but know in your heart you
will only do four, schedule four. The important thing now is to start. Later you can increase. For now, the
important thing is to practice scheduling.

Study hours for upcoming test seven days away

Day 1	Day 2	Day 3	Day 4	Day 5	Day 6	Day 7
_____	_____	_____	_____	_____	_____	_____

**C. To develop this as a habit, follow this procedure for each
upcoming test.**

Make several copies of this form, or enter your schedule in your weekly planner from Part II.

To keep track of your progress, put a ✓ each time you do the scheduled work.

A two-minute drill for exam time

Professional football teams have a set of plays they run in the last two minutes of each half, called the two-minute drill. They decide long before the game begins what they will do in those two minutes, so they don't have to make decisions while rushed. You should do the same for midterm and finals week, the ends of your halves.

S K I L L   B U I L D E R   15.2

Planning to study for a distant test

For a course in which you have only a midterm and/or final, work out a study schedule to span the time from now until the distant test. The goal is to do enough of the studying between now and the test that you will mainly be reviewing in the last days before the test.

If you know you won't do an hour, use shaping: start at a level you know you will do, then gradually increase.

A. Write the subject and the date of the distant test.

Subject: _____ Date of test :_____

B. Schedule one study hour for the subject for each week between now and the distant test.

Weeks leading up to the test

1 (now)	2	3	4	5	6	7	8

Scheduled study hour   ____ ____ ____ ____ ____ ____ ____ ____

C. Repeat this practice for a second subject or a second test. (Make more copies of this form if necessary.)

Subject: _____ Date of test: _____

Weeks leading up to the test

1 (now)	2	3	4	5	6	7	8

Scheduled study hour   ____ ____ ____ ____ ____ ____ ____ ____

D. Keep track of your progress.

Put a ✓ each time you do the scheduled work. If you find you are not doing the work, reschedule. What is interfering with your doing it?

If you see that you are *not* beginning, start by requiring an amount of time so low you know you can do it.

Example: "I'm going to study for that distant test ten minutes this week." Schedule that time. Then gradually increase the amount of time. Keep a record with ✓s on your schedule to ensure that you do begin.

Work out a study plan for midterms and finals before the time arrives, so you can be sure to allocate enough time to study everything you need to study.

Make a copy of your daily schedule from Part II, to work out your two-minute drill. Enter your exam times, work times, and any other scheduled events. Even though finals may be weeks away, it is good practice to work out a schedule for finals week and the days just before it.

Cramming

In spite of your best intentions, sometimes you end up cramming. Since you may have to do it some time, here are some ideas on how to cram better.

Rule 1: Try to avoid cramming. Material that is learned all at one time is less well remembered than material that is learned over a spaced-out period. Also, cramming makes you nervous, which means you won't think as well on the test. The best way to avoid cramming is to schedule study times earlier than the last minute.

Rule 2: To remember well, don't just read it, say it out loud or write it down. Look for connections to what you already know. As you learned in Part V, that leads to better storage of the material in your memory. Mark, a varsity basketball player, put it perfectly: "When you zoom through a chapter, not really getting the idea of what you just read, your brain is just not processing the information, and that makes it very hard to remember when it is time for the test." You only process the information when you elaborate it, so that should be your focus. Don't skim; elaborate, because that ties the new information into your mind.

Rule 3: Work on getting the big picture rather than acquiring little factoids. Try to get the outline of the material into your mind. Also, do not try to cover everything. It is better to understand some of it than skim all of it. If you go for quantity, there is a real danger that you won't remember anything at exam time, but if you go for quality, at least you will remember some of the material.

Rule 4: Don't cram right up until the last minute. Sometimes you see students frantically flipping the pages of their textbook thirty seconds before the test is given out. All that does is make them nervous, which increases the chances they will miss questions they might have gotten right if they were calm. Spend the last part of the time available before a test getting calm and relaxed.

Predict Test Questions

During the test is *not* a good time to find out you don't know something. Yet many students make that mistake. They think they have studied

QUESTIONS TO ANSWER AS YOU READ:

■ Where can you get ideas to predict test questions?

■ How can you develop this skill?

enough, but then they are completely surprised by a question on the test. At that point some people get nervous, which makes it harder to do any of the other questions on the exam. It would be nice to avoid this.

Being well prepared includes *predicting the questions* that will come on the test, and knowing the answers to them. If you are well prepared, there are no big surprises. "Oh, yeah, that question. Well, I'm ready for it." That's a great feeling.

Are there advantages to predicting questions?

There are strong advantages to predicting upcoming test questions. It makes the test less stressful. Students who often get nervous on tests benefit considerably from learning to predict what questions will be on a test.[1] It helps them stay calm. Also, students who do poorly on tests are often *overconfident* about their knowledge before the test.[2] Predicting test questions helps them see what they need to know.

> Corrine made a list of eighteen possible questions she might see on her communication exam. Her list included questions such as "Explain the difference between denotative and connotative meaning" and "Explain metacommunication." She outlined what her answer would be for each. This allowed Corrine to see what she needed to study. She realized that she understood denotative and connotative meaning, for example, but could not adequately explain metacommunication, so she studied that topic more.

What types of questions will be on the test?

The instructor should tell you whether the test will be, for example, essay questions or multiple choice. It is often better to study as if you were going to take essay questions, even when you are not. Studying for essay questions encourages you to organize your knowledge, and that helps you remember.

Where do you get your ideas on what questions to predict?

Notice your own thinking. As you read the text or listen to a lecture, you might think, "This is important." "That's a possible question for the upcoming test." If you're reading about the D-Day invasion in World War II, for example, and notice you're thinking, "Gee, that changed everything," then that's a clue that the material is important and might be on a test.

Textbooks often indicate what is important. They can do this by the use of headings—"Causes of World War II"—or *italicized* or **boldfaced** material. If the text is well organized, you can tell if something is important even if you don't know what it is. In Chapter 1 of a chemistry text[3] is a section headed "Law of Conservation of Mass." There are several paragraphs explaining the history of the idea and what it means, and an example showing the law in operation in the burning of magnesium in a flash bulb. There are also two exercises in measurement so the student can see how the law works, and five photographs. More than three pages are devoted to the topic. All this attention tells us this law is important. A test question on that chapter might be, "Explain the law of conservation of mass, and give an example of how measurement demonstrates it."

Instructors may tell you, directly or indirectly, what questions they think are important and therefore may be on the text.

> Jenny wrote "Many instructors tell you what is to be included on the test. I began highlighting that in my notes. I was taking a political science class on "the world's *isms*," including *liberalism, capitalism, communism, socialism*, etc. While discussing the final exam, the professor said the words, 'You better know socialism.' Wow! So I really studied up on socialism, and sure enough, it was on the final. I couldn't believe it."

Ask your instructor,

- "What is important?" or
- "What kind of questions will be on the test?"

Students who ask these questions often do better on tests than students who don't ask. You're not asking for special help, but you do want to know if something is important.

Copies of old tests are helpful because they give you an idea of the kind of questions an instructor likes. One instructor, for example, always has questions about psychology that begin, "Give an example from daily life of [some psychological concept]." If you know that, it helps you study the material.

The emphasis the instructor gives to topics in lectures is also a clue.

> Jenny, proud of her new ability to read instructors' minds, later wrote, "I was taking World Civ, and we got an entire hour lecture on Alexander the Great. Starting in Greece, his father, all his battles, devoted troops and generals, trips to India, with maps and so on. Later the professor mentioned him again. I got the message: Alexander the Great was Big. I thought he might be on the test, and sure enough, he was."

When you are making up practice test questions, don't just use definitions. If the test question calls for application or analysis, you can't just regurgitate the material; you have to understand it. "What is reinforcement?" would be a weak question on a psychology test. Try to think of questions that test your understanding, such as, "Which of the following is an example of reinforcement?" A question on a chemistry test like "What is the law of conservation of mass?" is less challenging than a question like "Explain the law of conservation of mass and give an example from the laboratory."

When studying, be sure you pay attention to what you don't know

It can be reassuring to work on a question you already know well, but it's the questions you *cannot* answer that will mess you up on the test. Even graduate students tend to study material they already know instead of working on the scary material they don't know.[4] Don't just make notes about questions you are able to answer. You need to know what you don't know so you can work on the material *before* the test.

When you try to predict multiple-choice items, think not only of the correct answer, but the alternatives you might have to choose between. You might be asked to make a difficult distinction. Suppose you predict the question on a history test is going to be "What is the date of D-Day?" You need to know specifically what year. It's not enough to just vaguely remember "In the 1940s" because your choices might be "1943, 1944, 1945, 1946."

Developing test prediction is a skill

Once you are good at this test prediction, it is *not* difficult to get yourself to do it because you see immediate results in the tests you take. When you are just beginning the skill you may not see dramatic effects right away, so you should take steps to get yourself to practice until your good work has results on the tests you take.

Remember the basic procedure: *Set goals, work out procedures to reach those goals, and keep track of how well you are doing.*

> Franklin decided to work on his skill at predicting test questions. He had two courses that had tests every Friday, so there was plenty of chance for practice. Midterms were coming also, and he hoped he could get good at the skill in time to help with them.
>
> "I usually don't try to predict any test questions, so I figured I should start small. I set a goal: predict four multiple-choice questions each week for each of the two quizzes I have to take—psychology and sociology. I would work up the answers for them too. My plan was to gradually increase the number of questions by two each week, so that after five weeks I would be predicting twelve questions." Franklin wrote down this

SKILL BUILDER 15.3

Predicting test questions

Practice predicting test questions. This form won't cover all the predictions you need to make, so make copies of it to use.

A. Predict three questions for an upcoming multiple-choice test:

Subject: _____

1. Predicted question with correct answer:

_____

_____

_____

Possible incorrect alternatives:

_____   _____   _____

2. Predicted question with correct answer:

_____

_____

_____

Possible incorrect alternatives:

_____   _____   _____

3. Predicted question with correct answer:

_____

_____

_____

Possible incorrect alternatives:

_____   _____   _____

B. Check your predicted questions above.

1. Are they more than just definitions? Do they test understanding or application of the concepts?

Yes _____   No _____

Predicting test questions

2. Do some come from the text?   Yes _____ No _____

3. Are some from lectures?   Yes _____ No _____

4. Are you testing yourself on material you don't know, not just on what you do know? Yes _____ No _____

C. Predict three questions for upcoming essay-question test:

Subject: _____

1. Predicted question:

_____

_____

_____

Outline of answer: _____

_____

2. Predicted question:

_____

_____

_____

Outline of answer: _____

_____

3. Predicted question:

_____

_____

_____

Outline of answer: _____

_____

S K I L L   B U I L D E R   15.3

Predicting test questions

D. Check your predicted questions above.

1. Are they more than just definitions? Do they test understanding or application of the concepts?

   Yes _____ No _____

2. Do some come from the text?   Yes _____ No _____

3. Are some from lectures?   Yes _____ No _____

4. Are you testing yourself on material you don't know, not just on what you do know?   Yes _____ No _____

E. Make predicting questions a habit.

To develop predictions as a study skill, you must practice. Follow the usual procedure: Set goals (start low and take small steps); keep records of your progress; reorganize if necessary; work out self-directions to encourage yourself to do the practice; and work out rewards to reinforce doing it. Be sure to adopt a skills-development attitude.

1. Record of the number of items predicted for the next several multiple-choice tests. Give the date of test and the number of items you attempted to predict. Set goals and try to gradually increase. Replan as necessary.

   _____   _____   _____   _____

   _____   _____   _____   _____

   _____   _____   _____   _____

schedule in his notebook and made a space where he could check off each week if he had done the required work.

"The first week went fine, but the second week I was too bored with the material to try to predict six questions. I had to regroup. I rearranged my schedule to only increase one question each week. Start with three; go up one at a time. I wrote the new schedule in my notebook. I would say to myself, 'Come on, Franklin, this is like medicine. It tastes bad, but it's good for you, so take your medicine,' and then I would do the work. I made sure I put a check mark in my book to show I had done it. And I had a great idea: if it was medicine, it would leave a bad taste in my mouth, so I let myself go get a frozen yogurt if—but only if—I did the work.

"I am in the sixth week now, and I will predict eight questions in each course this week. I can already see that my grades are getting better."

SKILL BUILDER 15.3

Predicting test questions

2. Record the number of questions you predicted, with an outlined answer, for your next several essay-question tests. Give the date and the number of questions. Set goals and try to gradually increase.

_____   _____   _____   _____

_____   _____   _____   _____

3. Write self-directions you could use to encourage yourself to do this work when the time comes:

_____

_____

Example: Roger tells himself, "I never predict test questions, but I would do better on the tests if I did. So, start. Predict at least two or three questions on this upcoming test."

4. Write rewards you could give yourself for doing the work:

_____

Example: Roger says to himself, "I won't go out to join the group until I've predicted at least two, even better, three, test questions when I'm studying for that upcoming test."

Franklin set specific goals, kept track of his progress, used reminders to prompt himself to do the work, used small steps, re-organized when he made mistakes in the first plan, and rewarded himself for doing the practice.

Take a skills-development attitude toward your ability to predict test questions.

Test results are feedback about how you are doing so far, but have no implications about your self-worth. If your skill at predicting questions improves, so will your scores on tests. Don't compare yourself with other people, because others' scores are not relevant to your goals. Think of the test results as an indication of your current level of skill at predicting the questions.

If you emphasize performance goals, on the other hand, you are more likely to fear tests and not do as well on them. Making high grades is hard, and if that is your only goal, you can get discouraged. But improving your skill at predicting questions from your current level is possible, and if that is your goal, you can feel optimistic about success.

Skill Builder 15.3 can help you practice predicting test questions.

Chapter 16

Staying Calm and Focused

PREVIEW WITH QUESTIONS TO ANSWER

Getting calm for tests
- What do you already know that will calm you?

Meditation
- What is a good procedure for meditating?

Muscle relaxation
- How do you do deep muscle relaxation, and what does it get you?

Staying mentally focused
- What can you do to stay focused on a test?

Getting nervous on tests is one of the main reasons students do not do well in school.[1] Becoming nervous is unpleasant, but even worse, it makes you perform poorly. It is like stage fright: the actor might know the lines, and perform well in rehearsal, but stage fright can ruin the performance. The same is true for getting nervous on tests. When you become nervous, your memories are jammed up, and you are not able to remember things that you would have remembered if you were calm. Also, you are not able to think as well, so you don't solve problems or think of solutions you might otherwise have done.

It is a shame to know the material but then not be able to think clearly on a test because you are too nervous. Our goal in this chapter is to learn how to stay calm both while studying and while taking tests. There are several different things you can do.

Getting Calm for Tests

Be prepared

One of the best things you can do to stay calm during a test is to be well prepared. Students often get nervous when taking a test because they know in their hearts that they are not well prepared.[2] It's nerve-wracking taking a test you are

QUESTION TO ANSWER
AS YOU READ:

■ What do you already know
that will calm you?

not ready for, so give yourself a break and walk into the room prepared. That should be step number one. The next step is to be sure you are calm.

De-stress yourself

People who do *not* take steps to reduce their stress on tests not only don't perform as well on the test, they also are more likely to get sick toward the end of each semester.

Exercise is calming. Chapter 4 has suggested practice for making exercise a part of your daily life. Exercise has the effect of changing your body's reaction to stress, so that you become less stressed when something upsetting happens *and* you get over the stress more quickly.

If you are having trouble with nervousness on tests, you definitely should increase your exercise.

Meditation

QUESTION TO ANSWER
AS YOU READ:

■ What is a good procedure for
meditating?

Students report using a variety of techniques for calming down just before a test: deep-breathing exercises, "letting my mind go blank," "closing my eyes and just relaxing," focusing on their breathing, or praying. These are forms of meditation.

Meditation helps you relax.[3] You can meditate to be calm either while you are studying or while you are taking a test.

Pay attention to your emotional state while you are taking a test or studying, so that you are not in full panic before you realize something is wrong. It is easier to calm yourself if you notice early that you are beginning to be nervous.[4]

"I can feel it as soon as I read a question I don't know the answer to. Sort of a jolt. Wham! Maybe my heart skips, I don't know. But then I begin to get nervous."

THINK PIECE 16.1   Exercise and nerves

If you are getting too nervous on tests, ask yourself, "What is the relationship between getting too nervous and not getting enough exercise?"

When was the last time you got too nervous on a test? _____

Did you get enough exercise in the week before that?   Yes _____   Probably not _____.

What should you do? Go back to Chapter 4, in the section on stress proofing, and work out a plan to get more exercise in the future. Don't go on reading this chapter until you've done the work in Chapter 4. The next sections teach other ways of calming yourself, but they will work even more effectively if you also get enough exercise.

The best approach to dealing with this reaction is to calm yourself *before* you begin the test.

> Mrs. DeFoe, a grandmother back in school for the first time in forty years, explained how she begins a test. "The first thing to do is get myself to calm down. Many years ago during Lamaze class [instruction in techniques for minimizing pain and the need for pain medication during childbirth] I learned deep breathing and focusing techniques, and I always practice these in any situation in which I might get nervous. After all, they got me through two childbirth labors! Once calm, I address the test."

There are at least nine different forms of meditation that have been developed around the world.[5] Here is one of the simplest techniques, developed in the United States by a medical doctor.[6]

The basic idea is to relax by reducing your attention to the outside world and focusing inward. Here is the procedure to follow:

1. Sit comfortably, away from noise and interruptions.
2. Try not to pay attention to things outside your body.
3. That is easier to do if you have something in your mind to focus on. Use the word *one.* Say it over and over to yourself, silently. Focus on it.
4. While you are doing this, other thoughts will come into your mind. But this is not the time for problem solving, so just let these thoughts drift out again, like water flowing down a river. When you realize you've been thinking about something else, gently go back to *one.*
5. Do this ten to twenty minutes, twice a day. Try it just before taking a test or before studying. Try it for a short time even during the test if you start to feel nervous.
6. People sometimes fall asleep when they do this, but that's not a problem. Normally people feel more awake yet calmer after meditating. Some people, in fact, feel very awake, so it's not a good idea to do this just before trying to go to sleep.

> Jennifer, returning to school after several years away, said, "Before every study period I check to see if I'm at all nervous, and if I am, I meditate. Before every test I spend fifteen minutes in the car in the parking lot, meditating and relaxing. When I get into the testing room, I close my eyes and meditate again, for a minute or two. If I begin to feel nervous while I'm taking the test, I put down my pencil and meditate for a minute or two, long enough to get calm again. When I took the GED test, I meditated between each part

while they were handing out the stuff. It always helps me get calm or stay calm.

"Some people asked me if I ever went to sleep in the car when meditating before a class. No, not for more than a minute. I've done it at home, when things were less pressing, but not really in the car just before a test."

Muscle Relaxation

QUESTION TO ANSWER AS YOU READ:

■ How do you do deep muscle relaxation, and what does it get you?

Once tension starts on a test, it is not likely to go away on its own. You have to take control and substitute relaxation for the tension. People use a variety of techniques—meditation, muscle stretching, martial arts, focus on breathing—to get themselves to relax.

Benefits of muscle relaxation

Deep muscle relaxation is a good method to use. We often tie up much tension in our muscles. Getting rid of that tension by relaxing the mus-

---

THINK PIECE 16.2 **Practicing meditation**

You get better at meditating through practice. Try meditation for two weeks to see if it helps you stay calm on tests.

Once or twice a day—before the day becomes stressful—set aside time to meditate for ten or more minutes:

Sunday	Monday	Tuesday	Wednesday	Thursday	Friday	Saturday
_____ ■	_____ ■	_____ ■	_____ ■	_____ ■	_____ ■	_____
_____ ■	_____ ■	_____ ■	_____ ■	_____ ■	_____ ■	_____

Keep a record of sticking to your schedule. Put a ✓ when you do the scheduled meditation.

Meditate before or during tests if you tend to get nervous on them. Keep a record of each test, and give yourself instructions just beforehand to be sure you meditate:

1. Write self-instructions to meditate just before a test:

_____

2. If you become nervous while taking a test, stop for a couple of minutes of meditation. Write directions to set your mind like radar to notice that you are getting nervous—pick up the first blip of panic—and want to take time out to meditate:

_____

_____

3. Keep a record each time you meditate before or during a test.

cles is a good way to feel less stressed-out. You won't feel tense if your muscles are relaxed.

Using this procedure really helps. One group of people who got very nervous on tests practiced this method for several weeks.[7] It reduced their nervousness on tests, and fifteen months later they were still *less* anxious when taking tests. In another experiment all but one student said they had benefited from the training, and students said that on the average they found two different ways that the relaxation helped.[8] They used relaxation not only for taking tests, but in social situations, with sleep problems, on job interviews, in the dentist's chair, on an airplane, and during sports competitions.

> A tennis player explained, "I used to get too tense in a tight game, and it would mess up my serve. Now I tell myself, 'Relax,' before every serve. It really helps my serve because I use proper form."

The procedure

Follow this procedure[9] for deep muscle relaxation. First tense a set of muscles. Then release that tension, so that the muscles relax more deeply than they were before, and softly say "Relax" to yourself. After some practice, you may find that you can make tension slide away just by saying "Relax."

You can work through the whole set of muscles, or focus just on those in which you feel tension. Repeat this as many times as necessary to get a set of muscles to relax.

For each muscle group, tense the muscles and hold for five seconds. Then relax the muscles, and say "Relax" to yourself. Notice the difference. Repeat for these muscle groups:

Hands. Make a tight fist; then relax.

Arms. Curl the arm and tighten the biceps and triceps.

Shoulders. Pull the shoulders back until the blades almost touch, and relax; then pull them forward all the way.

Neck. Incline the head forward and then back, relaxing after each movement.

Upper Face and Scalp. Raise the eyebrows as high as possible.

Center Face. Squint the eyes and wrinkle the nose.

Lower Face. Smile in an exaggerated way, and clench the teeth.

Abdomen. Make the abdomen tight and hard.

Buttocks. Tighten them.

Upper Legs. Stretch out the legs, tightening both the top and bottom.

Lower Legs. Curl the toes up toward you.

Feet. Curl the toes away from you.

Staying Mentally Focused

QUESTIONS TO ANSWER
AS YOU READ:

■ What can you do to stay
focused on a test?

There are three steps you can take to help yourself stay calm on tests. The first two are (1) be well prepared and (2) calm yourself with meditation or relaxation. Those you've already learned. The third step is to keep your mind focused on the test.

When you get nervous on a test, you begin to worry. This worrying—such as thinking, "Argh, I don't know any of this!"—distracts you from the test. People who get fairly nervous on a test spend only *about half* the test

THINK PIECE 16.3   Practicing muscle relaxation

You get better at muscle relaxation through practice. But don't wait until you get nervous on a test to practice. It is easier to relax if you have practiced beforehand. Take ten minutes each day as a test approaches to practice the whole set of relaxation exercises.

Keep a record to encourage yourself to do the necessary practice.

It is important to practice when you are feeling some tension, so that you learn how to get rid of the tension. Use muscle relaxation before or during tests if you get nervous on them, or during study periods if you begin to get tense. Give yourself instructions to remember to use the procedure.

Write your self-reminder here:

_____

_____

Keep a record with a ✔ each time you relax instead of remaining tense while studying or before or during a test:

Test _____ Relaxed? _____   Test _____ Relaxed? _____

Test _____ Relaxed? _____   Test _____ Relaxed? _____

Test _____ Relaxed? _____   Test _____ Relaxed? _____

Test _____ Relaxed? _____   Test _____ Relaxed? _____

Some people find that they get nervous in only one kind of course, for example, in math or science class but nowhere else. If so, that's the place to practice. Practice muscle relaxation in the *actual situations* that make you nervous.

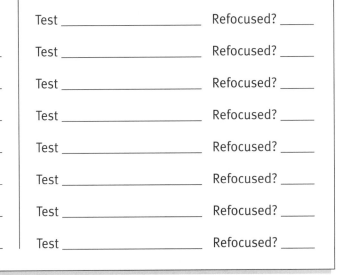

SKILL BUILDER 16.1

Keeping your mind on the test

When you start to worry while taking the test, use self-instructions to get your mind back on the test.

Examples: "Don't let yourself get distracted and worry. Just focus on the test." "Keep your mind in the groove." "Work now. Worry later." "Relax. Focus just on the test. Relax."

A. Write self-instructions to focus on the test.

First, notice when you are worrying, not thinking about the test. Then tell yourself to refocus on the test:

_____

_____

_____

_____

_____

_____

_____

B. Keep a record with a ✓ each time you use these instructions when you begin to get nervous on a test:

Test _____ Refocused? _____

Test _____ Refocused? _____

Test _____ Refocused? _____

Test _____ Refocused? _____

Test _____ Refocused? _____

Test _____ Refocused? _____

Test _____ Refocused? _____

Test _____ Refocused? _____

time thinking about the actual test. They spend the rest of the time worrying about what will happen if they fail.[10] They actually work on the test *less* than others because they spend so much time worrying.

When you begin to worry during a test, direct your attention to focus on the test, not on the worrisome thoughts. Use self-instructions to keep your mind focused on the test. This technique is similar to the procedure athletes follow to keep their mind on executing their game plan and not on worrying about the score. As soon as you notice you are worrying—"This is really hard" or "I'm not getting it" or "I'm ruined!" or "This is a catastrophe"—turn on your self-instructions to focus on the test. "No," you tell yourself, "this is not the time to worry. Concentrate on the test now." You can always worry later if you wish.

Myron wrote, "Negative self-statements have always been a problem for me. If I'm taking a test and think, 'I'm never going to pass this!' I change my thought to 'If I don't get the grade I want, next time I'll study more.' And I tell myself,

SKILL BUILDER 16.2

Checklist for getting calm on tests

A. Keep a record of the things you do to reduce nervousness on tests.

Test date:_____ Subject:_____

Rate your degree of nervousness: 0 = none; 1 = some; 2 = a lot; 3 = too much _____

How well prepared were you?

_____

How much had you exercised?

_____

Did you meditate before the test?

_____

Did you use muscle relaxation before or during the test?

_____

B. Keep this checklist for the next two tests you take. What do you learn from doing this?

Test date:_____ Subject:_____

Rate your degree of nervousness: 0 = none; 1 = some; 2 = a lot; 3 = too much _____

How well prepared were you?

_____

How much had you exercised?

_____

Did you meditate before the test?

_____

Did you use muscle relaxation before or during the test?

_____

Test date:_____ Subject:_____

Rate your degree of nervousness: 0 = none; 1 = some; 2 = a lot; 3 = too much _____

How well prepared were you?

_____

How much had you exercised?

_____

Did you meditate before the test?

_____

Did you use muscle relaxation before or during the test?

_____

C. Write what you learned:

_____

_____

_____

_____

'Never think about failing while taking a test. Get your mind back onto thinking only about the test!'

"What I do depends on what I notice about myself. If I'm taking a test and notice that I am feeling really emotional, almost panicked, then I do the relaxation exercises.

Maybe meditation also. If I notice, instead, that I'm not concentrating on the test, just worrying or having negative thoughts, then I direct my attention to focusing on the test materials. Sometimes I do both. I do whatever I need to do."

Skill Builder 16.1 will help you practice keeping focused on tests. Use Skill Builder 16.2 to keep a checklist for getting calm for tests.

Chapter 17

During and after Tests

Multiple-choice tests

What does *PIRATES* stand for?

Essay tests

What does *S-SNOW* stand for?

After the test

How should you analyze your errors on a test?

How should you feel about a bad grade? How can you learn from it?

There are two kinds of strategies you should pay attention to when you take a test:

1. Strategies that help you relax.
2. Strategies that help you do as well as possible.

The use of these two kinds of strategies is the best approach you can take to tests.[1] Chapter 16 outlined how to calm yourself, and this chapter teaches strategies for showing your stuff on the test.

Multiple-Choice Tests

Claude, the basketball player, has a system he follows, a set of steps to guide him as he takes a test. He explained, "When you have a multiple-choice test, there are several things to look for when answering the questions. If I am not sure of the correct answer, I look at the choices and try to eliminate the ones that are obviously not correct. If one of the choices has words like 'always' or 'never' in it, I know that's wrong. A lot of times the longest choice is the correct answer.

"Another thing I learned was to read the question very carefully. Sometimes you might misinterpret the question and not fully understand it.

QUESTIONS TO ANSWER AS YOU READ:

- What does *PIRATES* stand for?

"Also, if I don't know an answer, I don't let it upset me. That's a big mistake that a lot of students make. I just go on to the next one, and come back later to it."

Having a set of steps to follow keeps your mind focused, so you can do your best on the test.

Hughes and Schumaker[2] developed a system they call *PIRATES*. Their research showed that students who learn these skills show significant improvement in their test scores.[3]

Each letter (P–I–R–A–T–E–S) stands for one step you take as you work through a test.

P—*Prepare* to succeed

This first procedure should take less than three minutes. When you first begin the test, write down "PIRATES" to remind yourself what to do. Take a minute to get relaxed. Think a positive thought, such as, "I'm well prepared and relaxed for this test. I ought to do well."

If there is more than one section in the test, look over all the sections to decide which is easiest. Do the easiest one first.

I—*Inspect* the *Instructions*

Read the instructions and look for key words that will tell you exactly how to answer. Many students misread instructions on tests and get lower grades because they did not answer as they were supposed to answer. One experienced student noted that she always reads the instructions twice and often notices information the second time she didn't get on the first reading.

R—*Read; Remember; Remove*

Read the question. Then *before* you read the choices, *remember* what you know about the material in the stem of the multiple-choice item. Try to complete the stem of the item in your mind before reading the choices. This calls up information from your memory. It ties in your memory to the question, a warm-up, connecting the question to what you already know.

The next step is to *remove*—eliminate—any obviously wrong answers. Scratch a mark through them so you won't think about them any more.

For example, Ben is confronted with the following question on his psychology test:

The famous Skinner box was used to
a. study animals
b. confine B. F. Skinner
c. study operant conditioning
d. all of the above

Ben first reads the stem and *before* reading the choices tries to remember what he knows about the Skinner box. He remembers that the psychologist B. F. Skinner used it to study learning in pigeons. Ben then reads all four choices. He realizes that *b* is a silly choice and scratches through it. Choice *d* includes *b*, which is silly, so he scratches *d* also.

A—*Answer* or *Abandon*

If you know the correct choice, *answer* by marking the test sheet. If you do *not* know the answer, *abandon* the item. Mark the abandoned item with a ✓ and move on to the next one. You'll come back to it.

> Ben, from the example above, has to choose between choices *a* and *c*. In a way both *a* and *c* are correct. He decides that *c* is the better answer because it is more specific. He checks *c* on the scoring sheet.
>
> If Ben is not sure which is the correct answer, he should *not* answer at this point. Instead, he should mark the item for later return, abandon it now, and move on to the next item.

The R–A procedure is repeated over and over as you move through the test. For each item you

- Read/Remember/Remove it and then

- Answer/Abandon it.

If you encounter new instructions, repeat the I ("Inspect") part.

T—*Turn* back to answer

Once you've gone through the test, go back and deal with any marked items that you did not answer the first time. Your thinking about the topic may be jogged by later items, so that now you can figure out the correct answer.

> One older student noted, "I have found that many times other questions on the test will trigger my memory, or may even contain clues to skipped questions."

E—*Estimate* (guess)

Guess at an answer if you really don't know the correct choice. If you leave it blank, it's definitely counted as a wrong response.

Claude suggested that words like *never* or *always* are wrong. He's right, but guessing is not a precise science, and there can be exceptions to the rules. Some writers suggest several guessing strategies—go with the longest answer, pick the choice that is the most carefully qualified, choose "*c*" or "all of the above," pick between two choices that are very similar, or if given a range of numbers like "2, 8, 12, 20," choose one from the middle of the range. These ideas may be worth knowing, but they are usually *not* effective. Students who use them don't do any better than students who just guess randomly.[4]

There are, however, some things you can do to make your guessing more rational. Here are two rules for guessing:

Try to eliminate as many choices as possible. The odds are better if you're choosing between two instead of three or four choices. In the example above, if Ben knows that *b* and *d* are wrong, and eliminates them, he has doubled his chances of guessing the correct answer, or you could say, he has cut in half his chances of guessing wrong.

Look for something in the question that gives away the answer. If the test has been professionally constructed—a national test like the SAT or GED—the items won't contain giveaways, but if it has been made less carefully, there may be clues buried in the stem or choices.

For example, here's a question from a literature course. See if you can answer it.[5]

> The hungry coyote in Tippecanoe county was observed . . .
> a. sleeping in a ditch;
> b. stalking prey;
> c. looking for shelter;
> d. near the park.

When you first read this, you might think, "I have no idea. I never read that story."

But think about the item a minute. What do *hungry* animals do—sleep?—look for shelter? No, they look for something to eat. So the *hungry* coyote was probably stalking prey. This shows the benefits of reading the stems of items very carefully. If you skim over the word *hungry*, then you won't figure out the right choice, but if you read slowly and carefully, you may think, "Wait a minute . . ."

Let's go back to PIRATES for the last step.

S—Survey

Look over the test when you are finished. Check to be sure you haven't made any clerical errors and that each question has an answer. This sounds really simple, but an amazing number of students miss items on

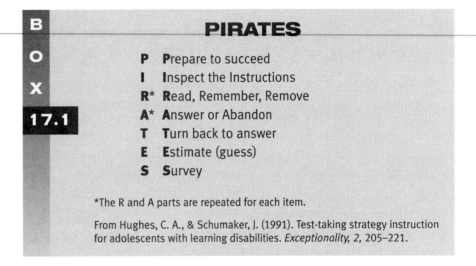

From Hughes, C. A., & Schumaker, J. (1991). Test-taking strategy instruction for adolescents with learning disabilities. *Exceptionality, 2,* 205–221.

tests just because they don't give an answer to them. It is good to have a reminder to do it.

Use Skill Builder 17.1 to practice making PIRATES a habit.

Essay Tests

QUESTION TO ANSWER AS YOU READ:

■ What does *S-SNOW* stand for?

The basic rules you learned for any test also hold for essay tests: be relaxed and be well prepared. Do the easy questions first to be sure you get them right.

The acronym for the procedure to follow in writing essay exams is *S-SNOW,* adapted here from work by Scruggs and Mastropierri.[7] The object is to "snow"—an old-fashioned slang word meaning to make a tremendous impression on—your instructor. *S-SNOW* stands for:

S-S—*Study* the instructions, and *study* the questions

- Study the whole test to allocate your time.
- Study each question to be sure you answer all of it.

S number one When you first *study* the test, allocate your time. If the test period is fifty minutes, for example, and there are three questions on the test, divide 3 into 50 to allocate the time you will give to each question, in this case approximately fifteen minutes each. Keep track of the time as you work through the test so you will know what question you should be working on.

Juanita notes, "When I first started taking essay tests in college I would drive myself crazy by spending too much time on the first question. I would look at the clock and see

SKILL BUILDER 17.1

Making PIRATES a habit

The best way to get the PIRATES working on your ship is to use self-instructions and to practice. Good students typically talk themselves through tests more than poor students do.[6] When you sit down to take the test, murmur "PIRATES" to yourself. "Use the PIRATES system." For each step, remind yourself what to do: "PIRATES. Okay, I'm at *R*. Read; remember; remove. *Read* the item, try to *remember* what I know about it, and *remove* any wrong choices. [Pause while you do that.] Right. Okay, now I'm at *A*—answer or abandon. I don't know the *answer* to this one, so *abandon* it. Move to the next."

A. Work out self-instructions in your own words to remind yourself to use PIRATES. Write the self-instructions here:

_____

_____

_____

_____

_____

_____

_____

_____

_____

B. Keep a record with a ✓ each time you use PIRATES on a test:

Test_____ Used PIRATES?_____

Test_____ Used PIRATES?_____

Test_____ Used PIRATES?_____

Test_____ Used PIRATES?_____

Test_____ Used PIRATES?_____

Test_____ Used PIRATES?_____

Test_____ Used PIRATES?_____

Test_____ Used PIRATES?_____

Test_____ Used PIRATES?_____

Test_____ Used PIRATES?_____

I had spent half the time, but still had three questions to go. So, I started organizing my time as soon as I began the test: twelve minutes for this, twelve minutes for that. It was a little harder to keep track of the time, but it paid off, because I had plenty of time to write out my answers."

S number two *Study* the individual questions. Students often miss part of a question and lower their grade with a partial answer. Read the instructions and the question for an essay test slowly, very carefully. *Twice is a good idea.* A question on a history test might be "Describe the causes of World War II. Which do you think were most important? Why?" If you named the important causes but didn't say which were most important or why, you would lower your grade.

SKILL BUILDER 17.1

Making PIRATES a habit

C. Think about your practice.

If you used only part of PIRATES, what parts? What are your plans to use the whole system? You can gradually increase the number of parts you use. Keep a record of your use and of your increase.

1. Write your plan.

   _____

   _____

   _____

   _____

   _____

   _____

2. Record your practice.

   Test_____ What parts? _____

   Test_____ What parts? _____

   Test_____ What parts? _____

   Test_____ What parts? _____

   Test_____ What parts? _____

   Test_____ What parts? _____

   Test_____ What parts? _____

   Test_____ What parts? _____

3. Write your reflections: What parts worked best for you? What can you do to fit this technique to your individual style?

   _____

   _____

   _____

   _____

   _____

   _____

   _____

   _____

   _____

   _____

   _____

N—*Note* important points of each question

Essay questions in college often do *not* ask you merely to list points or events. They ask you to think about the events in some way. You might be asked to *analyze* or to *evaluate*, to *draw conclusions*, or to *compare* or *contrast* events.[8]

These are the *command words* in an essay question that tell you what to do.[9] For example, a history question would not be simply "What were the causes of World War II?" Instead, it might be "*Compare* the causes of World War II with the causes of World War I." Or you might be asked to evaluate the importance of the causes: "*Discuss* the causes of World War II." If you only listed the causes, but did not "discuss"—that is, "provide reasons for and give different points of view"—your answer would be incomplete and your grade would be lowered.

When you notice a *command word* in a question, *underline* it. That should be the focus of your answer. When you read the instructions for an essay question, remind yourself to "look for the command words."

Here are some command words that appear frequently in test questions:

Analyze. Break a topic into its parts and discuss the relationships between the parts.

Compare. Show how events, items, ideas are similar.

Contrast. Show how events, items, ideas are different.

Discuss. Provide the reasons for or give different points of view about something.

Evaluate. List the positives and negatives of something; then judge it.

Trace. List the order in which events occurred.

O—*Organize (outline)* your answer

It's a mistake to start writing right away. Before writing, get your answer organized. Jot down notes on any important points; then *outline* or *organize* your notes. Before answering the question on the causes of World War II, Juanita writes notes to herself—"economic depression, rise of Hitler, German feeling of being cheated in WWI"—then she arranges these in a good order before writing.

This step takes a minute or two, but it is time very well invested, because your answer ends up well organized. Organizing your answer also helps you remember all the important points you want to cover.[10]

W—*Write* your answer

Your goal is to show the instructor that you really know this stuff. Two things you can do to accomplish this:

- Skip your introduction. Don't have any wind-up.

- Put your answer to the main part of the question in the first sentence.

Juanita's first sentence could be "There were several causes of WWII, and each of these has to be considered in relation to the others." That's wind-up. It's filler. It doesn't tell the instructor anything about what Juanita knows. Suppose, instead, she first organized her answer and then wrote, "The four major causes of WWII were 1, 2, 3, and 4 [listing them]." By the end of the first sentence she would have shown the instructor that she knew this stuff, making a good first impression. Then she could discuss each cause and show how it related to the others.

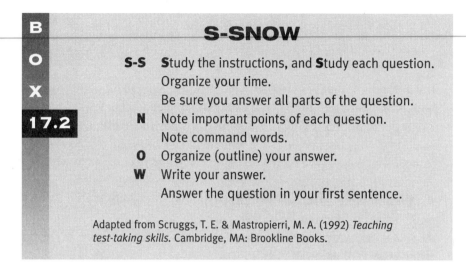

Adapted from Scruggs, T. E. & Mastropierri, M. A. (1992) *Teaching test-taking skills*. Cambridge, MA: Brookline Books.

Starting with a bang like that is a skill, so you should expect to have to practice it. Really great writers spend hours practicing their skill. Ernest Hemingway, the great twentieth-century American novelist, could spend all day on one sentence, and Erich Segal, the author of *Love Story*, a wildly successful romance of the 1960s, spent a week on the opening paragraph. You don't have that kind of time when taking an exam, which means *you have to think about what you are writing as you go*. Don't ramble. Even if you ramble into a good answer, the meandering you go through to get there makes your answer look bad. Don't spend all the test time writing words on paper. Stop to think, and follow your outline.

Use Skill Builder 17.2 to practice the S-SNOW technique for essay questions.

This seems minor, but this last point is actually important because it affects the *impression* you make on the instructor. Keep your paper really neat and easy to read. Don't scribble. If you can, write on only one side of the page. The easier you make your paper to read, the better your chances that you will get a good grade on it.

After the Test

The test you just finished is not the last test you are ever going to take. If you want to get better at tests, it is a good idea to learn from the ones you've taken. Learn from your mistakes, and feel good about your successes.

Analyze your errors

A baseball batter is having a bad time and has struck out several times lately. He asks his coach, "What's wrong?"

The coach replies, "What kinds of errors do you make? Maybe you're taking your eye off the ball just before it gets to the plate. Maybe you're

SKILL BUILDER 17.2

S-SNOW falling on essay tests

The best way to make S-SNOW a habit is to use self-talk to guide your actions, and to practice over and over. As you sit down to begin an essay exam, remind yourself: "S-SNOW. It's snowing. Use snow." Say to yourself, "Okay, S-S-N-O-W. The S steps are *study* the instructions and *study* the questions. Be sure I *note* all parts of the question and look for command words. Then *organize* my time. Then *write*. First sentence summarizes. Right, now do the first step." Make plans now as to what you will say to yourself.

A. Work out and write down self-instructions in your own words to remind yourself to use the full S-SNOW:

_____

_____

_____

_____

_____

_____

_____

_____

_____

_____

B. Keep a record with a ✓ each time you use S-SNOW on a test:

Test_____ Used S-SNOW?_____

Test_____ Used S-SNOW?_____

Test_____ Used S-SNOW?_____

Test_____ Used S-SNOW?_____

Test_____ Used S-SNOW?_____

Test_____ Used S-SNOW?_____

Test_____ Used S-SNOW?_____

Test_____ Used S-SNOW?_____

Test_____ Used S-SNOW?_____

Test_____ Used S-SNOW?_____

C. Think about your practice. If you used only part of S-SNOW, what parts?

Example You might have organized your time well, but not have noticed important command words in the instructions.

What are your plans to use the whole system? You can gradually increase the number of parts you use. Keep a record of your use and of your increase.

1. Write your plan:

_____

_____

_____

_____

_____

_____

_____

_____

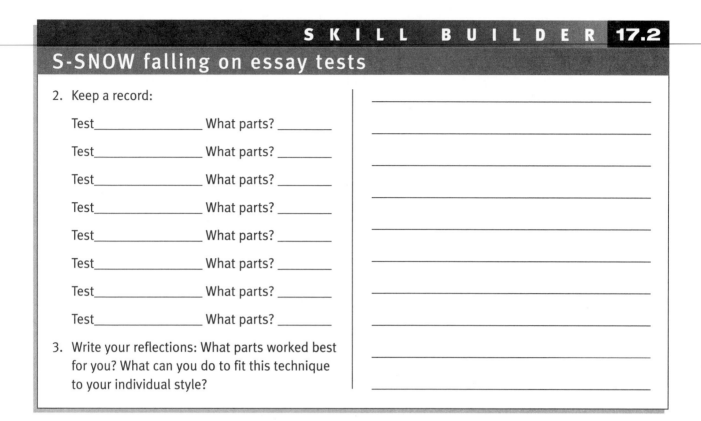

SKILL BUILDER 17.2

S-SNOW falling on essay tests

2. Keep a record:

   Test_____ What parts? _____

   Test_____ What parts? _____

   Test_____ What parts? _____

   Test_____ What parts? _____

   Test_____ What parts? _____

   Test_____ What parts? _____

   Test_____ What parts? _____

   Test_____ What parts? _____

3. Write your reflections: What parts worked best for you? What can you do to fit this technique to your individual style?

going for pitches outside the strike zone. Maybe you're swinging for homers too much. If you know what type of error you're making, that helps to correct it." The coach is right. The same thinking applies to your test taking.

After you get your test paper back, spend a few minutes going over it. Feel good about the ones you got right, and analyze the ones you got wrong. Why did you get them wrong?

Carla writes, "During the test I was not nervous; and I went through the questions quickly. In analyzing my mistakes later, I found that some of the questions were missed because I was going too fast and did not pay close attention to the question. I did all the easy ones first and went back to the ones I didn't know, but I missed several of them. To be honest, I missed these because of lack of information. I just didn't know the right answer. Of the eight questions I missed, I think three were from careless, quick reading and the others were from lack of information. I've gone over two of my tests now, and in both cases I missed some because of careless reading and the majority because of lack of info."

Carla's findings are typical. Students often miss questions because of quick or careless reading of the question, and also because of simple lack of information.[11] A batter needs to know if he's going for pitches outside the strike zone. You need to know why you are making errors on tests.

> Carla concluded, "I need to slow down during the test and put more energy into reading the information provided carefully. The obvious remedy for lack of knowledge is to put more energy into understanding the text. I also need to focus more on predicting test questions."

> Another student, Gwen, noted, "I missed information and facts mainly from the last part of the chapter. I think this is caused by lack of concentration and rushing through the last parts of the assigned readings. I don't think I was aware of this before."

> Hideki analyzed his errors and decided he was "second guessing" himself. "I need to stop changing the answer I know to be right." (Some students improve their answers by taking a long second look, but others, like Hideki, often make things worse.)

> Hideki also noted, "I think I'm not abandoning items I don't know fast enough. I tend to linger over them, hoping the right answer will pop out, but all this does is make me nervous. So, I'm going to concentrate on that for the next test."

> Another student said, "I still don't write the answer to the question in the first sentence when I do essay tests. I need to work on that more."

You cannot come to these kinds of conclusions if you don't analyze your errors.

It may take a bit of courage to get yourself to do this. You may want to avoid thinking about your errors. But then you are doomed to repeat them. If you figure out what kinds of errors you are making, you can avoid them in the future.

Use the strategies

Many errors on tests occur because the student is *not using* some of the test-taking strategies you've been reading about here. Strategies don't work if you don't use them. After a test, de-brief yourself by working through the checklist in Skill Builder 17.3.

Take a skills-development attitude about bad grades

If you got a bad grade, it is hard to force yourself to review the test to find the source of your errors. Sometimes it seems easier to tell yourself you don't care. Remember the idea of a skills-development attitude. ~~You're not going to pay attention to the grade now. You just want to~~ figure out what skills you need to work on. If you work on the skills, the grades will improve.

From a skills-development viewpoint, a bad grade means that

- You did not put enough effort into preparing for the test.

- You did not use enough test preparation strategies.[12]

Success comes from the use of effort and strategies. Also, the test may be more challenging than those you've been used to. This is often true as you move from high school to college. It is not some lack of ability that you have, but simply a lack of practice. Your test preparation skills need practice.

A bad grade does *not* mean there is something wrong with you.[13] There may be something undeveloped about your test-taking skills— you're not using them, or you're making mistakes. For example, you might not be predicting test questions, or you might not be relaxed enough on the test. Those are skills you can practice. There may even be holes in your previous education—but those holes can be filled in.

If you think that academic skill is like talent—you either have it or you don't—then you will see no point in trying to improve your test-taking skills. They are fixed for life. But if you realize that all skills are developed through practice, then a bad grade merely gives you the information that . . .

You need more practice.

If you do the work outlined in the Skill Builders in Chapters 15, 16, and 17, you will get plenty of practice, and you will see definite improvement. Keep a skills-development attitude, not a performance attitude. Don't fret about your grades now; just try to develop your test-taking skills.

Talk with your instructor

It can be hard to force yourself to go talk to the instructor when you've made a bad grade. It's embarrassing, and you don't want the instructor to think you are polishing the apple. But most instructors are really pleased when a student who has made a bad grade comes to talk with them. The reason we became instructors, after all, is because we like to teach people.

And you need not be embarrassed: your instructor has seen many cases of bad grades before and knows it is just part of learning to be a good college student. We have even made bad grades ourselves: your author once made a D in freshman English. (No cracks about how that explains the writing in this book!)

It does not have to be a long talk, so you can get in and out pretty quickly. What should you talk about with the instructor? Here are ideas for a script to follow.

1. Find out what you can do to perform at a higher level next time. Take a skills-development approach: you are here to learn, to improve your skills. Ask the instructor how to do that.

2. Ask questions about

   - Aspects of the test or assignment you did not understand.

   - How you should prepare.

   - How much time students who did well prepared.

3. Don't argue about the grade. That shows you are less interested in learning and merely interested in the grade.

Your instructor may ask you questions about how and how much you prepared. Listen carefully to what she says about this, because you might not be preparing for the test in the optimal way.

Go over Skill Builder 17.3 before talking with your instructor. That way, some of the basic issues are answered, and you will be prepared to learn more.

SKILL BUILDER 17.3

Checklist of test-preparation activities

Here's a checklist to help you spot sources of errors on tests. Answer these honestly, and the problem is often revealed to you.

A. Review your preparation before the test.

1. Were you well prepared for the test?

   Yes_____ No_____

   Partially_____ or fully_____?

2. Did you predict test questions and their answers?

   Yes_____ No_____

   How many?_____

B. Review your practice during the test.

1. Were you calm before and during the test?

   Yes_____ No_____

2. Do you think you stayed focused on the test?

   Yes_____ No_____

3. Did you use PIRATES or S-SNOW?

   Yes_____ No_____

   Partially_____ or fully_____?

4. Do you think you have a skills-development attitude about this test?

   Yes_____ No_____

Part VII

Improving Verbal Skills: Gaining Control over Words

One of the world's leading authorities on writing, Peter Elbow, writes, "Many people are now trying to become less helpless, both personally and politically trying to claim more control over their own lives. One of the ways people most lack control over their own lives is through lacking control over words."[1]

Words are so important that according to the Bible everything began with them: "In the beginning was the word."

Learning to write better, spell correctly, have a good vocabulary, and speak effectively will give you much greater control over words, and over your own life.

We are judged by the words we use. If you applied for a good job but could not write well or spell correctly on the application, you probably would not get the job. If your speech in the job interview were stumbling, you would make a poor impression. People form impressions of us based on our skill at using words. Use them well, and people think we are smart and well educated. Use them poorly, and it's bad for our team.

Being good with words is a skill, verbal skill. Like all skills, it is based in knowledge but developed through practice. How good do you feel you are at these four skills?

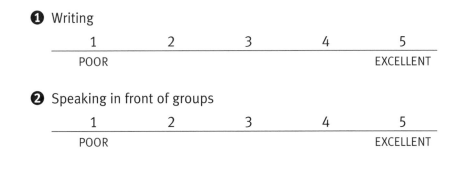

❶ Writing

1	2	3	4	5
POOR				EXCELLENT

❷ Speaking in front of groups

1	2	3	4	5
POOR				EXCELLENT

❸ Using vocabulary

1	2	3	4	5
POOR				EXCELLENT

❹ Spelling

1	2	3	4	5
POOR				EXCELLENT

If you feel that you don't rate highly enough in one or more of those verbal skills, try the chapters here that teach you how to get better at them. These chapters are absolutely up to date in how to improve each skill, and they provide practice so you can improve.

Is working on these skills worth it to you? You'll have to read, think, and do the practice. If you do, you will get better. Is that worth the effort it will take?

Chapter 18

Gaining Control over **Written** Words

PREVIEW WITH QUESTIONS TO ANSWER

Powerful news about writing
- What are your chances of improving your writing with practice?
- How is good writing related to good time management?
- What is the PoWeR system for improving your writing?

PoWeR Step One: *P* for *Planning*
- What are the four parts of the Know—AGO system for planning your writing?
- What is the TREE system for organizing an essay?

PoWeR Step Two: *W* for *Writing*
- What are good techniques to get started?
- What are some ideas about what to say?
- What are some good rules about sentences and paragraphs?
- How does planning fit in during writing?

PoWeR Step Three: *R* for *Revising*
- What is the SCAN system for revising an essay?
- What are the benefits of keeping the reader in mind?

Powerful News about Writing

There is good news about improving your writing: Good versus poor writers show little or no difference in intelligence or motivation. But there is a large difference in how much they have *practiced* writing.[1] Good writers have written a lot more. The difference between a good and a not-so-good writer is practice, not anything else.

This implies that with practice you can improve your writing significantly. If you are not yet a good writer, you can expect to get better if you

QUESTIONS TO ANSWER
AS YOU READ:

- What are your chances of improving your writing with practice?

- How is good writing related to good time management?

- What is the PoWeR system for improving your writing?

practice. Using these techniques, you can "elbow" your way into the ranks of good writers.

We are not talking about getting better at grammar or punctuation. You may have found writing instruction discouraging in the past because the emphasis was too much on all the rules of grammar or punctuation. The purpose of this chapter is *not* to teach you more about grammar or punctuation. The purpose is to provide *practice in conveying meaning*, to gain better control over words.

Why improve your writing? Better writing is directly related to better grades.[2] Most good jobs require writing—memos, summaries, proposals, outlines, and so on. If you can explain something well—if you can clearly convey your meaning—you will advance. Writing well makes you seem smarter. If you can persuade through writing—selling—you will advance.

Can you improve your writing? Definitely. After receiving training similar to what we will follow here, a group of learning disabled students were able to write so well that their writing could no longer be told from that of other students.[3] Students and teachers who have followed these procedures say it has helped their writing, and that they would be glad to do it again. You can expect improvement in the quality, length, and structure of your writing,[4] and in your confidence about your writing.[5]

Setting the stage for writing well

Part of good writing is good time management. You have to schedule the time to write. Waiting until the last minute, when the paper is due in a few hours, does *not* give you the time to write well. You should schedule times for writing. As before, keep a record of your time on task. Don't interrupt yourself, and don't let others interrupt you. If you intend to write for thirty minutes, try to come close to using all that time.

The place where you write is also important. Trying to write in a room with other people talking, the TV on, and people coming and going is pretty inefficient. If you can't control the noise and interruptions in one place, don't write there. Find some quiet place such as the library where you can concentrate well enough to write.

Use Skill Builder 18.1 to practice setting the stage for writing.

Mistakes writing novices make

What do beginning writers do that experienced writers have learned not to do?[6] Novice writers tend to list everything they know about a topic, but do not organize the material. The person just writes ideas until the supply is exhausted, then stops.

Typically, novices do not write *enough* about a topic. They don't give enough details, and they don't ask themselves if they are being clear.

Setting the stage for writing

You should set a schedule for writing, pick a quiet place to do it, get started on time, and keep track of your time on task.

A. Decide your writing times.

Some weeks you will need to write, but others, you won't. Let's assume you are making up a weekly study schedule, as you learned in Chapter 2. For weeks in which you need to write, set aside some of your study time for writing, or create other times for it. Start small and increase gradually.

Write down your writing times:

S_____   M _____   T _____   W _____   T _____   F _____   S _____

S_____   M _____   T _____   W _____   T _____   F _____   S _____

S_____   M _____   T _____   W _____   T _____   F _____   S _____

B. Record your actual use.

Place a ✓ beside your schedule each time you do the work. If you don't meet your schedule, change your schedule, take smaller steps, and use self-instructions and rewards.

C. Keep a record of your time on track.

For each scheduled session, how much of the allotted time were you actually working on your writing?

S_____   M _____   T _____   W _____   T _____   F _____   S _____

S_____   M _____   T _____   W _____   T _____   F _____   S _____

S_____   M _____   T _____   W _____   T _____   F _____   S _____

D. Analyze your writing place.

Is it free of distractions? _____ If not, what would be a better place?

_____

E. Write self-instructions to get started:

_____

_____

F. Write rewards for doing the practice:

_____

Example: "I'll go to the library and write on my paper for thirty minutes before starting the weekend social activities."

Novices spend too little time on their writing. And novices tend not to revise their writing. They turn in their first draft, but unfortunately that is usually not a person's best effort at conveying meaning.

We need strategies to overcome these problems.

Writing with PoWeR

There are three steps in the writing process:[7]

- Planning what you will write.

- Writing.

- Revising what you have written.

The memory aid for this process is PoWeR—*Plan, Write, Revise.* The rest of this chapter is devoted to practicing the *PoWeR* system. Students who follow this system in their writing learn to write better and make significantly better grades.

PoWeR Step One: P for Planning

QUESTIONS TO ANSWER AS YOU READ:

- What are the four parts of the Know—AGO system for planning your writing?

- What is the TREE system for organizing an essay?

Novices don't do enough planning before they write. They sit down without planning, write what they remember, then quit. Consequently their writing does not do justice to what they actually can do, because they don't fully activate their memories or creativity.[8] Their approach leads to writing that is less organized and less interesting than it could be.

Expert writers spend a lot of time planning.[9] They start writing and then return to planning again. In their planning they generate information to use and they organize the information. They set goals in terms of the purpose of their writing and the audience for whom they are writing.

You can learn to do the same things, using a simple system, the Know—AGO procedure, *four* steps to follow when planning your writing:

Know—Ask yourself, What do I need to *Know?*

AGO—Who is the *Audience?*

What are my *Goals?*

How should the writing be *Organized?*

A memory aid to help remember this: "What did I know long ago?"

Know—What do I *Know?* What do I need to *Know?*

Generate information from your memory, and decide what information you don't yet have that you need to get. Ask yourself,

- What do I already know?

- What else do I need to know?

> Jackie is planning a term paper in history. "I wanted to write about Alexander the Great. I first wrote down what I already knew about him, such as his family background, his education, his early conquests. I spent a good amount of time on that, to be sure I got down everything I already knew. That got me a lot of information, but I realized I needed more. I needed dates and places to flesh out the early stuff, and I needed a lot of info on the later conquests, as I was fuzzy about them. For example, why did he die so young? I made a note to consult my text and at least one book on Alexander from the library."

A good technique to get ideas flowing is to talk out loud to yourself, or scribble things rapidly on a paper. Some of what you say or write will be nonsense, but some will stimulate ideas you might not have had if you were silent. Good writers try to get their ideas flowing, so they can choose the best ones.

A—Audience

The tone you take when writing a letter to a friend is different from the tone you take in a term paper. In your planning, think about who your audience will be. What do they know? What do they need to know? Should you write more or less, depending on the audience?

> Jackie continues, "My audience for this paper is Dr. Elliott, my history prof. My problem is, she knows a lot more about Alexander the Great than I do. I can't write a whole book about Alexander. What should I do?
>
> "First, I decided I better consult three or four books instead of one. And I should write more than I originally intended. I realized that just listing all of Alexander's battles would get pretty boring, and Elliott probably knew all that anyway. So, I had a problem, but at first I wasn't sure what to do about it."

G—Goals

If your only goal is to get the paper finished, you're making a mistake. For a better paper, set more interesting goals. "What would I like to accomplish in this paper?"

Try personalizing the assignment to fit your interests. If you can get interested in the topic, your writing will be better,[10] so look for an angle that interests you.

> Jackie writes, "I'm a psych major. History is sort of interesting, but not totally, so I tried to find a psychological angle to write about. An interesting question was, How did Alexander the Great get that way? What made him want to conquer the world? In other words, why was he so ambitious? That interested me, so I focused part of my paper on that."

Jackie took what could have been a dreary listing of the battles of Alexander and gave the subject a twist that made it interesting for her.

What kinds of goals should you set for your paper? They could address the following:[11]

- The *purpose* of the paper, as Jackie's focus on the causes of Alexander's behavior.

- The *completeness* of the paper—"I want to write a really thorough paper, really get into it" or "For this paper, I want to take a narrow focus and deal with just one issue."

- The *length* of the paper—"I've never written a ten-page paper, and I decided I would try this time" or "This is a minor paper, so I think I'll just do four pages on it."

- *Interesting writing,* such as using certain vocabulary words, or having variation in your sentences—"I made a list of words I want to use in my paper: *empowerment, achievement, role models, psychological development,* and others."

Setting goals helps you plan what you will write. Jackie, for example, could set the goal of covering all of Alexander's major battles, or she could set the goal of focusing on his education to see how that might have influenced his personality and life. Each of these goals starts her paper off in a different direction, and gives it a focus that will make it better organized.

O—Organization: Use TREE

Organize the flow of ideas in a paper before you write. That will help you see any holes in your organization—where more information is needed— and will help the paper have good structure.

TREE is a memory aid for an organizational structure developed by Harris and Graham.[12] Think of "the tree of organization." Almost any essay paper can be organized using TREE, and *students' papers improve considerably* if they use TREE in their planning. The system works well for essays, but not well for fiction.

T—Topic sentences. Begin what a statement of what the paper is about.

R—Reasons to believe the statement in the topic sentence. Now give your reasons—facts, opinions of others, and so on—for believing the topic statement.

E—Examine Examples and *Evidence.* Present the reasons to support your topic statement. Discuss your reasons. How well supported by facts and *evidence* are they? How strong is the evidence? Also give *examples,* as they often make things clearer. (Notice how there are many cases of actual students in this book, providing examples of the abstract principles.)

E—Ending. State your conclusions. Wrap up your arguments. Often it is best to end with a concluding sentence that summarizes what you have said and presents the conclusion to it.

> Here is a (shortened) example from Jackie's paper on the psychological causes of Alexander the Great's ambition to conquer the world. When she first made notes for the paper her notes were disorganized:
>
> Aristotle was Alexander's tutor
>
> no record of what the tutoring was about
>
> Alex's father was King Philip who had conquered all of Greece
>
> He hired Aris from Athens
>
> Aris was famous as a philosopher and scientist, most imp. of his time.
>
> Alex must have learned ambition from his father and Aris

If she had written directly from her notes, her paper would not have been well organized. She sorted the ideas, with main topic and supporting ideas, and came up with the following:

> "Alexander the Great set out to conquer the known world of his era, demonstrating great ambition. Where did this ambition come from? Possibly he learned it from his father, King Philip, and his personal tutor, Aristotle the philosopher."
>
> Those first sentences present Jackie's topic. Now she can go into the reasons she believes as she does.
>
> "Alexander's private tutor was Aristotle, a famous Greek philosopher and scientist. Alexander's father, King Philip, sent to Athens to hire Aristotle to come to his court to educate the young prince. Aristotle himself must have been a

very ambitious man because he had risen to be the most important thinker of his era. King Philip seemed to feel that only the best was good enough for his son. King Philip was certainly ambitious, because he had conquered all of Greece."

Jackie then examines the reasons for her topic statement, and evaluates the evidence.

"What do we know about what Aristotle taught Alexander? The historical record about this is nonexistent. There are no records of what happened during the actual tutoring."

From this beginning she discusses how ambition is learned—which she gets from her psychology books—and looks to Alexander's life to see if it is reasonable that he learned it that way. At the end she concludes:

"Alexander may have learned ambition from his father and his tutor. We will never know for sure because the evidence is lacking. But it's an interesting possibility!"

Summary: Steps to follow when planning your writing

Ask, What did I *know* long *ago?*

- Ask yourself, What do I *Know?* What do I need to *Know?*

- Ask yourself, Who is the *Audience?* What are my *Goals?* How should the writing be *Organized?*

Use the TREE of organization:

- Write a *Topic* sentence.

- Give *Reasons* to believe it is true.

- *Examine* the reasons and the *Evidence* and give *Examples.*

- Write an *Ending*—Have a conclusion.

Skill Builder 18.2 will help you plan a paper using Know—AGO.

QUESTIONS TO ANSWER AS YOU READ:

- What are good techniques to get started?

- What are some ideas about what to say?

- What are some good rules about sentences and paragraphs?

- How does planning fit in during writing?

PoWeR Step Two: W for Writing

Novice writers tend to write too little, while experts write more words than they finally use. They throw some away. A writer's best friend is the Delete button on the computer. Novices often stop writing too soon, before they have said all they intended to say.[13] While writing, novices don't refer back to their plans—if they have any—but experts let their plans guide them, and also change their plans as they write.[14] Novice college writers tend to think about avoiding errors in spelling, grammar, and punctuation while they are writing—"Did I spell that right? Should this be a comma?"—while more expert college student writers think about conveying their meaning—"Did I explain that well? Do I need to say more?"[15] The experts don't think about punctuation, spelling, and grammar until they revise their writing later.

There is no set of rules to follow that will guarantee good writing, and great writers sometimes break all the rules. Here are some ideas that can improve your writing. For most students, using these ideas considerably improves their writing.

Getting started

Mechanics. Set your computer to double-space, because you will want to go back to make notes and changes. If you are writing by hand, use only every other line of the sheet so you can pencil in changes.

Just as you would not try to study amid a lot of distractions, don't try writing under those conditions.

Getting words to flow. A good way to get started writing is "free writing," in which you write anything that comes to mind. Tell yourself to write anything for at least five or more minutes, to get your juices flowing.

> Peter sits down at the computer and begins typing. "I have to start writing this history paper. It's about Napoleon. What am I going to say? Interesting guy. A great general, very tricky in his battles. He understood how to be good to his men, and they loved him. Did he say something like, 'An army travels on its stomach?' What does that mean? What else am I going to write about this. Let's see . . ."

Peter wouldn't turn in the paper that way—it's disorganized—but by just starting to type, he starts to get into the topic, and he is producing words. Already he has ideas for paragraphs on Napoleon's battle plans and his care of his men.

Use standard sentence openers to get started.[16] When you are stuck, begin a sentence with one of these to get moving.

"I believe . . ."

"One reason . . ."

"For example . . ."

"I think . . ."

For example: "I believe . . . uh . . . I believe . . . that the people Napoleon conquered must have been resentful. Or were they? Maybe they hated their government and were glad Napoleon kicked it out." From here the writer can make notes on this interesting question.

SKILL BUILDER 18.2

Planning a paper with Know-AGO

For the next paper you have to do, in any course, unless you are writing fiction, work through the steps for planning outlined here.

Topic of the paper: _____ Course: _____

Know

1. What do I know about this? (facts, ideas)

   _____

   _____

   _____

   _____

   _____

   _____

   _____

   _____

   _____

2. What do I need to know? (And where do I find out?)

   _____

   _____

   _____

   _____

   _____

   _____

_____

_____

_____

_____

_____

Jackie's work, above, is an example.

AGO

A. Plan for your *Audience:*

1. Who is the audience for this paper?

   _____

2. What does this imply for the paper?

   _____

   _____

Example: Audience: "Steve, the graduate teaching assistant in history, will grade it." What that implies: "I have to be complete, and I have to not be boring. He hates boring writing. I have to use footnotes."

B. Plan your *Goals.*

1. What can I do to make this paper interesting to write?

   _____

   _____

   _____

Planning a paper with Know-AGO

Example: "Make it psychological; tie it to what I am interested in."

2. What are my goals about?

a. The purpose of the paper?

_____

_____

b. The completeness of the paper?

_____

_____

c. The length of the paper?

_____

_____

d. Any good writing I want to do, or good words I want to use?

_____

_____

_____

_____

_____

_____

Example: "Use words like *era, historical record, evidence.*"

C. Plan your *Organization*—using the TREE of organization.

1. T.—What is the *topic* statement of the paper?

_____

_____

_____

_____

_____

_____

Example: "Some people believe that Picasso could not draw well, which they use to explain his style, but he was actually quite accomplished as a draftsman."

2. R.—What *reasons* will I give to support my topic statement?

_____

_____

_____

_____

_____

_____

_____

_____

_____

Example: "Here is a photocopy of a painting Picasso did when he was only sixteen years old. You can clearly see that he has already mastered representational painting. He could draw exceedingly well."

Planning a paper with Know-AGO

3. E.—What is the *evidence* concerning my reasons? How do I *evaluate* them? What *examples* should I give?

_____

_____

_____

_____

_____

_____

_____

_____

_____

_____

4. E.—Don't forget to wrap up my thinking with an Ending: Concluding statement:

_____

_____

_____

_____

D. Analyze your time spent. Be honest with yourself here. What could you do to improve?

1. What is the total time you spent planning this paper? _____

2. Is that enough? _____

3. Write a possible schedule to increase the planning time for papers:

_____

_____

_____

_____

(Note: Some writing instructors teach never to use "I" in a class paper. If that's your situation, just change the wording in these starters or write with "I" but then change the words before you turn in the paper.)

What to say?

Start with the main idea, the topic sentence. Often you don't discover your topic sentence until you have written several sentences or even paragraphs. When you do realize, "Hey, that sentence I just wrote is the major idea behind this whole paper," move that sentence to the front of the essay.

In the middle of his third paragraph, Peter writes, "One of the reasons Napoleon was successful was that he was devoted to his men and they were devoted to him." Bang!

That's the topic of the whole paper, he thinks, so he moves that to be the first sentence of the whole essay.

Write lots of details. Giving more detail often makes writing more interesting and understandable. For example, here's a story: a young man and woman from two families that dislike each other fall in love. This makes for a lot of trouble, and the two actually die as a result. Is that interesting? No. It is empty of detail; it's too abstract. But Shakespeare's *Romeo and Juliet,* a play, and Bernstein's *West Side Story,* a musical, which follow that same story line, are very interesting, because they are full of detail.

Give yourself instructions to write more, to provide more detail. When they are writing, good writers ask themselves, "Am I giving enough detail? Do I need to say more?"

Write more. Write more. Write more. Remember that one of the biggest mistakes novices make is *not* writing enough. Not enough detail, not enough reasons, not enough examining the reasons, not enough examples. Tell yourself, "Don't quit. Write more. Give more details, more reasons, more examination of the reasons, more examples."

Keep the reader in mind. Think about the person or persons who will read the paper.

- Will they understand?

- Are you being clear?

- Is it interesting?

When writing, stop now and then to ask these questions. Change your writing depending on your answer.

How to say it?

Pay attention to sentence length. If a sentence is long, it is difficult to control it. Great writers like Henry James or Ernest Hemingway could write very long sentences, but for most of us it's hard not to lose the reader. If you have a sentence much longer than fifteen or twenty words, look for places where you can break it into two.

Build sentences into paragraphs. When you write a paper, each paragraph is one building block of the total construction. Put your paper together with paragraphs.

Each paragraph has only one main idea in it. All the rest in the paragraph supports that idea. If your paper has nine main ideas, you should have at least nine paragraphs.

The first sentence in a paragraph is usually the main idea, and the rest of the sentences are supporting ideas. A person should be able to read through your whole paper, just reading the first sentence of each paragraph, and get all your main ideas. If you have a main idea in the middle, either put it first or start a new paragraph.

> Peter writes, "An army travels on its stomach. Napoleon's troops were devoted to him. If they were, it was because he was pretty good to them. He always made sure they were well fed. And he promoted men quickly if they were good in battle."
>
> Looking at this he sees that the *second* sentence is really the main idea here, so he moves it to be first, and places the "stomach" sentence in a better place after the "well fed" sentence.

Use transitions. To make your writing smoother for the reader, it helps to alert her where you are headed, so she won't be surprised when you go there. You know where you are going, but your reader does not. Therefore, gently guide her thinking so when you go to the next topic the change does not seem too sudden.

To accomplish this, tie paragraphs together with transition sentences. That way, the change from one paragraph to the next is not too abrupt.

> For example, here is the end of Peter's paragraphs about how well liked Napoleon was by his troops, and the beginning of his paragraphs about Napoleon's military victories:
>
> "And so we see that Napoleon did several things to make his men like him, want to follow him.
> "Napoleon won many battles."

> But when revising, Peter realizes that the change from Napoleon's men liking him to the battles is too abrupt. The reader's mind is still on the men liking him. Peter needs to gently switch the reader to the next topic. To do this, he could write a transition sentence something like, "And where did his men follow him? Into battle." Then he can move into the paragraphs about Napoleon's battles.
> The reviewed material reads like this:
>
> "And so we see that Napoleon did several things to make his men like him, want to follow him.
> "And where did his men follow him? Into battle.
> "Napoleon won many battles."

There's a trick to creating these transition sentences. Look at the words in the paragraphs you have to make the transition between, and use one or more of them to create your transition. In the example, Peter used the word "follow." If you take the time to create these transitions, your writing will seem smoother.

Keep planning

Keep your outline in front of you as you write. The purpose of the outline—remember *TREE*—is to guide your writing. As you are writing, keep asking yourself, Am I putting in all the information called for by my outline? Am I writing what I intended to write?

Keep thinking as you write. In the middle of writing the paragraph above, Peter asks himself, "How much do I want to focus on Napoleon's relationship with his men? Am I neglecting his battles?" He tinkers with his plan, to improve the paper. Keep developing new ideas. Keep making changes in the organization. Keep on planning. The planning isn't finished until the paper is.

Skill Builder 18.3 will help you practice writing like an expert.

PoWeR Step Three: R for Revising

QUESTIONS TO ANSWER AS YOU READ:

- What is the SCAN system for revising an essay?
- What are the benefits of keeping the reader in mind?

College students who are good writers revise their writing several times before turning in a paper, while novices usually turn in their first draft. When novices do revise, they tend to focus on grammar, spelling, and punctuation, not on the quality of the writing,[17] but good writers save proofreading until last, and focus on quality first. Revising is not just proofreading, not just searching for errors.

Revising means asking, "Did I convey my meaning?" It means finding and solving problems about clarity or interest.

Keeping the reader in mind

People who are good at revising think about the needs of the reader as they revise.[18] Sometimes it helps to read your writing out loud, so you don't just skim over parts, but listen to it as though you are a reader. Skimming is the enemy.

Try asking another person to listen as read the material so you see how a reader responds. Or a friend can read your draft to give you feedback on it. You don't want just to hear "It's good," as sweet as that is, because your paper will get better only if you learn the places in it where the reader does *not* get your meaning. Every athlete knows that a good coach tells you what you are doing wrong, not just what you are doing right. Of course, you don't want all the focus on what you do wrong, but a little bit is helpful.

SKILL BUILDER 18.3

Writing like an expert

For the next paper you have to do, in any course, practice the steps outlined here for good writing. Use this as a checklist.

Course: _____ Paper _____

A. Work on your writing.

1. Practice getting words to flow. Keep a record with a ✓ if you use *free writing* or *starter sentences*. Record a ✓ plus what technique you used.

   _____

   _____

   _____

   _____

2. Start your paper with a *topic statement,* or find it later and move it into the starting position. Write the topic statement for the paper:

   _____

   _____

   _____

   _____

3. When writing, remember to *increase the details*. Keep a record with a ✓ and the date if you remember to do this.

   _____

   _____

   _____

   _____

4. *Write more.* If you thought about quitting, but didn't, give yourself a second (✓) in the space under ✓ above.

5. Think about the *reader*. What would make your writing clearer or more interesting? Write your ideas:

   _____

   _____

   _____

   _____

   _____

   _____

   _____

6. Arrange or rearrange sentences and paragraphs to create a *good structure*. If you thought about leaving your writing as it was, but didn't, give yourself a third (✓) under ✓ above.

7. Follow your plan—and if necessary, *make changes* in it—as you are writing. If you did this, give yourself a fourth (✓).

B. Make writing practice a habit. For any part of the checklist that you are *not* doing, write out self-instructions to encourage yourself to do it:

1. _____

   _____

2. _____

   _____

SKILL BUILDER 18.3

Writing like an expert

3. _____

_____

**C. Analyze your time spent.
Be honest with yourself here.
What could you do to improve?**

1. What is the total time you spent writing this paper? _____

2. Is that enough to do the things you have to do?_____

3. Write a possible schedule to increase writing time:

_____

_____

_____

_____

_____

_____

Many colleges have writing workshops where you can take your paper and get feedback from the people there. They can be very helpful, and you won't feel as if they are putting you down. Almost all those personnel truly want to help you improve your writing.

If you are not a native English speaker, definitely ask someone who is a native speaker to go over your paper with you.

For each sentence in your paper, ask yourself these questions:

- Is this clear? Will people understand it?
- Is this interesting?
- Do I need to add more?
- Do I need to change anything?

Using SCAN

Harris and Graham developed a system which suggests what to do as you revise each sentence in your paper. Students who learn to use this system make more meaningful revisions of their writing. Their writing tends to be better, longer and more convincing, and to have fewer errors.[19]

First, read your draft and find the topic sentence that gives your primary thought. Is it clear? To fill out your topic sentence, add more reasons why you believe it. Tell yourself to stop and do this before moving on.

Second, read each sentence and SCAN it.

S stands for *Sense?* Does it make *sense?* What do you need to change to have it make sense?

THINK PIECE 18.1   Record of grades on papers

Are you improving? If you practice the full PoWeR system, you can expect to improve. Keep a record of your grades on papers:

_____   _____   _____   _____   _____

_____   _____   _____   _____   _____

C is for *connected ?* Is it *connected* to the other sentences? If not, connect it, by adding more or changing some words.

A is for *Add ?* Should you *add* more? more detail? more reasons to support your main idea?

N is for *Note.* Be sure to *note* any errors of spelling, punctuation, grammar, or capitalization and correct them. *Notice that this is the last step.*

Follow the SCAN procedure for every sentence in your paper.

When you make changes, what kinds of changes should you make? Often, you will need to say more. Sometimes you need to say something in a different way, so it sounds right. Sometimes you drop something. You connect things better, or emphasize them more. Or, you use different words to make the writing more interesting.

Here is an example from pages 000—000 of this book. Many of the changes were made because the writer was thinking of the reader. The numbers indicate spots where something was changed in the revising, and the changed material is underlined. When it was first written, the passage went like this:

> **Keeping the reader in mind.** People who are good at revising think about the needs of the reader as they revise.
>
> (1) They ask themselves, Is it clear? Is it interesting? Do I need to add more? Does it make sense?
>
> (2) Sometimes it helps to read your writing out loud, so you don't just skim over parts, but listen to it as though you are a reader. (3) Skimming is the enemy.
>
> (4) Sometimes it helps to ask another person to listen as read the material so you see how a reader responds.
>
> (5) If you are not a native English speaker, definitely ask someone who is a native speaker to go over your paper with you.
>
> (6) For each sentence in your paper, ask yourself these questions: Is this clear?

(7) <u>Will people understand it?</u> Is this interesting? Do I need to add more?

(8) <u>Does it sound right?</u> Do I need to change anything?

The reasons for the changes: (1) These questions were dropped because they are repeated just below. It would have been boring to repeat. (2) Dropping the sentences reduced that paragraph to only one sentence, too short, so the next material was moved up. (3) This sentence was added to emphasize the point about skimming, to be sure the reader got it. (4) The first part of the sentence was changed to "Try asking" because it sounded just like the first part of the earlier sentence. (5) Two whole paragraphs on using other people to give feedback on the paper were added. Other people's opinions can be very helpful, and this technique did not have enough emphasis before. (6) The first part of this sentence was later italicized to give it emphasis so the reader would be sure to get it. Notice how the reader is kept in mind. (7) This sentence was added for greater clarity. (8) This question was dropped because there were too many questions for the reader to remember.

Use Skill Builder 18.4 to help you practice revising your writing.

Summary: The complete PoWeR system for writing

Step One: Planning

Know — Ask yourself, What do I need to *Know*?

AGO — Who is the *Audience*?

What are my *Goals*?

How should the writing be *Organized*?

Use the TREE of organization:

Topic or theme

Reasons for it

Examine reasons; give *Examples*

Ending

Step Two: Writing

Getting words to flow.

Start with the main idea; give details; write more; keep the reader in mind.

Use good sentence and paragraph structure.

Continue to plan.

S K I L L   B U I L D E R 18.4

Revising: SCAN your sentences

Revising is new for most novice writers, so go carefully, building in each part of the procedure one small step at a time. Better to start low and gradually increase than never to finish at all.

A. Step one: Find the sentence that conveys your topic, your main idea.

1. Ask, Is it clear? Check ✓when you do this. ___

2. Make changes to make it clear. ___ (✓)

3. Add at least one more reason to support your main idea. (Two is better.) Put these in your paper:

   a. _____

   b. _____

4. Write self-instructions to get yourself to do this:

   _____

   _____

   _____

   _____

B. Step two: Use the SCAN technique.

Do this for each sentence in your paper.

1. If you don't do it for all sentences, work out a gradual shaping process to increase how many sentences you SCAN.

   _____

   _____

   _____

   _____

Example: "Start with two sentences. Then four, then six, then one page, then two pages, and so on, gradually increasing."

2. Write self-instructions to tell yourself to SCAN sentences:

   _____

   _____

   _____

   _____

3. Write your rewards for SCANning

   _____

   _____

   _____

   _____

Example: "I won't turn on the TV until I have done whatever level of SCAN my schedule calls for." Or "If I do the required level for SCAN, I can do whatever I want for the rest of the day."

C. Analyze your time spent. Be honest with yourself here. What could you do to improve?

1. What is the total time you spent revising this paper? _____

2. Is that enough to do the things you have to do? _____

3. Use the shaping process of gradually increasing, above, to increase the amount of your papers that you revise.

Step Three: Revising

Find your main idea sentence and ask, Is it clear?

Add at least one more reason to support the main idea.

SCAN each sentence:

S—Ask, Does it make *Sense?*

C—Ask, Is it *Connected* to the others?

A—Do you need to *Add* anything?

N—*Note* errors in spelling punctuation, grammar, or capitalization.

Chapter 19

Gaining Control over **Spoken** Words

PREVIEW WITH QUESTIONS TO ANSWER

Dealing with nervousness and stage fright

- What should you do to reduce nervousness?

Organizing your speech

- How can you plan an effective, well-organized speech?

Practice, practice, practice

- How can you get enough practice?

Giving the speech

- What will help you deliver the speech well?

> After only eight months on his new management training job, Kenji's boss told him to "go out to the Salem store and work for a couple of weeks and then come back and give us a report on how we might get more sales moving out there."
>
> "What kind of report?" Kenji asked.
>
> "Oh, you know, a verbal report. A little talk. We'll just get all the managers together, and you can tell them what you've found. Later you can write it up."

Being able to speak in public is a very good skill to have. Bosses tend to evaluate us in terms of our self-confidence. If we can speak in public, they think we have a lot, and that's good as far as the boss is concerned. Even if you are never asked to give a verbal report at work, there are many opportunities in life to speak to groups: at church when the new budget is being discussed, orienting a group of volunteers who want to help in a public school, in your club when elections come around, or in a political group discussing an issue in city government.

If you want to influence others, if you want to be any sort of leader, if you want your voice to be heard throughout life, it's good to learn to speak in public.

Don't worry, it's not as hard as you fear.

Keep a skills-development attitude about this. If you are just beginning to learn to speak to groups, then you should not worry much about how you will appear to people. You're a freshman at this, so the only question is, Are you improving? Everyone who bothers to learn to speak to groups notices that it gets much easier the more they practice.

There are certain specific issues to deal with in developing this skill:

- Dealing with nervousness or stage fright.
- Organizing your speech.
- Getting enough practice.
- Actually delivering the speech.

We will deal with each of these in turn.

Dealing with Nervousness or Stage Fright

QUESTION TO ANSWER AS YOU READ:

- What should you do to reduce nervousness?

The reason most people worry abut speaking in public is their fear of making a poor impression on the audience. This is a performance orientation, not a skills-development attitude. People get so worried about what the audience will think about them that they perform poorly and, sure enough, the audience is unimpressed. There are several solutions to this problem.

Be well prepared

Just as it helps to reduce anxiety on tests to know your material inside out, it greatly reduces anxiety about public speaking to really know what you are talking about. This is absolutely the best thing you can do to give yourself confidence: really know your stuff. Often people are nervous because they know in their hearts that they are not well prepared. If you are well prepared, you gain great confidence.

Realize that your fear is almost certainly exaggerated

Most people worry far more about the impression they are going to make than is warranted. Frankly, the audience is usually more interested in your message than they are in you, and they will pretty much ignore you if the message is interesting. Typically, the audience is not aware if the speaker is nervous, unless he faints or tells them he is nervous (which is a mistake).

Whatever anxiety you have about making a talk will go away in the first two minutes. It's like parachuting from an airplane: very frightening before you do it, but once you do it you are too busy doing things to be scared any more.

A good technique to keep yourself from getting too nervous is to think about your audience and your message, not yourself. The important questions are, Are you getting your message across? Does the audience understand it? Is it interesting to them?

Use self-reminders to focus on the audience and their needs, not yourself

Watch them and keep their needs in mind, and you won't be aware of yourself, and so won't worry about what they think about you.

> Sitting in her chair in communication class, listening to others give their talks, Sandra is saying to herself, "Don't worry. Don't get nervous. Just focus on giving this talk. I know this stuff, and they don't, so I just have to get the ideas across to them. Think about them; watch them to see if they understand."

Use the stress reduction activities you know to calm yourself before your speech

A man who was going to give a speech before a group that might hire him went for a long jog beforehand, to be sure he was relaxed. Go to the bathroom just beforehand so you won't have to worry about that.

In Chapter 16, on getting calm for tests, you learned about meditation and muscle relaxation, as well as other stress reduction techniques. Use them to relax whenever you are going to give a talk.

> Just before his speech in sociology class, Jaime went into a stall in the men's room and did a complete muscle relaxation procedure, so he would be calm.

> June was in the ladies room the same day practicing meditation.

> Shane didn't drink any coffee that morning so he wouldn't be tense.

The more you practice your speech, the more relaxed you will be when you give it.

Try to spot and cut off thoughts that make you nervous

"This is going to be a disaster" is *not* a helpful thought to have just before giving your talk. Substitute thoughts like, "No, it will be okay. I am well prepared, I've rehearsed, and besides they are not interested in me, they are interested in what I have to say. Relax."

Organizing Your Speech

QUESTION TO ANSWER
AS YOU READ:

■ How can you plan an effective,
well-organized speech?

A well-organized speech is much easier for the audience to follow. Use an outline form for your notes. Don't write so much on each page that you cannot easily read the notes. You should be able to glance at your notes and tell what to say next.

When you are first preparing your talk, check with the instructor to be sure you are following directions for what to cover and how to do it.

Most talks should start with a clear statement of your main ideas, followed by a group of supporting statements, and ending with a summary that reviews what you said. A good outline for your talk goes like this:

1. Tell them what you are going to tell them.
2. Tell them.
3. Tell them what you told them.

The outline seems simple-minded only when you see it in writing. When an audience hears the speech, it seems well organized and the organization helps listeners remember the major points.

> Mazie is going to give a talk to her Biology and Habitat class on birds, specifically cardinals. Her first lines are, "Northern cardinals, the familiar red bird with the crest, used to be rare in North America, but today are very common. Why? Because cardinals live at the edges of woods, and in the old days woods extended unbroken across the eastern part of the continent, but today the forest is broken into thousands of small forests and lots, and these have many edges where cardinals can live." In just a few words she has set the theme for her whole talk. Now she goes into a summary of several research studies about cardinals, their habitat and food preferences, mating and chick rearing, and so on. At the end, she summarizes, "So, cardinals, our old red favorite, live in the suburbs because there are lots of forest edges there. They have prospered greatly in the last one hundred years."

Don't try for too many major points in your talk. About *five* is enough. Emphasize each of them so the audience can tell them apart from the details. For each major point, provide examples and pertinent details.

If you can, use visual aids, such as charts and pictures. When Mazie gave her talk on cardinals, she showed a picture of a Northern cardinal, then a picture of a forest broken up into small woods, then a picture of a cardinal on its nest. Make any signs you use very, very neat, computer-printed if possible, for this gives your talk a professional air.

Mazie was trying to give a balanced picture of the life of cardinals, but sometimes you want to present one particular point of view. For example, you might want to give a strong pro-environment, antidevelopment speech.

There are special considerations here. Start with a fairly strong statement of the point of view you want to endorse, but then quickly anticipate some of the questions and objections that may occur to your audience. If you don't do this, the audience will spend their time thinking of counterarguments to what you are saying, instead of listening to you.[1]

Suppose your assignment in history is to talk about who you think was the greatest person in the last one hundred years. You might start by saying, "I think the South African political activist Nelson Mandela, who fought apartheid, is the greatest person of his century. Oh, of course, other people come to mind: Winston Churchill, Gandhi, Einstein, Eleanor Roosevelt, Martin Luther King, Jr., but let me explain why I think Mandela should get the prize." By mentioning the others, you keep your audience from thinking "Who do I think is the most important?" instead of listening to your ideas about Mandela. Anticipate questions, objections, and points against you so the audience will listen to your thinking.

Practice, Practice, Practice

QUESTION TO ANSWER AS YOU READ:

■ How can you get enough practice?

Great speakers practice their speeches over and over. Demosthenes, a famous ancient Greek orator, used to practice with pebbles in his mouth so he would be sure to enunciate every word well. What appears to be spontaneous in the speeches of great orators like Martin Luther King, Jr., and Winston Churchill was actually the result of much practice.

Practice allows you to see what is missing in your talk, perhaps an example here or a new fact there, and teaches you how to speak in a comfortable manner. You can practice by giving your talk to a friend, or just give it to a bare room. Some students talk into a tape recorder and play it back to see how they sound. Practice speaking loudly, as you might do in a classroom, so you will be used to talking that way.

If you practice several times you will know your material very well and will not have to use your notes much. This will make you seem relaxed in your delivery, as though you were just talking to the audience. Practice also teaches you how to stay within the time limit of your talk, an important skill.

Check out the place where you will give your talk. If you have never before been in the front of the class, or behind the podium, go there and feel what it's like before the time for your talk. You might even imagine you are there, giving your talk, so you feel familiar with the place beforehand.

SKILL BUILDER 19.1

Planning an excellent talk

Use this to plan an upcoming speech.

Topic: _____ Date of speech _____

A. Step 1. Be well prepared.

Estimate the hours you will need to work on developing the talk: _____.

Schedule work times to do this:

Sunday _____ Monday _____ Tuesday _____ Wednesday _____ Thursday _____ Friday _____ Saturday _____

Place a ✓ when you do it. Add more hours if necessary. Remember that being well prepared is the best guard against stage fright.

B. Step 2. Outline your talk.

1. Introductory statement:

   _____

   _____

2. Main ideas:

   a. _____

   b. _____

   c. _____

   d. _____

   e. _____

3. Summary statement:

   _____

   _____

C. Step 3. Deal with nervousness or stage fright.

1. Be well prepared. See above, and don't fool yourself. It's worth the effort.

2. Write self-reminders to hold a skills-development attitude about this talk:

   _____

   _____

Your skills inventory

Example: "Okay, remember I'm not a pro at this yet, so I will just do my best and see if I can improve from one time to the next. I will use all the strategies I know to give a good talk."

3. Write self-reminders to focus on the audience, on getting your message across:

_____

_____

Example: "Don't think about how I look; think about them: do they understand? do I need to go slower? do I need to give more examples?"

4. Use stress reduction techniques (exercise, caffeine reduction, meditation, muscle relaxation). Specify the techniques and when they will be used:

_____

_____

D. Step 4: Practice.

Schedule several practice times.

Sunday _____ Monday _____ Tuesday _____ Wednesday _____ Thursday _____ Friday _____ Saturday _____

Place a ✔ when you do it. Practice more if necessary. Remember that much practice makes the speech go better.

Giving the Speech

When Evelyn was in her second year of medical school she had to give a talk about a particular patient in front of the whole group of medical students and faculty who worked with that kind of patient. "I'm nervous about doing it," she told her advisor. "When the faculty do it, they seem so knowledgeable, so totally in command of the subject."

"Here's what to do," counseled the advisor. "When it's your turn at the head of the table, *play the role of someone who is totally in command of the subject*. Just play the role, and you will do fine." Evelyn was amazed to find this was true. Play the role of the relaxed, confident speaker and you will be.

Some technical points: Don't read your talk, that's boring. Try to have a normal tone to your voice. Make eye contact with the audience. Relax.

Don't be stiff in your body; control any nervous motions. Give yourself instructions to do all these things.

Afterwards, get feedback from others on things you can do to be better next time. Remember, you are just now developing this skill, so don't worry about your performance, just try to get better and better.

Try using Skill Builder 19.1 to plan a talk.

Chapter 20

Increasing Your Vocabulary

PREVIEW WITH QUESTIONS TO ANSWER

What are the advantages to increasing your vocabulary?

- How important is it to have a large vocabulary?

Learning new words

- How are new words learned?
- What is the best procedure for enlarging your vocabulary?
- What is the keyword method?

The importance of reading

- How is reading important for vocabulary?

What are the Advantages to Increasing your Vocabulary?

The single most important thing you can do to increase your IQ (intelligence quotient) is increase your vocabulary.[1] The bigger your vocabulary, the greater your intelligence. Vocabulary is measured both directly and indirectly on IQ tests and so contributes to your total score. When you increase your vocabulary, you open yourself to the benefits that go with greater intelligence. Business and political leaders almost always have large vocabularies.

Words give us tools to think with. Without the tools, it is harder to think. Suppose a speaker says something that is "dull and trivial, but said as though it is really deep." It is cumbersome to use that whole phrase in quotes to think about the speech, so we don't communicate about it as well as we might. "What did he sound like?" "Oh, it was kind of stupid." If you know the word *platitude,* on the other hand, it becomes easy to describe the speech. A platitude is a dull or trivial remark uttered as though it were profound. "What was his speech like?" "Oh, it was full of platitudes."

**QUESTION TO ANSWER
AS YOU READ:**

■ How important is it to have a
large vocabulary?

Vocabulary is not taught enough in school, with the result that many of us would be helped by increasing our vocabularies.[2] College is a good time to increase it. In college you learn both entirely new words and new definitions of old words. College students average learning two or three new words a day.

Learning New Words

**QUESTIONS TO ANSWER
AS YOU READ:**

■ How are new words learned?
■ What is the best procedure for
enlarging your vocabulary?
■ What is the keyword method?

Most new vocabulary is learned in context. You figure out the meaning of a word by noting how it is used. Children learn up to thirteen new words a day, and the primary way they do this is by noting the context. For example, a three-year-old, wanting to be helpful, brings some trash he found on the floor to his mother. The mother says, "Put it in the trash can over there, honey" and gestures to the corner of the kitchen. The child looks to the corner and sees only two things: (1) the cat—he already knows the name for that—and (2) a large, hollow object with a plastic liner. He figures this must be the "trash can." He has learned a new word.

A few minutes later the child is about to pick up an interesting looking object from the table, and his mother says, "No, honey, leave the candle there." Now he's learned another word, *candle*. Of course, he may have to hear it more than once before he learns it well. We learn *via* practice.

Step one: *Notice words you don't know, and try to figure out their meaning from the other words in the sentence*

The enemy is skimming over the word, not stopping to notice it. Suppose you read in a story, "He was *pallid*, no color in his face at all." You don't know *pallid*. You could just keep on reading, not noticing pallid, or you could stop and try to figure out its meaning.

Judging by the other words in the sentence, it might mean "colorless," or it might mean "sickly," or perhaps "nervous." It surely does not mean "strong" or "happy" or "angry" because they don't fit the rest of the sentence. Try substituting your guess, to see if it makes sense. "He was colorless, no color in his face at all." That fits.

Sometimes other sentences in the story will help you rule out certain definitions. For example, if there has been nothing in the story that would make the character "nervous," you could rule that out. Studying the context and then substituting like this can give you a general idea of the meaning of the word. If your guess fits well, you've learned the word.

Sometimes the precise meaning cannot be guessed from the context. In our example, "sickly" works, too. Other parts of the story might not give a clue about whether "sickly" is a good guess or not.

Sometimes we guess the wrong meaning from context, and continue to think of the wrong meaning for some time. A student confided, "I used to think that the word *mosaic* was some kind of picture of Moses on the floor or wall. Finally, I ran into a situation where that definition of *mosaic* just didn't fit at all, and realized that *mosaic* has nothing to do with Moses."

The student's instincts were not all wrong. A mosaic is a picture made by piecing together bits of material, for example, by cementing colored tiles onto a surface. But *Mosaic* with a capital *M,* is an adjective meaning "relating to Moses" as in "Mosaic teachings." The two words have entirely different orgins; mosaic without a capital M comes from a Latin word for *artistic.*

If it's important, you need to look it up.

Step two: *Make a list of words you don't know to look up in a dictionary*

The basic ideas are these:

- Start a list of words to learn.

- Set a goal of how many you will look up each week.

- Schedule times to do this.

- Devise self-instructions to encourage yourself to do this.

- Reward doing it.

To avoid having to go to a library to do this, buy a dictionary. A small paperback dictionary is probably not large enough, because some of the words you want to look up will not be in a paperback. You don't need a giant dictionary. One called a "collegiate" is big enough.

Step three: *Be sure you learn the word*

You can look up a word and read its definition, but still not learn it. Words that children learn, like *cat* or *trash can,* are easy to learn because they stand for physical objects, but words like *pallid* or *horrid* are harder to learn and remember because they don't stand for physical objects, and they are not used often. To learn a word, you have to use it.

Make up a sentence or two with the word when you first read it in the dictionary. "Okay, *pallid* means 'deficient in color.' No color. Let's see, a sentence. Okay. 'I don't like this painting. It is pallid.' Or 'He was sick; his face was pallid.'"

Sometimes you look up a word, but then several days later realize you have forgotten what it means, which can be frustrating.

The *keyword method* is a powerful technique to avoid forgetting newly learned words. The system is basically a way of using elaboration—see Chapter 12—to increase your chances of remembering a word. People who use this technique remember about 50 percent more words that they have just learned.[3]

Here's how it works: To remember a new word; think of a word you already know that sounds like part of the new word, then think of a connection between them. If the connection is strange, all the better. For example, our student wanted to remember the meaning of *mosaic*—a wall or floor decoration made by inlaying small pieces of colored material to form a picture. The student thinks of a picture of Moses on the floor made out of tiny pieces of colored glass.

More examples: To remember the meaning of *gastric*—which means anything related to the stomach—a student said to herself, "*Gas*tric—gas. I've got gas on my stomach." To remember *pallid*, a student thinks of the word *pale*. To remember *replete*, which means "completely full, gorged, filled," a student thought of her friend Pete, who was rather overweight. "Pete is replete."

It is definitely worth taking out a moment to think of an association like this to help you remember a new word.

Learning foreign language vocabulary. The keyword technique is very helpful in learning vocabulary words when you are studying a foreign language. The trick is to use elaboration, just as you do when you want to learn something in English. This greatly helps you remember vocabulary words. If you try just brute memorization, many of the words will fade from memory, but if you tie them to other parts of your mind, they are less likely to fade.

Here's an example. Suppose you are taking beginning Spanish and have to learn these words for tomorrow:

mesa (table)

gallo (chicken)

pinto (spotted)

You've heard the word *mesa* before, as a name for large, flat-topped mountains in the West. In fact they are called "mesa" because they are shaped like a table, flat on top. You picture a gigantic mountain shaped exactly like a table with legs and a flat top; it's a "mesa." By tying together a picture of a table, the word *mesa* you already know as a mountain in the West, and the Spanish word *mesa*, you elaborate on the Spanish word and make it more likely you will remember it.

Use the same procedure for all the Spanish vocabulary words you need to learn. "Gallo" sounds in English like "*guy*-oh." You picture a guy, dressed like a cowboy, riding a huge chicken. *Gallo*. Get along, little chicken.

You know pinto beans, of course; you just never realized they were called "pinto" because they are spotted. Now you think of pinto beans when you see the word *pinto*. Later a friend from Costa Rica tells you that their national dish of rice and beans is called "gallo pinto," spotted chicken, which is easy to remember because it has no chicken in it. It's vegetarian chicken. Easier to remember because the association is weird.

The need for practice. If you don't use it, you may lose it. You will remember words if you practice with them, and you are less likely to remember if you don't. Set your mind to use the word. "I always tell myself to use the new word within a day or two of looking it up. I look for some way to fit it into the conversation."

Some words, of course, are difficult to fit into the conversation without seeming pretentious. Most of us know words we recognize when we see them written, but we never use them in our speech. That's normal. If you can't find another way to use it, you can always say, "Hey, I found this great word. *Pallid.* Means without color." If you use it, you don't lose it.

As part of his College Success course, Grant decided to increase his vocabulary. "When I am reading, I keep a list by my side and write down any words I run into that I can't define. I first try to figure out the meaning of the word from its context, but if I cannot, or if I'm not sure, I write it down. Sometimes I write down where I saw the word so I can go back later and understand how it was used. For example, on page 139 of *Captain Blood* by Sabatini, I came across the word *impasse*. I wanted to know what that sentence meant, because it was important for the story, so I wrote down all the information. To avoid feeling overwhelmed, I write down only the first three unfamiliar words I see on any given day.

"I decided to look up the definition of one word per day. I did this at the beginning of my scheduled study period. After a week, one word seemed too little, so I upped it to two words per day. It only takes a few minutes.

"I also scheduled reading so that I would do more of that, because people who read more have better vocabularies. I started by scheduling just two half-hour periods per week, but toward the end was reading as much as three and a half hours per week, a half hour each day. To gain the extra time for reading, I cut down on my TV viewing some. I would say to myself, 'Okay, Grant, before you watch TV, do a half hour's reading. It will expand my vocabulary, which will make me smarter, and that's what I want.' I've noticed that smart people have large vocabularies, so I remind myself of that.

"To be sure I remembered the words I looked up, I made up a sentence with the word in it when I first read it. I set a rule to use the word at least once a day for several days after

S K I L L   B U I L D E R   20.1

Increasing your vocabulary

A. Part one. Recognize unknown words.

1. Write self-instructions to notice and make a record of words you can't define:

   _____

   Example: "Set my mind like an alarm clock. Notice words I can't define."

2. How often will you notice new words as you read? Set a goal.

   _____

   Example: "I will find and record at least one new word a day."

4. Keep a record with a ✓ and the date each time you meet your goal

   S_____ M_____ T_____ W_____ T_____ F_____ S_____

   S_____ M_____ T_____ W_____ T_____ F_____ S_____

   S_____ M_____ T_____ W_____ T_____ F_____ S_____

   S_____ M_____ T_____ W_____ T_____ F_____ S_____

   S_____ M_____ T_____ W_____ T_____ F_____ S_____

   S_____ M_____ T_____ W_____ T_____ F_____ S_____

5. If you are not meeting your goal most weeks, why not? Ideas for problem solving: (Possibilities: no goal, goal too high, lack of commitment to the goal, lack of self-instructions, lack of rewards for doing it.)

   _____

   _____

B. Part two. Look up words in a dictionary.

1. Write your list of words:

   _____ _____ _____ _____

   _____ _____ _____ _____

   _____ _____ _____ _____

   _____ _____ _____ _____

   _____ _____ _____

   Goal (words to look up per day and week):_____

   Remember to start low and gradually increase the goal.

SKILL BUILDER 20.1

Increasing your vocabulary

2. Write your schedule. When will you look up words? At a specified time?

S_____ M_____ T_____ W_____ T_____ F_____ S_____

Before or after some event such as your daily study period?

_____

Example: "One word before studying each day and one before watching TV."

3. Record your actual use. Place a ✓ beside your schedule each time you do the work. Continue for several weeks.

4. Write self-instructions to get started looking up words:

_____

_____

C. Part three: Follow a procedure to learn the word.

1. *When you look up the word:*

    a. Read the definition.

    b. Make up a sentence with it.

    c. Put a ✓ beside it.

2. *Use the keyword method.* To remember the meaning of the word, think of a word that sounds like part of it, then imagine some association between them. For example, you look up *gastric* which means "relating to the stomach," and you think, "*Gas*tric—gas. I've got gas in my stomach." For each word in your list for which you form a keyword, put a K—for "Keyword"—beside it.

    Write self-reminders to form keywords:

    _____

    Goal: For how many words will you form a keyword? _____

3. *Use the new words.* Try to use each new word several times in the days after you first look it up. Put a U—for "Used"—beside it, above, each time you use it in daily conversation or in your writing.

    Goal: How often will you try to use each new word?

    _____

    Write self-reminders to use the new words:

    _____

S K I L L   B U I L D E R   **20.1**

Increasing your vocabulary

4. *Reward yourself for looking up words and for using them.*

Example: "Every day I will look up the meaning of at least one word. I won't have my evening cup of herb tea until I have done this."

_____

_____

It is important to fit these ideas to a way of learning that feels comfortable to you, so adapt these procedures to yourself.

Example: "I will look up a word in the dictionary and then make up a sentence with the word after I've read the definition. I will then use the word at least once per day for the next week. I will keep track of this."

_____

_____

_____

I learned it. My girlfriend was doing this same project, so we made a game out of it, to see who could use new words the most.

"I really liked this project. At the end of eight weeks I learned more than one hundred new words. Once in class my religion professor used the word *nefarious,* which I never knew before, but I knew it, and I felt great about that."

Use Skill Builder 20.1 to practice increasing your vocabulary.

The Importance of Reading

QUESTION TO ANSWER AS YOU READ:

■ How is reading important for vocabulary?

Most vocabulary learning comes from learning in context. The child is told to put something in the trash can, and thereby figures out what a trash can is. You will *not* learn new vocabulary from context if you are *not* exposed to the context. For adults the major context for learning new vocabulary is reading.

The more people read, the larger their vocabulary[4]. You can read books, newspapers, magazines, the Web, whatever. The evidence from a large number of educational studies is "simply overwhelming" that people learn new vocabulary from reading, and later telling about what they have read.[5] The more you read, the bigger your vocabulary. The vocabularies of people who read increase throughout their lives, so effectively they get smarter and smarter.

The more people watch TV, incidentally, the smaller their vocabulary. This is because the level of vocabulary on TV is set around third grade so that everyone can follow it. In fact, if five-year-olds watch a lot of TV, they have a good vocabulary for their age—because it's at third-grade level—but if they continue to be heavy viewers, their vocabulary falls behind that of other children after third grade.

Chapter 21

Spelling: Putting Your Best Foot Forward

PREVIEW WITH QUESTIONS TO ANSWER

Steps to better spelling
- What are the steps to follow?

The best spelling study procedure
- What are the three steps to learn how to spell a word?

Searching for the right spelling
- What are the strategies to remember how to spell a word?
- What are the Reliable Rules?

Spelling consciousness
- What is spelling consciousness? How can you develop it?

Being a poor speller is *not* good for your social image. Spelling poorly is associated with lack of education.[1] "I only got my job because I was so persistent," one student said. "After I was hired my boss told me he wasn't going to hire me because my spelling was bad. He thought that meant I was not smart enough." There are advantages to improving your spelling skills.

There is good news and bad news about spelling. The bad news first: Many students believe that they spell badly. Students says things like, "I'm a horrible speller," "My spelling is a catastrophe," or "All my life spelling has been a problem for me." The bad news is, they are right. At least a lot of people believe so. Newspaper articles report that bosses think new employees don't spell very well.[2] Educational researchers agree. Spelling is not taught enough in schools, and when it is, it is not taught very well.[3] That tends to make us bad spellers.

You can rely on spell-check programs when you are writing something on a computer, but you won't always be working that way, and then problems will show up. One student remarked, "The instructor sent me to the blackboard, and I was so embarrassed because I couldn't spell some of the words he dictated."

Finally, the good news: It is not very difficult to fix the situation. One authority writes, "Good spelling requires a relatively small amount of learning."[4] Only three hundred words account for 49 percent of all spelling errors.[5] A few minutes a day spread over several months will make you a much better speller. In fact, you should *not* spend more than fifteen minutes a day on it, and can get by with less.[6] You can improve with as little as five minutes a day. This means working on two or three words at a time, not some huge list.

Steps to Better Spelling

QUESTION TO ANSWER AS YOU READ:

■ What are the steps to follow?

Start a list of words you want to learn how to spell

Some students have trouble with particular words, and put these on their list. "I've always had trouble with *syllable* and *privilege,* so I started my list with them." Some people note down words in lectures or textbooks that they can't spell. "Whenever the instructor uses a word I can't spell, I put a box around it in my notes. Later I go back and add that word to my to-learn list." You will find words in your reading. When you run into a word you can't spell, jot it down.

Don't make a huge list: that's discouraging. As soon as you have a couple of weeks' worth of work, hold off adding words until you've reduced the size of the list. Add new words later.

Set a goal

Set your goal in terms of the number of minutes per day you will work *or* the number of words per day you will learn. An advantage of using number of minutes is that you know exactly when you can stop. An advantage to using number of words is you know exactly how much you will accomplish each day. Be realistic and start small.

> "I didn't want to start with ten words a day because I knew that in a couple of days I might give up," Bill explained. "So I started with three words a day and thought I could increase if that was too easy."

> "I thought I would start by working on spelling for ten minutes four days a week," Anna said.

> "I will study spelling five minutes a day from Sunday to Friday."

> Paolo began at bedrock. "I will learn a minimum of one word per day."

Many students begin with five to ten minutes per day devoted to spelling. Learning to spell just one word a day five days a week will mean seventy-five words over the course of a full semester. In four semesters, that's three hundred words. Two words a day would increase that to six hundred words.

THINK PIECE 21.1   Basic rules to save face

There are a few frequently misspelled words that really separate the sheep from the goats. If you get them right, you look socially okay, but if you don't, it's sad. Truly, it is hard to exaggerate how much better you look to bosses, instructors, and others if you get these right. If you are not sure you are spelling these correctly, put them at the top of your to-do list.

For each of these three sets, ask yourself, "Do I always get these right?" If not, fix it. Put the misspelled words on your initial list of words to learn in Skill Builder 21.1.

Set 1: there, their, they're.
There means "in or at that place" as opposed to "here": "Put the stuff down over *there*."

Their is the possessive form of *they*. "Put *their* stuff down over there."

They're is a contraction of *they are*; the *a* in *are* is dropped: "*They're* going to be happy if you put their stuff down over there."

Do you always get these right? Yes _____ No _____ If not, write plans to fix it:

_____

_____

Set 2: its, it's.
Its is the possessive for *it*: "This is the dog's house. And this is *its* drinking bowl. I think the dog wants you to stay away from *its* things."

It's is a contraction of *it is*; the *i* in *is* is dropped. "*It's* too bad the dog bit you. I told you to leave its things alone."

Do you always get these right? Yes _____ No _____ If not, write plans to fix it:

_____

_____

Set 3: To; too.
Too means "also" or "besides." He says, "I love you." She says, "I love you, too." Don't confuse this with *to*.

To means "in the direction of" or "toward" or ideas like that. "He gave the gift *to* her. They traveled *to* Detroit."

Do you always get these right? Yes _____ No _____ If not, write plans to fix it:

_____

_____

S K I L L   B U I L D E R   21.1

The joy of spelling

A. Write your initial list of words to learn (be sure to spell them correctly here):

_____ _____ _____ _____

_____ _____ _____ _____

_____ _____ _____ _____

_____ _____ _____ _____

_____ _____ _____ _____

B. Write your goal (words per day and week or amount of time per day and week)

_____

Write a possible schedule of work (start low and take small steps):

_____

_____

Example: "Start with one word per day; then increase to two; then see if I want to increase it. Could increase just on the weekends."

Set a schedule

Just as you schedule your study time, you should schedule the times when you will study spelling.

"Every day at 4:00 P.M. I will study spelling for ten minutes."

"Each day, when I get out of the shower, I will study spelling for ten minutes."

"I'm going to study spelling for five minutes at the beginning of each scheduled study period each day, whenever that falls."

"I'll study three words each evening just before supper."

Use self-instructions to remind yourself to do it

Remind yourself that you want to do this, and that it will not take much time. Remind yourself of your goals.

SKILL BUILDER 21.1

The joy of spelling

C. Schedule when the practice will happen. At a specified time?

S_____ M_____ T_____ W_____ T_____ F_____ S_____

Before or after some event such as supper?

_____

S_____ M_____ T_____ W_____ T_____ F_____ S_____

Example: "Before TV on Sunday, Monday, and Tuesday; after dance class on Friday."

D. Record your actual use. Place a ✓ beside your schedule each time you do the work. If you don't do it enough, change your schedule, take smaller steps, and use self-instructions.

E. Write self-instructions to get started:

_____

_____

F. Write your reward for doing the practice:

_____

"Sit up and open your spelling notebook, and concentrate on that for twelve minutes. It won't take long."

"You won't always be able to write with the spell-check program. Doing this will make me a better student and help me look smart."

"This is about practice. If you're not good at something, you practice it over and over and after a while you're good at it."

Find a reward for doing the weekly work

If you reinforce your spelling practice, you are more likely to do it. The reward can be anything that follows the spelling practice, but only happens *if* you do the spelling practice. For example, one student didn't let herself eat breakfast until she had done her seven minutes practice several days a week. Another worked out a deal so that her mother would do her dish-washing duties one day if the student did her spelling practice all week. A third bought herself small items each Saturday if she stuck to her spelling practice schedule all week. One young dancer gave herself extra time to dance if she put in the time on her spelling. Rewards will help you do the weekly practice.

Note that the reward is not for learning to spell a certain number of words. *You get it for doing the practice time.*

The Best Spelling Study Procedure

QUESTION TO ANSWER AS YOU READ:

■ What are the three steps to learn how to spell a word?

Suppose you want to learn to spell *amateur.* The procedure many people follow is to spell the word out loud over and over. "Amateur: A-M-A-T-E-U-R. A-M-A-T-E-U-R. A-M-A-T-E-U-R." This is *not* a very effective procedure. You can say it over and over, but not learn it because it never gets into your long-term memory. There's a better way.

It's a three step process:

1. *Look* at the word carefully.
2. Close your eyes and *visualize* its correct spelling.
3. Then *write* it down and *check* your spelling.

Step one: Look

We sometimes misspell words because they are not spelled the way they sound. Take *laboratory.* In American English it often sounds like "LAB-ra-tory." If it were spelled like that, it would be *l-a-b-r-a-t-o-r-y,* but that is *not* correct. Also, some words have silent letters in them that are not pronounced, such as *muscle.* It is easy to miss that silent *c.* Silent letters sometimes get dropped when the ending of the word changes. For example, *move* becomes *moving.*

When we read, our eyes skim along rapidly, reading the word as we would hear it, and not noticing individual letters. That is great for reading, but it makes spelling difficult if the word is not spelled just as it sounds.

To conquer these problems, the first step in learning to spell a word is to

■ Look at it carefully, noticing each letter in the sequence of letters.

■ Pronounce the word as it is actually spelled.

For example, "lab-or-a-tory." Use it in a sentence that way. "Come up to the lab-or-a-tory and see what's on the slab."

Try that for these words:

gourmet

jeopardize

pneumonia

Step two: Visualize

The task is to get the correct spelling into your long-term memory. The best way to do this is to use imagery. Students who use imagery to learn spelling end up better spellers than those who do not, and their ability persists for a longer time.[7] Read the word carefully and then imagine the word in your mind's eye.

To visualize a word's spelling, close your eyes and "see" the word in black letters against some background such as a screen.[8] If the word wavers or you can't get a clear image, try "nailing" it down. Exert mental effort to get it visualized. Some people visualize with eyes open, some with eyes closed. Some visualize against a white background. One woman said she always thought of the blue sky. Hold the visualization for a second or two. Then check if your image of the word is correct.

When you first try this procedure, the visualization will be weak, but if you practice a bit you will be able to visualize words readily. Don't give up if after five minutes the visualization is weak. It takes more practice than that.

Step three: Write and check

Now open your eyes, cover the word, and write it down. Then check your spelling.

If your spelling is not correct, repeat the procedure from step one. It could be that you have not yet noticed the correct arrangement of all the letters, or that you did not visualize all of them in their correct order.

Work on the whole word, but pay particular attention to the difficult parts. If you were learning to spell *anthropology,* but got it wrong the first time, pay attention to the parts you got wrong. "Oh, yeah, it's in the middle where I'm missing it." Give the difficult parts special attention so you are sure you get all the letters in their correct sequence. Be sure to visualize those parts.

If necessary, break long words into parts and learn one part at a time: *anthro* first, then *pology.* In your final work, of course, put them back together to learn the whole word.

If your spelling is correct, cover the word and write it out two more times. This "overlearning" of the correct spelling will help you remember it. When you do these extra two times, pay close attention. If you just dash them off, they won't help your overlearning. Pay particular attention to any parts of the word you have been getting wrong.

Use Skill Builder 21.2 to practice learning to spell.

Make adaptations to fit your individual study style

Make any changes in the procedure that you feel will help you learn. One student made up little stories for words to help her remember the

SKILL BUILDER 21.2

Look—Visualize—Write and Check

A. Write self-instructions to remember to use the three-step process:

_____

_____

B. Record your use of the process:

1. For the first time, record each step in the process; ✓ if you do it.

Word _____   Word _____

Looked carefully _____   Looked carefully _____

Visualized _____   Visualized _____

Covered, wrote, checked _____   Covered, wrote, checked _____

Word _____   Word _____

Looked carefully _____   Looked carefully _____

Visualized _____   Visualized _____

Covered, wrote, checked _____   Covered, wrote, checked _____

Remember to repeat the whole process if the word is incorrect the first time.

2. For later times, keep a record of using the process; ✓ when you do.

Date _____ Used the three-step process? _____

Date _____ Used the three-step process? _____

spelling: "*Opportunity*: There is this seaport called *Port Unity*. Just add *op* and you've got *op-port-unity*." Another student tries to hear the word in his head when he visualizes it. Some write out the to-be-learned words on flip cards and test themselves over and over.

Many students like to give themselves weekly spelling tests to check on the words they have practiced that week. This ensures that you can still spell the words you practiced earlier and contributes to remembering them later. Work with another person who reads the word to you. "My roommate and I would test each other each week on our spelling lists for the week."

Summary: Best spelling study method

1. Look carefully at the word.
2. Visualize it in your mind.

SKILL BUILDER 21.2

Look—Visualize—Write and Check

Date _____ Used the three-step process? _____

Date _____ Used the three-step process? _____

Date _____ Used the three-step process? _____

Date _____ Used the three-step process? _____

Date _____ Used the three-step process? _____

Date _____ Used the three-step process? _____

Date _____ Used the three-step process? _____

Date _____ Used the three-step process? _____

C. Write the changes to make to improve the process.
Write here your ideas on adapting the process to your style:

_____

_____

D. Keep a record of your weekly tests: ✓ if you do a self-test;
give the percentage correct:

Week 1 _____   Week 2 _____   Week 3 _____   Week 4 _____

Week 5 _____   Week 6 _____   Week 7 _____   Week 8 _____

Week 9 _____   Week 10 _____   Week 11 _____   Week 12 _____

3. Write it out and check your spelling.
4. If it is correct, write it carefully two more times.
5. If it is incorrect, go back to step 1.

QUESTIONS TO ANSWER AS YOU READ:

■ What are the strategies to remember how to spell a word?
■ What are the Reliable Rules?

Searching for the Right Spelling

Sometimes you're not trying to learn a word, you're trying to remember how to spell it, but you don't have a correct version to check. For example, you're writing on an essay exam and aren't sure how to spell a particular word. Don't panic. There are strategies to follow, problem solving for spelling.

Good spellers don't necessarily have the correct spelling of every word on the tip of their tongue. Instead, when they can't spell a word, they use the strategies they know to figure out how to spell it. The first thing to do is to remind yourself to use the strategies listed below. "Ah, wait, I don't know how to spell this. Yeah, okay, use the strategies."

If getting the spelling right is important, it will help to relax for a moment. You can give yourself instructions to do that, too. Remember the relaxation instructions in Chapter 16.

Use several strategies. That is what good spellers do. The ones here are adapted here from the work of Vera Woloshyn and Michael Pressley.[9]

Strategy one: Check the Reliable Rules

There are certain rules of spelling in English that are quite reliable. See Box 21.1. For example, "*I* before *E* except after *C*" is part of a reliable rule. "I believe this receipt is correct." When in doubt, remember the Reliable Rules and check to see if one is relevant.

You need to learn the rules. Learn these one at a time, perhaps one each day. If you try to learn too many at once, you may confuse them and not learn any.

Strategy two: Use visualization to try to remember the word

Suppose you need to spell *dolphin*. You are not sure if it ends with *phin* or *fin*. But you have seen this word many times before. Try closing your eyes and calling up a visualization of how it is spelled. Does one visualization feel better than the other?

Try to remember everything you can about the word. "How do you spell *Miami Dolphins?* Can I visualize that? It feels like there ought to be something other than an *F* in the middle of the word. I don't think it's *Miami Dolfins.* Must be *ph.* Miami Dolphins."

As you practice visualizing this way, it becomes easier and easier.

Some people are confused about visualization. You cannot lose weight just by visualizing how you will look when you are slim. But you can visualize how a word is spelled if you have seen it spelled before. That's really just using your memory, and that's the kind of visualization recommended here.

Strategy three: Use the Rhyming Rule

If the last part of two words rhyme, they are often spelled the same. For example, *rhyme* and *thyme, know* and *snow, lake* and *flake, conceit* and *deceit.*

Suppose you were trying to remember how to spell *thyme.* The problem is, it rhymes with *rhyme* but also with *lime.* Use visualization to see

B
O
X

21.1

Reliable Rules for Spelling

Rule	Example

General

1. Old Faithful: *I* before *E*, except after *C*,   *believe*, but *conceive*
   or when sounded like "ay" as in *neighbor* or *weigh*.   *weight*

2. No word in English ends in *V*.   *move*, not *mov*

3. In English *Q* is always followed by *U*.   the duck goes *quack*, not *qack*

4. To show a plural, add *S*,   cup—*cups*
   but if the word already ends in *S*, add *ES*.   glass—*glasses*

5. Use apostrophe and *S* to show possession.   the *children's* coats
   But if the word already ends in *S*, just add
   the apostrophe. (Not for proper nouns
   such as names.)   the *boys'* coats

6. To show a letter left out, use an apostrophe.   *We're* = we are

7. Abbreviations usually end with a period.   September = Sept.

Rules about the root word

8. *E* rules:
   - *E* plus vowel, drop the *E:*
     If a word ends in *E*, drop the *E* when   *drive* becomes *driving*
     adding an ending that starts with a vowel.   *line* becomes *lining*

   - *E* plus consonant, keep the *E:*
     If a word ends in *E* and you're adding an
     ending that starts with a consonant,   *move* becomes
     keep the *E*.   *movement*

9. *Y* rules:
   - *Y* with consonant before it, change   *dry, dries; fly, flies*
     Y to *I* when adding something,
   - unless the ending begins with *I*, then keep the *Y*.   *dry, drying; fly, flying*

which feels like a better fit. "I remember the herb word is spelled funny. So it is probably not like lime because then it would be *t–i–m–e*. Must be *t–h–y–m–e*."

Strategy four: Focus on the root word

Divide the word into the root and the ending, and think how to spell each.

Endings and pronunciation change, but the root word usually doesn't change much. For example: "sign" is the root word for "signature." "Signa-

---

SKILL BUILDER 21.3

Search techniques

Use the four strategies when you are searching for the correct spelling.

A. Write self-reminders to use the strategies:

_____

_____

B. Write self-instructions to relax when searching, and list things you will do to relax:

_____

_____

C. Use Reliable Rules:

Learn the rules one at a time. Check here with a ✔ when you have *really* learned each rule.

Rule 1 _____   Rule 2 _____   Rule 3 _____   Rule 4 _____   Rule 5 _____

Rule 6 _____   Rule 7 _____   Rule 8 _____   Rule 9 _____

D. To develop the habit, keep track of using the four strategies when you need to search for the spelling of a word.

Occasion _____   Strategies used _____

Occasion _____   Strategies used _____

Occasion _____   Strategies used _____

Occasion _____   Strategies used _____

Occasion _____   Strategies used _____

Occasion _____   Strategies used _____

ture" is pronounced differently, but the spelling of the root is actually the same. Even "pronunciation" doesn't change much from its root, "pronounce." When changes in pronunciation are made it is often because the longer word sounds strange if it is pronounced the same as the root word. Try saying "signature" but keeping the pronunciation that goes with "sign."

Rules number 8 and 9 in the Reliable Rules, the *E* and *Y* rules, are about the root word.

Use Skill Builder 21.3 to help you practice spelling search techniques.

Spelling consciousness

QUESTION TO ANSWER AS YOU READ:

■ What is spelling consciousness? How can you develop it?

People who are good at spelling pay more attention to spelling.[10] They pay attention to their own writing, checking for misspelled words. When reading, they notice words they don't know how to spell. This spelling consciousness allows them to correct misspellings when they occur in their own writing and to learn new word spellings.

The idea of *knowing when you don't know* came up before. Recognizing when you don't know how to spell a word is a strong step toward being an educated person. It will help you improve your spelling, which will help you present yourself to others in a favorable light.

There are two parts to the process of spelling consciousness.

Part one: Check your own work

After you have written something—an e-mail to a friend as well as a homework assignment—stop for just a minute to read through your writing, checking for misspelled words. Tag misspellings by underlining, circling, or otherwise marking them. Then look up the word in the dictionary.

How do you look up a word in the dictionary if you don't know how to spell it? Sound out the first part of the word carefully, to give yourself an idea how to spell it. If the word, for example, is *amateur*, sound out the first part, "a-ma" and look that up. There are not too many words that start *a-m-a*, and you can scan them looking for your word.

If it's the first part of the word you don't know how to spell, that's harder, as there may be more than one way to spell it. The best procedure still is to sound out the beginning of the word carefully. Take *fantasy*. The first part is "*f-a-n*." Look that up. Suppose you are not sure if it starts with a *F* or a *PH*? If you don't know, try both ways of spelling the first sound in the word.

Some words, of course, defeat this process, for example, *pneumonia*. These you just have to remember. Remembering "It's weird. Doesn't start with *neu*," is a help.

You can gradually introduce this procedure into your life. Start with the goal of tagging and looking up only one word; then gradually increase. "Once a day I will mark one word I didn't spell right and look it up." "Once for each set of notes, or letter or paper I write."

There are dictionaries for the spelling challenged in which words are listed as they might be spelled, not as they are actually spelled. The words are listed as we poor spellers think they might be spelled. If you are spelling challenged, get one of those.

Part two: Recognize and learn new words

This procedure is similar to that for learning any new spelling, except now you have to *recognize* that you have run into a word you can't spell. This is the process:

1. Stop when you recognize a word you can't spell.
2. Look at it carefully.
3. Visualize its spelling.

Set your mind to notice when you encounter words you can't spell. For example, your eyes are skimming over the sentence, "Originally, she hoped to play as a professional, but after several years realized she would be happier as an amateur." Bang! You notice *amateur.* "I can't spell that," you think. You stop.

The enemy is skimming without thinking. It can be overcome with practice. Set your mind, as you set an alarm clock, to notice new words.

Practice setting your mind to stop, and you will begin to notice things you have never noticed before. This is true for any skill. When you are first learning to ski, for example, you speed down the hill hardly noticing anything, just trying not to fall. But after much practice you notice many things: the condition of the track, the condition of the snow, other people, the rushing wind, and the whir of your skis.

Remind yourself you don't have to do this all the time, just enough to meet your goal. That way, you won't frustrate yourself by stopping too often.

Look carefully at the word. Pay attention to each letter and to the sequence of letters. Notice the confusing parts. "*A-M-A-T-E-U-R.* Oh, it ends *T-E-U-R.*" You have to get the correct spelling into your mind.

THINK PIECE 21.2   Building spelling consciousness

Develop the habit of checking your own work. Set a goal: how often will you check yourself. Once a day? Start at a low level and increase gradually. Keep a record of doing the checks, so you will hold yourself to your goal.

Also set your mind to notice when you encounter words you cannot spell. Set a goal for how often you will do this. And, set goal for learning new words you notice, such as one per day. Then keep records to be sure you stick to your plan.

Visualize the correct spelling of the word. Visualizing works exactly as it does when you are learning to spell a word. See the correct spelling in your mind's eye.

You can go on and write out the correct spelling a couple of times, for practice.

This can be gradually practiced by setting a goal to do it once per day, or once per reading assignment. Make it easy to do; don't frustrate yourself; increase gradually.

Reading: Just a word

All aspects of verbal skill are improved by reading. If you read more, your spelling, vocabulary, writing, and reading skill itself improve. Reading improves your spelling because it gives you exposure to correctly spelled words and because it gives you practice in going from the words on paper to words in your mind. Reading makes you literate.

Part VIII

Lifelong Learning

The education of a man is never completed until he dies.

—*Robert E. Lee, Confederate general*

The object of education is to prepare the young to educate themselves throughout their lives.

—*Robert Maynard Hutchins, educator*

The most important lessons that we can teach our [students] are the skills and attitudes that will be required of life-long learners.

—*Patricia Cross, researcher and educator*

People who do not educate themselves, and keep educating themselves, will be the peasants of the information society.

—*Harlan Cleveland, businessman and diplomat*

Chapter 22

Lifelong Learning

What does lifelong learning mean?

■ Why should you expect to learn all your life?

Transfer of skills

■ How can you use the skills you have learned in this course to deal with other courses? What is the problem of transfer?

■ What is the A-P-Q approach to dealing with the problem of transfer?

Developing new skills

■ What other learning skills should you develop?

■ How do you stack up on development of basic job skills?

Home schooling yourself

■ How can you structure learning for yourself?

■ What is Walkabout? What could be your Walkabout?

What Does "Lifelong Learning" Mean?

Some people think that learning stops when you finish school, but the wise ones have always known that learning goes on throughout life.

> Tamika, age twenty-six, is one year out of nursing school, an officer in the Army, and daily learning hundreds of things about patients, doctors, diseases, treatments, medical procedures, the health system, and being a lieutenant in the United States Army.

QUESTION TO ANSWER AS YOU READ:

■ Why should you expect to learn all your life?

Oscar, age thirty-seven, emigrated to the United States eight years ago and now has a good job as a computer specialist, where daily he is learning more about computer hardware, software, working cooperatively with other people, life in the United States, English, and getting along with his wife of a different ethnic background.

Kristen, age fifty-two, is at the "top of her life," running her own business—daily learning how to do the business well; keep the books; deal with employees, customers; and suppliers; manage her now very nice income; cope with her two late-teen kids; explore a new relationship with a nice man; take care of her aging mother from a distance; and begin to think about retirement planning.

Phil, age seventy-one, is retired, and daily learns about plants because he volunteers as a docent—a guide—at a city garden, learns about reading and teaching because he volunteers to teach seven-year-olds, learns about children again as he plays with his grandson, learns about nutrition and exercise as he takes care of his body, learns about lots of interesting places in and out of the United States as he takes several Elderhostel trips each year, and wonders that his days are so busy.

Eric Hofer, a longshoreman and writer, once said that human beings are "perpetually unfinished." We never stop learning, we never stop changing. You are always a freshman at something, and you are always getting better even at the things you have mastered.

College is the beginning, not the end. Why do you think they call graduation "commencement"? Planning and managing your learning outside school is a common human activity. The Canadian researcher Allen Tough spent years interviewing people about the learning they did outside school.[1] He found that people did much learning, often without calling it "learning." Learning was a larger part of their lives than most people realized. It was just something they did.

Tough found that the average person carried out five learning projects each year and spent an average of one hundred hours on each. These included projects at work, but also at home in hobbies, interests, or necessities. A person might be learning new techniques on her job in a service company, learning about her hobby of orchid growing in her little greenhouse, and learning about household repairs in her old home. People used a variety of learning strategies. About three-quarters of the projects were not in classes, and were planned by the learner.

The pace of learning may even be quickening. Many people think that the pace of needed learning is speeding up in our society. We are becoming a "learning society" in which constant change will mean constant learning. There are many articles in newspapers and magazines about what the worker of the future will be like, and they all agree that she or he will have to be a learner.

You should expect that you will always be learning. That's good, not bad. The people who are bored with life are the ones who are *not* learning. Our minds are restless. The more you learn at work, the higher your job satisfaction is. If you have a job running a cash register, for example, after a few months you have mastered the job, and there is little new to learn. It becomes boring. If you were the store manager, on the other hand, there would be much more to learn, and it would take much longer to master that job, which would make it interesting. Mastering learning tasks is interesting.

Through this book you've been developing learning strategies you can use to plan and manage your own learning. They are *not* just for college, they are for life. The same strategies you used to learn material from a textbook, the same strategies you used to manage your time, the same strategies you used to improve your writing can be used in many different settings throughout your life. You can use them at work, at home, doing your hobbies, dealing with your clubs, any time you need to learn. The question is, Will you remember to use the skills you have learned here?

Transfer of Skills

QUESTIONS TO ANSWER AS YOU READ:

- How can you use the skills you have learned in this course to deal with other courses?
- What is the problem of transfer?
- What is the A-P-Q approach to dealing with the problem of transfer?

Strange as it seems, people often learn a skill in one situation but do not remember to use it in another situation. *Transfer of skill* means learning a skill in one situation, such as the course in which you are reading this book, and then using the skill in another situation, such as a new course you take next term. People often do *not* transfer their skills. In education this is called the "problem of transfer." People may not see that the skill is relevant to the new situation, or they simply may not remember it, but the effect is the same: they fail to benefit from knowing the skill.

> Penny learned to use time management at school, but was astounded one day when someone pointed out to her that she would benefit from time management in her household work. She had never thought of that. She was well organized at school, but not at home.

> Jamal took an entire five-week backpacking course, which taught him every skill he needed for the wilderness, so he was appalled on a day hike when his friend fell and cut her-

self and he had not brought first aid supplies. He hadn't transferred the skills learned from five weeks overnight in the wilderness to a one-day hike.

This kind of thing is a very common occurrence. You may think, "Of course I will remember to use some skill I have learned if it is going to help me in another situation," but in fact many people do not.[2] Students learn to improve their writing in one course, but don't use the skill in another, or they learn to study effectively in one course, but still use inferior methods for another.

Lack of transfer of learned skills from one situation to another is such a common problem that you need to take steps to avoid it. It would be a shame to develop a skill that serves you well in one class, but not use it in another, or not use it at work. You don't want to just "learn and hope" that the new skills will transfer to new situations. There are concrete steps you can take to increase the chances you will remember to use your new skills later.

This last chapter deals with a very important step in your development as a sophisticated learner. *You must take charge of your own learning*, spotting issues and problems and dealing with them by using the learning strategies you know. Throughout your life, you will be learning, and if you manage your own learning well, you will learn more, and more easily. A very important part of managing your own learning is remembering to use the strategies you already know.

Using your learning skills in other courses

Will you use the learning strategies you developed in this course in other courses?

> The semester after Mark read this book he was sitting down to write his first paper in his World Religions course and he suddenly thought, "Hey, I should use the PoWeR approach that I learned last term." He began to sketch out the steps he would follow and began thinking how he would *Plan*, the first step in PoWeR.

> A year after she took this course, Shayna was taking botany and had to learn the four steps in photosynthesis. "The four steps are important," she said to herself, "I know they are going to be on the test. But I don't really understand why they occur in the order they do." Then she remembered mnemonics, from Chapter 14. "Hey," she thought, "I should make up a mnemonic to remember this."

Learning skills are problem-solving skills. Each course you take presents little problems to be solved for you: how to study for this course, how to write a paper for that one, how to take lecture notes in another. The learning skills you have developed through this book are problem-solving skills. You can use the skills you have learned to deal with the various problems presented to you by other courses. If you have a problem with reading the material in a course, use the reading chapters in this book to find solutions to the problem. If you have a problem memorizing basically meaningless material in another course, use the ideas on memorizing you've learned here.

Skill builder 22.1 asks you to list your courses and the problems you meet in each, and think of strategies you have learned that will help.

Looking to the future

Think of future courses you will take: will you recognize learning problems when you meet them, and will you remember to use the learning strategies you have developed here? If you are bored and can't get yourself to go to class, if you don't have the confidence to study systematically for a challenging course, if you don't understand some of the assigned material—these are all learning problems about which you have been reading. Any time you are having a problem in a course, it is probably some sort of learning problem, in which case there are solutions to be found in this book.

Here are steps you can take to increase the chances your skills will transfer to new courses.[3] Use the letters *A–P–Q* to remember them.

A—Be *Aware.*

P—*Practice.*

Q—Ask *Questions.*

A—Be *Aware* that transfer will not occur automatically. You have to pay attention to the question, Am I using the learning skills I know? Do they fit this situation? If you don't think about transferring skills, transfer is less likely to occur, so it pays to think about it whenever you are in a new learning situation.

P—*Practice* your already developed skills over and over. This is the easiest path to transfer. The more you practice a skill, the more readily will you use it in new situations. Keep on practicing the skills you developed in this book, and keep on practicing the skills you knew before you read this book.

To encourage yourself to practice, continue to keep records of using the strategies. If you don't keep the records, you might stop using the strategies, but keeping the records is enough to keep you practicing. Peo-

SKILL BUILDER 22.1

Applying your skills to various courses

Thinking about the problems presented in each course you take and how to use learning strategies to deal with them will help you transfer your skills from one situation to another.

A. List your courses here. What kinds of study issues or problems do you encounter in each?

1. _____

_____

_____

_____

_____

2. _____

_____

_____

_____

_____

_____

3. _____

_____

_____

_____

_____

4. _____

_____

_____

_____

_____

_____

_____

_____

5. _____

_____

_____

_____

_____

_____

B. For each course, which of the learning skills from this book might help you deal with the course? Write them in the list above.

Example: "Sociology. Problem: The instructor lectures fast and my attention wanders, so I miss stuff in the notes. I should work on concentrating in class and getting good notes."

Example: "English. There is a lot of reading to do. I could use time management to get more done. I should try the bootstrapping idea to get myself started doing the reading."

Example: "Chemistry. We have lab study groups, but one of the guys keeps showing up not having done the prep reading, so he is clueless, no help at all. I should read the material on working with others and see if I can ask him to come prepared."

ple who do all sorts of self-change, such as losing weight, stopping smoking, or breaking some bad habit, find this is true: they continue to be good only as long as they keep records.[4] The events of the day crowd our lives, we are busy coping with them and can forget to use newly developed skills. We want to use them; we are just too busy to remember.

Keeping records helps overcome this problem. For example, you might feel you need self-explanation to understand the material in your science text, so you keep a record chart in your science notebook, "Did I use self-explanation?" and make a note whenever you use the technique.

Do not avoid this idea because it seems simple. It works. Many students find that all they have to do to remind themselves to use truly helpful learning strategies is keep a record of using the strategy. When they don't keep the record, they slide back to their old, inefficient study methods, but keeping the record is enough to keep them efficient.

Q—Ask *Questions*. Whenever you are in a new learning situation—taking a course, reading a how-to manual or book, doing on-the-job training, in any novel learning situation—ask yourself these questions:

Have I seen this kind of learning situation before? How is the new situation like old situations you have dealt with? What learning strategies did you use in a past, similar situation?

> Ramon had recently moved to the United States and was now working on English. In Catholic school back home, he had studied Latin and had worked out several strategies for learning vocabulary. He realized that learning English was similar—basically, it was language learning—so he consciously began using the strategies he had used on Latin in school to pick up English in the street.

What is the learning problem here? Once you see whatever the issues are—lots to memorize, poor organization of the material, nonunderstandable text, boring or frightening material—you can bring to bear your learning strategies to deal with the problem.

> Natasha was taking a noncredit computer course because she thought it would help her get promoted at work. The course was frustrating, and Natasha was getting pretty upset at those darned computers. "What is the problem?" she asked herself. "I get really frustrated. How have I dealt with frustration in the past?" She realized she had done that, so she began using the same strategies for dealing with frustration that had worked for her in earlier, frustrating courses.

What learning strategies do I know that could apply to this situation? For future courses, you should ask yourself, What strategies do I know that would help me deal with this course? Often the learning strategies you know can be very helpful in some new situation, if only you remember to use them.

> Stephen had started the English course thinking it would be very easy—"All I have to do is read novels!"—but pretty soon realized it wasn't going to be so easy. "How should I cope?" he asked himself; "What strategies do I know?" He had used time management in the past, so he began that again. He had also intended to work on his reading skills, and now realized this would be a good time to do that. He realized class participation was important, and he had previously begun to develop those skills, so he began to work more on them. Finally, he thought he should get to know this instructor, so he began dusting off his instructor-relating skills, too. "I can cope," he thought, "if I use the strategies I know."

It's almost always best to try to apply strategies you know, even if they don't fit perfectly. People sometimes joke that if all you have is a hammer, you try to hammer everything, but on the other hand if all you have is a hammer, it's a lot better than a rock.

Developing New Skills

QUESTIONS TO ANSWER AS YOU READ:

- What other learning skills should you develop?
- How do you stack up on development of basic job skills?

Remember Eric Hofer's notion that we humans are "perpetually unfinished." Even as students we are unfinished. Have you learned well all the skills developed in this book? Perhaps not. Would it help you if you did learn them? Almost certainly. Remember the research finding that the more students learn strategic learning skills, the better they do in their college courses. You may have come to the end of the course in which you use this book, but that doesn't mean you should stop learning new skills.

Keep this book and work on new skills. The more you learn, the better off you will be. You can expect that your grades, your education, and your future job prospects will all improve if you learn more skills.

THINK PIECE 22.1   Aware—Practice—Questions

The letters outlining the three steps are A–P–Q. To remember these three steps, make up your own mnemonic and commit the three steps to memory. Tomorrow, test yourself to see if you can list the three steps, and the questions for step three. Then test yourself a week later. Can you still remember all the details? If not, repeat the process. If you can, test yourself a month later. If you still remember all, congratulations. If not, repeat the process. The point is to fully commit A–P–Q to long-term memory.

THINK PIECE 22.2   The honor roll of strategies

Just below is a list of all the major strategies you have read about in this book. Look it over and ask yourself, How does each of these apply to the courses I am taking? How could I use these in my course? For each course, go down the list and ask yourself how that skill would help in that course. Make notes for yourself as new goals pop into your mind.

A list of learning strategies

Time management	Motivating yourself *via* goals
Class attendance	Note taking
Participating in class	Thinking
Problem solving	Concentrating
Making material meaningful	Organizing for better memory
Self-explanation	PQRSR
Elaboration	Mnemonics
Preparing for tests	Writing well
Staying calm	Speaking well
Taking tests	Increasing vocabulary
Adapting learning to your own style	Having a skills-development attitude
Reading well	Working well with others

Which ones to learn? *First* develop skills that will help you right away. Ideally, you have already worked on the ones you most badly needed, but there may be others that would be a great help if you learned them now. Time management, for example, is a skill that is helpful in every aspect of life, and the better you are at it, the more control you gain over life.

Second, develop skills you *know* will help you in the future. For example, you might never have been confident of your people skills, so you want to work on material from Chapter 5. Or, you might have always wanted to be a good public speaker, so you work on Chapter 19. Or you know you have to take an especially challenging course in the next couple of semesters, so you decide to work on your study skills in Part V beforehand.

What skills will you need in future jobs? Some, of course, are specific to the job, but there are general job skills that will help in almost all jobs. Several authors have prescribed lists of skills future workers will need, and there is considerable agreement. Two economists studied the job market and developed a short list of basic skills that will benefit every worker:[5]

■ Basic math

■ Problem solving

■ High-level reading

- Ability to work in groups

- Good writing and speaking

- Ability to use computers for word processing.

It's not a long list. Most of them are covered in this book.

Work on any of those skills on which you are *not now* at least average. Just getting up to average on such skills gives you a big boost, because the competition is not terribly strong. Many job applicants have weaknesses in one or more of those skills. If you become pretty good at them, you will have a very secure future in the job world. Success is what comes when you think you are only keeping up with the others.

It's important to be a little brave here. You might get nervous about math, for example, or computers, but make a distinction: you are not going to try to be a master at those skills; you are just going to get better at them than you now are. (That's the skills-development approach.) And remember, we almost always fear things more than it's really worth fearing them.

<table>
<tr><td>**QUESTIONS TO ANSWER AS YOU READ:**</td></tr>
<tr><td>

- How can you structure learning for yourself?

- What is Walkabout? What could be your Walkabout?

</td></tr>
</table>

Home Schooling Yourself

Home schooling, as you know, means that children learn at home instead of going to school. To learn throughout life, you have to home-school yourself, learn without school or a teacher.

If you follow a structured approach, home schooling becomes easier. Your structure organizes for you what you will learn, and if necessary even

---

THINK PIECE 22.3   Your skills appraisal

For each of those skills—

   basic math,

   problem solving,

   high-level reading,

   ability to work in groups,

   good writing and speaking, and

   ability to use computers for word processing—

make an honest appraisal of your own level of skill now. Are you very good, good, average, poor, or pretty poor? Does that tell you where you should be focusing? Try to get even better at the ones you are already good at, but also try to get up to average on the ones on which you are currently weak. If you can just get to average on all, you will be far ahead of the competition.

organizes your learning time. Malia Watson, the author of Chapter 10, worked out a three-component plan for learning topics. She would

- Read about the topic from a reading list she prepared.

- Do something creative centered on the topic.

- Do some volunteer work centered on the topic.

For example, she was interested in housing and architecture. She made a reading list, and began with the first book on the list. She built a compost bin as her creative project, and she volunteered to work with Habitat for Humanity, a nonprofit organization that builds homes for people. Sometimes we learn easily *without* providing much structure. Sometimes we need the structure, or we won't do the work.

> Jen wants to learn about the history of Japan, so she checks a book out of the library and begins to read it. She also checks out Japanese historical movies, such as *Shogun, Rashomon,* and some samurai movies, to provide extra interest. But when Jen decided she wanted to get better at reading Japanese, she took a course. She knew she just wouldn't sit around the house learning written Japanese. She needed the structure the course provided.

Sometimes the only structure we need to do the learning is to set a goal.

> Deborah said she wanted to "get more culture into my life," so she set a goal: to do one "cultural thing" per month—such as go to a play, concert, or art movie, or go to an art gallery or museum.

> Rich wanted to know more about painting, so he set a rule for himself, that he would read any article about painting he encountered in *Time* or *Newsweek*. He made himself read the article even when he didn't think he would find it interesting. After a period he realized it was all interesting to him now.

Providing structure

If your desired learning is progressing without much structure, fine. If it is *not*, provide structure. Follow these steps:

1. Set goals and subgoals.
2. Provide practice.
3. Keep a record of your progress.
4. Use problem solving to overcome obstacles.

For several years Sandy had wanted to learn about investments, but had never gotten around to it. Finally, she set a goal: "By the end of the semester I'm going to learn some stuff about investing." Her first subgoal was "to ask the reference librarian for some books and articles to read." An action goal was to read one article or chapter per week. She set up a notebook in which to keep notes on what she was learning, and in the front kept a record of doing her reading each week. One problem she ran into was that some of the reading was very technical. So she gave herself permission not to read technical material she encountered, but to be sure to read something each week. Also, she found out that the public TV station had a Friday night program on investing, so she began watching that.

How will you know if you need to provide structure or not? Easy. If there is something you keep wanting to learn, but don't, try providing some structure to encourage yourself to do it.

The best way to develop your skills at home schooling is to practice them. Like everything else, you get better with practice. Here's a chance to practice.

Walkabout

The aboriginal people of Australia have a traditional procedure in which young men pass from childhood to full manhood. They call the procedure "Walkabout." For six months the youth lives by himself in the desert, living entirely off the land without aid from his tribe. During this time he conquers his fears, develops many important skills, and becomes a man. In the 1970's a movie was made about this, called *Walkabout*.

Maurice Gibbons, an educator in British Columbia, Canada, saw the movie and wondered, What would be an appropriate Walkabout in our society?[6] A modern student doing a walkabout should have the chance to develop skills appropriate to her life, just as the aboriginal youth does. Gibbons developed the Walkabout idea for the high schools in British Columbia, and for many years any high school senior had to do one.

In the modern Walkabout the student chooses one of five kinds of learning projects:

- *Adventure*, a challenge to daring and endurance.

- *Creativity*, exploring and cultivating the imagination.

- *Service* to the community.

- Developing a practical *skill*.

- Carrying out a *learning project*—formulating a question and answering it.

Students often come back months after learning about Walkabout to ask, "What were the five elements again?" so it may help you to have a mnemonic to remember the five later. Try *CLASS:*

C—Doing something *creative.*

L—*Learning* new things.

A—Having an *Adventure.*

S—Being of *Service* to others.

S—Developing a practical *Skill.*

The project has to be a balance of reflection and action. The student sets goals, provides action, reflects on progress, makes adjustments and solves problems. It has to be a challenging project, not something small. It has to be something new, not already learned. In British Columbia, the project takes up the entire last semester of the student's senior high school year.

The students loved it. Many felt that it gave their education meaning, it gave them a chance to do something exciting, and it helped them tie together what they had learned in school with the rest of life.

The final Skill Builder: Walkabout. Your final Skill Builder assignment, should you choose to accept it, is to do your own Walkabout. Show some *CLASS.* You will love it if you try it. Think about yourself and what you would like to learn. Pick one of the topics above, follow the rules, and develop a large home schooling project for yourself. It has to be new for you, challenging, not small potatoes. It might involve learning more about your work, your schooling, your leisure interests, or important life skills. It's not important which.

The more you put into this, the more you get out of it. Students who have really gotten into the project say things like, "It changed my life," or "I found myself" or "I really learned what I want to do." Students sometimes say, "I realize I've been doing Walkabout projects all my life." Many students say they would like to do other Walkabout projects and intend to continue this way of thinking. It gives learning a focus.

Here are a few examples of Walkabout projects done by your author's college students, organized by CLASS:

Creativity

- Writing poetry, then making a movie about that
- Learning to draw birds
- Learning oil painting

- Learning to photograph horses beautifully
- Making a large hooked rug
- Making Christmas ornaments to give away

Learning

- Researching a trip to Europe
- Finding and researching a new town to move to
- "Getting deeply into bird watching . . ."
- Learning how to invest in mutual funds
- Learning retirement and estate planning
- Finding out what to do to get into and complete graduate school

Adventure

- Going to a remote part of Alaska on a camping trip
- Taking a trip to Lebanon
- Driving from Phoenix to Alaska in an old car
- Running the Honolulu marathon
- Playing paint ball ("It frightened me, so I ought to do it.")
- Snow boarding ten spots in Colorado

Service

- Being an AIDS awareness instructor in the university
- "Spreading the word of Allah in my community"
- Creating an organization to distribute public service messages
- Setting up a nonprofit organization to get inner city children to the country for a vacation
- Volunteering at a senior care center
- Establishing litter clean-up days

Skill

- Learning to drive a car
- Becoming better as a teacher

- Learning to sail a large sloop
- Learning to play ice hockey
- Making a quilt
- Gardening

Now it's your turn. Let the learning begin.

Notes

Part I

Chapter 1

1. Bransford, J. D., Vye, N., Kinzer, C., & Risko, V. (1990). Teaching, thinking, and content knowledge: Toward an integrated approach. In B. F. Jones & L. Idol (Eds.), *Dimensions of thinking and cognitive instruction* (pp. 381–413). Hillsdale, NJ: Erlbaum.

2. Rosenbaum, J. (1999). Unrealistic plans and misguided efforts: Are community colleges getting the right message to high schools? *CCRC Brief*. No. 4. Oct. 1999. New York: Columbia University, Teacher's College Community college research center.

3. (1999, December 12). Report says high schools fail to prepare graduates. *Honolulu Advertiser*, G8.

4. Pintrich, P. R. (1995). Understanding self-regulated learning. In P. R. Pintrich (Ed.), *Understanding self-regulated learning* (pp. 3–12). San Francisco: Jossey-Bass.

5. Corno, L. (1994). Student volition and education: Outcomes, influences, and practices. In D. H. Schunk & B. J. Zimmerman (Eds.), *Self-regulation of learning and performance* (pp. 229–254). Hillsdale, NJ: Erlbaum.

6. J. Naisbett & Aburdene, P. (1985). Re-inventing the corporation.

7. Azar, B. (1996, June). Schools the source of rough transitions. New York: Warner Books. Washington, D.C. *APA Monitor*, p. 14.

8. Zimmerman, B. J. & Martinez Pons, M. (1990). Student differences in self-regulated learning: Relating grade, sex, and giftedness to self-efficacy and strategy use. *Journal of Educational Psychology, 82,* 51–59.

9. Hatie, J., Biggs, J., & Purdie, N. (1996) Effects of learning skills interventions on student learning: A meta-analysis. *Review of Educational Research, 66,*(2), 99–136.

10. Schunk, D. H., & Zimmerman, B. J. (Eds.). (1994). *Self-regulation of learning and performance.* Hillsdale, NJ: Earlbaum.
    Schunk, D. H., & Zimmerman, B. J. (Eds.). (1998). *Developing self-regulated learners: From teaching to self-regulated practice.* New York: Guilford Press.

11. McKeachie, W. J., Pintrich, P. R. & Lin, Y. G. (1985). Teaching learning strategies. *Educational Psychologist, 20,* 153–160.

12. Hofer, B. K., Yu, S. L., & Pintrich, P. R. (1998). Teaching college students to be self-regulated learners. In D. H. Schunk & B. J. Zimmerman (Eds.), *Self-Regulated Learning.* (pp. 57–85). New York: Guilford Press.

13. Weinstein, C. E. (1998). Presidential address. *Newsletter for Educational Psychologists, 22,* Nov. 1998. Washington, DC: American Psychological Association.

14. Lan, W. Y. (1998). Teaching self-monitoring skills in statistics. In D. H. Schunk & B. J. Zimmerman (Eds.), *Self-Regulated Learning.* (pp. 86–105). New York: Guilford Press.

15. Hofer et al., above.

16. Ford, M. (1992). *Motivating humans.* Newbury Park, CA: Sage.

Part II

Introduction

1. Lakein, A. (1973). *How to get control of your time and life.* New York: New American Library.

2. Zimmerman, B. J., Greenberg, D., & Weinstein, C. (1994). Self-regulating academic study time: A strategy approach. In D. H. Schunk & B. J. Zimmerman (Eds.), *Self-regulation of learning and performance.* Hillsdale, NJ: Erlbaum.

3. Britton, B. K., & Tesser, A. (1991). Effects of time management practices on college grades. *Journal of Educational Psychology, 83,* 405–410.

4. Zimmerman et al., above.

5. Tice, D. M., & Baumeister, R. F. (1997). Longitudinal study of procrastination, performance, stress, and health: The costs and benefits of dawdling. *Psychological Science, 8,* 454–458.

Chapter 2

1. Lakein, A. (1973). *How to get control of your time and life.* New York: New American Library.

2. Baumeister, R. F., Heatherton, T. F., & Tice, D. M. (1994). *Losing control: How and why people fail at self-regulation.* San Diego, CA: Academic Press.

3. Jamis, I. L. (Ed.). (1982). *Counseling on personal decisions: Theory and research on short-term helping relationships.* New Haven: Yale University Press.

4. Farmer, R., & Nelson-Gray, R. (1990). The accuracy of counting versus estimating event frequencies in behavioral assessment: The effects of behavior frequency, number of behaviors monitored, and time delay. *Behavioral Assessment, 12,* 425–442.

5. Mace, F. C., & Kratochwill, T. R. (1985). Theories of reactivity in self-monitoring. *Behavior Modification, 9,* 323–343.

6. Fixen, D., Philips, E., & Wolf, M. Achievement place: The reliability of self-reporting and peer-reporting and their effects on behavior. *Journal of Applied Behavior Analysis, 5,* 19–30.

7. Locke, E. A., & Latham, G. P. (1990). Work motivation and satisfaction: Light at the end of the tunnel. *Psychological Science, 1,* 240–246.

Locke, E. A., & Latham, G. P. (1994). Goal setting theory. In H. F. O'Neil & M. Drillings (Eds.), *Motivation, theory, and research.* Pp. 13–29. Hillsdale, NJ: Earlbaum.

8. Anderman, E. M., & Maehr, M. L. (1994). Motivation and schooling in the middle grades. *Review of Educational Research, 64,* 2, 287–310.
Zimmerman, B. J., & Kitsantas, A. (1996). Self-regulated learning of a motoric skill: The role of goal setting and self-monitoring. *Journal of Applied Sport Psychology, 8,* 60–75.

Chapter 3

1. Connelly, K., DuBois, N., & Staley, R. (1998, April). *Structured interview study of the long term effects of a college study skills course: Traces and self-report measures.* Paper delivered at the annual convention of the American Educational Research Association, San Diego, CA.

2. Zimmerman, B. J., Greenberg, D., & Weinstein, C. (1994). Self-regulating academic study time: A strategy approach. In D. H. Schunk & B. J. Zimmerman (Eds.), *Self-regulation of learning and performance.* Pp. 181–202. Hillsdale, NJ: Erlbaum.

3. Heffernan, T., & Richards, C. S. (1981). Self-control of study behavior: Identification and evaluation of natural methods. *Journal of Counseling Psychology, 28,* 361–364.

4. Dush, D. M., Hirt, M. L., & Schroeder, H. (1983). Self-statement modification with adults: A meta-analysis. *Psychological Bulletin, 94,* 408–422.

5. D'Zurrilla, T. J., (1986). *Problem solving therapy: A social competence approach to clinical intervention.* New York: Springer.

Chapter 4

1. Watson, D. (1993). *Psychology.* Pacific Grove, CA: Brooks/Cole.

2. DeLongis, A., Folkman, S., & Lazarus, R. (1988). The impact of daily stress on health and mood: Psychological and social resources as mediators. *Journal of Personality and Social Psychology, 54,* 486–495.

3. Cohen, S., & Syme, S. L. (1985). *Social support and health.* New York: Academic Press.

4. Feuerstein, M., Labbe', E. E., & Kuczmierczyk, A. R. (1986). *Health psychology: A psychobiological perspective.* New York: Plenum.

5. Pincomb, G. A., Lovallo, W. R., Passey, R. B., Brackett, D. J., & Wilson, M. F. (1987). Caffeine enhances the physiological response to occupational stress in medical students. *Health Psychology, 6,* 101–112.

6. Watson, above.

7. Perri, M. G., & Richards, C. S. (1977). An investigation of naturally occurring episodes of self-controlled behaviors. *Journal of Counseling Psychology, 24,* 178–183.

8. Gould, R. A., & Clum, G. A. (1993). A meta-analysis of self-help treatment approaches. *Clinical Psychology Review, 13,* 169–186.

9. Putnam, D. E., Finney, J. W., Barkley, P. L., & Bonner, M. J. (1994). Enhancing commitment improves adherence to a medical regimen. *Journal of Consulting and Clinical Psychology, 62,* 191–194.

Part III

Chapter 5

1. Covington, M. V. (1992). *Making the grade.* Cambridge: Cambridge University Press. Garcia, T., & Pintrich, P. R. (1994). Regulating motivation and cognition in the classroom: The role of self-schemas and self-regulatory strategies. In D. H. Schunk & B. J. Zimmerman (Eds.), *Self-regulation of learning and performance.* Hillsdale, NJ: Erlbaum.

2. Dweck, C. S., & Elliot, E. S. (1983). Achievement motivation. In P. H. Mussen & E. M. Heatherington (Eds.), *Handbook of child psychology. Vol. 4. Socialization, personality, and social development.* Pp. 643–691. New York: Wiley.

3. Harakiewicz, J. M., Barron, K. E., & Elliot, A. J. (1998). Rethinking achievement goals: When are they adaptive for college students and why? *Educational Psychologist, 33,* 1–22.

4. Butler, D. L., & Winne, P. H. (1995). Feedback and self-regulated learning: A theoretical synthesis. *Review of Educational Research, 65,* (3) 245–282.

5. Schunk, D. H., & Zimmerman, B. J. (Eds.). (1994). *Self-regulation of learning and performance.* Hillsdale, NJ: Earlbaum.

6. Ames, C. (1992). Classrooms: Goals, structures, and student motivation. *Journal of Educational Psychology, 84,* 261–271.

7. Schommer, M. (1990). Effect of beliefs about the nature of knowledge on comprehension. *Journal of Educational Psychology, 82,* 498–504.

8. Sternberg, L. J. (1985). *Beyond IQ: A triarchic theory of intelligence.* New York: Cambridge University Press.

9. Biemiller, A., Shany, M., Inglis, A., & Meichenbaum, D. (1998). Factors influencing children's acquisition and demonstration of self-regulation on academic tasks. In D. H. Schunk & B. J. Zimmerman (Eds.), *Self-regulated learning.* Pp. 203–224. New York: Guilford Press.

10. Chi, M. (1996). Constructing self-explanations and scaffolding explanations in tutoring [Special issue] *Applied Cognitive Psychology, 10,* S33–S49.

11. King, A. (1995). Cognitive strategies for learning from direct teaching. In E. Wood, V. Woloshyn, & T. Willoughby (Eds.), *Cognitive strategy instruction for middle and high schools.* Pp. 18–65. Cambridge, MA: Brookline Books.

12. Watson, D. (1992). *Psychology.* Pacific Grove, CA: Brooks/Cole.

13. Astin, A. (1993). *What matters in college?* San Francisco: Jossey-Bass.

14. Zimmerman, B., & Risemberg, R. (1993). Self-regulatory dimensions of academic learning and motivation. In G. Phye, *Handbook of academic learning.* Pp. 106–127. San Diego: Academic Press.

15. Karabenick, S. A., & Knapp, J. (1991). Relationship of academic help seeking to the use of learning strategies and other instrumental achievement behavior in college students. *Journal of Educational Psychology, 83,* 221–230.

Chapter 6

1. Woehr, D., & Cavell, T. (1993). Self-report measures of ability, effort, and nonacademic activity as predictors of introductory psychology test scores. *Teaching of Psychology, 20,* 156–160.

2. Green, G. (1993). *Getting straight A's.* New York: Carol Publishing Group.

3. King, A. (1992). Comparison of self-questioning, summarizing, and notetaking-review as strategies for learning from lectures. *American Educational Research Journal, 29,* 303–323.
   King, A. (1995). Cognitive strategies for learning from direct teaching. In E. Wood, V. Woloshyn, & T. Willoughby (Eds.), *Cognitive strategy instruction for middle and high schools.* Pp. 18–65. Cambridge, MA: Brookline Books.

4. Pauk, W. (1997). *How to study in college* (6th ed.). Boston: Houghton Mifflin.

Chapter 7

1. King, A. (1995). Cognitive strategies for learning from direct teaching. In E. Wood, V. Woloshyn, & T. Willoughby (Eds.), *Cognitive strategy instruction for middle and high schools.* Cambridge, MA: Brookline Books.
   Also see A. King (1995). Facilitating elaborative learning through guided student-generated questions. *Educational Psychologist, 27,* 111–126.

2. King, A. (1994). Inquiry as a tool in critical thinking. In D. Halpern (Ed.), *Changing college classrooms.* San Francisco: Jossey-Bass.

3. In these questions, numbers 2, 4, and 6 are the author's modification of Dr. King's work, and number 3 is entirely Dr. King's.

4. Wheeler, D. D., & Janis, I. (1980). *A practical guide for making decisions.* New York: Free Press.

5. Nezu, A. M., & D'Zurilla, T. J. (1989). Social problem solving and negative affective states. In P.C. Kendall & D. Watson (Eds.), *Anxiety and depression: Distinctive and overlapping features.* Pp. 285–315. New York: Academic Press.

6. D'Zurilla, T. J. (1986). *Problem solving therapy: A social competence approach to clinical interaction.* New York: Springer.

Part IV

Chapter 8

1. Carter-Wells, J. (1990). Raising expectations for critical reading. *New Directions for Higher Education. 96,* 45–54.

2. Pressley, M. & McCormack, C. B. (1995). *Advanced educational psychology.* New York: Harper Collins.

3. Roitblat, H. (in press). *Power tools for the mind.* Honolulu, HI: University of Hawai'i.

4. Pressley, M., El-Dinary, P., Wharton-McDonald, R., & Brown, R. (1998). Transactional instruction of comprehension strategies in the elementary grades. In D. H. Schunk & B. J. Zimmerman (Eds.), *Self-regulated learning.* New York: Guilford.

5. Carver, R. (1990). *Reading rate: A review of research and theory.* San Diego, CA: Academic Press.

6. Pressley, M., & McCormack, C. B. (1995), above.

7. Wade, C., & Tavris, C. (1998). *Psychology.* New York: Longmans.

8. The need to read. (1999, April 25). *Honolulu Advertiser,* p. E1.

Chapter 9

1. Clay, M. M., (1993). *An observational study of early literacy achievement.* Portsmouth, NH: Heineman.

2. Perry, W. (1981). Students' use and misuse of reading skills. *Harvard Educational Review.* Reprinted in G. Gibbs, (1995) *Teaching students to learn: A student-centered approach.* Milton Keynes, England: The Open University Press.

3. Roitblat, H. (in press). *Power tools for the mind.* Honolulu, HI: University of Hawai'i.

4. Schunk, D. H., & Rice, M. J. (1987). Enhancing comprehension skill and self-efficacy with strategy value information. *Journal of Reading Behavior, 19,* 285–302.

5. Watson, D. L. (1992). *Psychology.* Pacific Grove, CA: Brooks/Cole. P. 156.

6. Above, p. 156.

7. Above, p. 175.

8. Flavell J. H. (1976). Metacognitive aspects of problem solving. In L. B. Resnik (Ed.), *The nature of intelligence.* Hillsdale, NJ: Earlbaum.

9. Pressley, M., & E. S. Ghatala (1990). Self-regulated learning: Monitoring learning from text. *Educational Psychologist, 25,* 19–33.

10. Hacker, D. J. (1998). Self-regulated comprehension during normal reading. In D. J. Hacker, J. Dunlosky, & A. C. Graesser (Eds.), *Metacognition in educational theory and practice.* Pp. 165–191. Mahway, NJ: Earlbaum.

Chapter 10

1. 6565 Frantz Road Dublin, Ohio 43017-3395
   TEL: 1-800-848-5878 (North America) FAX: +614-764-2344
   mailto:watsonm@oclc.org http://www.oclc.org/

Part V

1. Pressley, M., & Van Meter, P. (1996). Memory: Teaching and assessing. In E. DeCorte & F. E. Weinert (Eds.), *International encyclopedia of developmental and instructional psychology.* Pp. 431–436. Oxford: Pergamon Press.

2. Dembo, M. H., & Eaton, M. J. (1997). School learning and motivation. In G. D. Phye (Ed.), *Handbook of academic learning.* Pp. 66–105. San Diego, CA: Academic Press. Zimmerman, B. (1998). Academic studying and the development of personal skill: A self-regulatory perspective. *Educational Psychologist, 33,* 2/3, 73–86.

Chapter 11

1. Voeks, V. (1970). *On becoming an educated person* (3rd ed.). Philadelphia: W. B. Saunders Co.

2. Above.

3. Lan, W. Y. (1998). Teaching self-monitoring skills in statistics. In D. H. Schunk & B. J. Zimmerman (Eds.), *Self-Regulated Learning.* Pp. 86–105. New York: Guilford Press.

Chapter 12

1. Klein, M. (1981). Context and memory. In L. D. Benjamen & K. T. Lowman (Eds.), *Activities handbook for the teaching of psychology.* Pp. Washington, DC: American Psychological Association.

2. Chi, M., DeLeeuw, N., Chiu, M-H., & LaVancher, C. (1994). Eliciting self-explanations improves understanding. *Cognitive Science, 18,* 439–477.

3. Chi, M., Bassok, M., Lewis, M., Reiman, P., & Glaser, R. (1989). Self-explanations: How students study and use examples in learning to solve problems. *Cognitive Science, 13,* 145–182.

4. Roitblat, H. (in press). *Power tools for the mind.* Honolulu, HI: University of Hawai'i.

5. Pressley, M., & Woloshyn, V. (1995). Learning facts: The value of always asking yourself Why and other mnemonic strategies. In M. Pressley & V. Woloshyn (Eds.), *Cognitive strategy instruction that really improves children's academic performance* (2nd ed.). Pp. 234–243. Cambridge, MA: Brookline Books.

6. Meese, J. (1994). The role of motivation in self-regulated learning. In D. H. Schunk & B. J. Zimmerman (Eds.), *Self-regulation of learning and performance.* Pp. 25–44. Hillsdale, NJ: Erlbaum.

7. Winne, P. (1995). Inherent details of self-regulated learning. *Educational Psychologist, 30,* 173–188.

8. Lan, W. Y. (1998). Teaching self-monitoring skills in statistics. In D. H. Schunk & B. J. Zimmerman (Eds.), *Self-regulated learning.* Pp. 86–105. New York: Guilford Press.

9. Langer, E. J. (1989). *Mindfulness.* Reading, MA: Addison-Wesley. Weinstein, C. E., & Hume, L. M. (1998). *Study strategies for lifelong learning.* Washington, DC: American Psychological Association.

10. Pressley, M., & McCormick, C. B. (1995). *Advanced educational psychology.* New York: Harper Collins.

11. Ebbing, D. D. (1998) *General chemistry* (4th ed.). Boston: Houghton Mifflin. P. 59.

12. King, A. (1992). Comparison of self-questioning, summarizing, and notetaking-review as strategies for learning from lectures. *American Educational Research Journal, 29,* 303–323.

Chapter 13

1. Pressley, M., & McCormick, C. B. (1995). *Advanced educational psychology.* New York: Harper Collins.

2. Ciborowski, J. (1992). *Textbooks and the students who can't read them.* Cambridge, MA: Brookline Books.

3. Robinson, F. (1970). *Effective study* (4th ed.). New York: Harper & Row.

4. Green, G. W. (1985). *Getting straight A's.* New York: Carol Publishing Group. P. 53.

5. Roitblat, H. (in press) *Power tools for the mind.* Honolulu, HI: University of Hawai'i.

Chapter 14

1. Mastropierri, M. A., & Scruggs, T. E. (1991). *Teaching students ways to remember.* Cambridge, MA: Brookline Books.

2. Willoughby, T., & Wood, E. (1995). Mnemonic strategies. In E. Wood, V. Woloshyn, & T. Willoughby (Eds.), *Cognitive strategy instruction for middle and high schools.* Pp. 5–17. Cambridge, MA: Brookline Books.

3. Schunk, D. H. (1998). Teaching elementary students to self-regulate practice of mathematical skills with modeling. In D. H. Schunk & B. J. Zimmerman (Eds.), *Self-Regulated Learning.* Pp. 137–159. New York: Guilford Press.

4. Roth, K. J. (1990). Developing meaningful conceptual understandings in science. In B. F. Jones & L. Idol (Eds.), *Dimensions of thinking and cognitive instruction.* Pp. 130–176. Hillsdale, NJ: Earlbaum.

5. Pressley, M., Symons, S., McGoldrick, J. A., & Snyder, B. L. (1995). Reading comprehension strategies. In M. Pressley & V. Woloshyn (Eds.) *Cognitive strategy instruction that really improves children's academic performance.* Pp. 57–100. Cambridge, MA: Brookline Books.

Part VI

1. Hofer, B. K., Yu, S. L., & Pintrich, P. R. (1998). Teaching college students to be self-regulated learners. In D. H. Schunk & B. J. Zimmerman (Eds.), *Self-Regulated Learning*. Pp. 57–85. New York: Guilford Press.

2. McKeachie, W. J., Pintrich, P. R., & Lin, Y. G. (1985). Teaching learning strategies. *Educational Psychologist, 20,* 153–160.

Chapter 15

1. McInerny, V., McInerny, D. M., & Marsh, H. W. (1997). Effects of metacognitive strategy training within a cooperative group learning context on computer achievement and anxiety: An aptitude-treatment interaction study. *Journal of Educational Psychology, 89,* 686–695.

2. Hacker, D. J., Bol, L, Horgan, D., & Rakow, E. A. (1998, April). *Test prediction and preparedness.* Paper presented at AERA, San Diego, CA.

3. Ebbing, D. (1993). *General chemistry.* Boston: Houghton Mifflin.

4. Lan, W. Y. (1998). Teaching self-monitoring skills in statistics. In D. H. Schunk & B. J. Zimmerman (Eds.), *Self-Regulated Learning.* New York: Guilford Press. Pp. 86–105.

Chapter 16

1. Pintrich, P. R., & DeGroot, E. V. (1990). Motivational and self-regulated learning components of classroom academic performance. *Journal of Educational Psychology, 82,* 33–40.

2. Wood, E., & Willoughby, T. (1995). Cognitive strategies for test-taking. In E. Wood, V. Woloshyn, & T. Willoughby (Eds.), *Cognitive strategy instruction for middle and high schools.* Pp. 245–258. Cambridge, MA: Brookline Books.

3. Shapiro, D. H. (1985). Meditation and behavioral medicine: Applications of a self-regulation strategy to the clinical management of stress. In S. R. Burchfield (Ed.), *Stress: Psychological and physiological interactions.* Pp. 307–328. Washington, DC: Hemisphere.

4. Scruggs, T. E., & Mastropierri, M. A. (1992). *Teaching test-taking skills.* Cambridge, MA: Brookline Books.

5. Smith, J. C. (1985). *Relaxation dynamics: Nine world approaches to self-relaxation.* Champaign, IL: Research Press.

6. Benson, H. (1975). *The relaxation response.* New York: Morrow.

7. Deffenbacher, J. L., & Michaels, A. C. (1981). Anxiety management training and self-control desensitizaton training—fifteen months later. *Journal of Counseling Psychology, 28,* 459–462.

8. Sherman, A. R., & Plummer, J. L. (1973). Training in relaxation as a behavioral self-management skill: An exploratory investigation. *Behavior Therapy, 4,* 543–550.

9. Adapted from Paul, G. L. (1966). *Insight vs. desensitization in psychotherapy.* Stanford, CA: Stanford University Press.

10. Sarason, I. (1972). Experimental approaches to test anxiety: Attention and the uses of information. In C.D. Spielberger (Ed.), *Anxiety: Current trends in theory and research* (Vol. 2). New York: Academic Press.

Chapter 17

1. Zeidner, M. (1995). Adaptive coping with test situations: A review of the literature. *Educational Psychologist, 30,* 123–133.

2. Hughes, C. A., & Schumaker, J. (1991). Test-taking strategy instruction for adolescents with learning disabilities. *Exceptionality, 2,* 205–221.

3. Scruggs, T. E., & Mastropierri, M. A. (1992). *Teaching test-taking skills.* Cambridge, MA: Brookline Books.

4. Wood, E., & Willoughby, T. (1995). Cognitive strategies for test-taking. In E. Wood, V. Woloshyn, & T. Willoughby (Eds.), *Cognitive strategy instruction for middle and high schools.* Pp. 245–258. Cambridge, MA: Brookline Books.

5. Scruggs & Mastropierri, above.

6. Biemiller, A., Shany, M., Inglis, A., & Meichenbaum, D. (1998). Factors influencing children's acquisition and demonstration of self-regulation on academic tasks. In D. H. Schunk & B. J. Zimmerman (Eds.), *Developing self-regulated learners.* Pp. 203–224. New York: Guilford.

7. Scruggs & Mastropierri, above.

8. King, A. (1995). Cognitive strategies for learning from direct teaching. In E. Wood, V. Woloshyn, & T. Willoughby (Eds.), *Cognitive strategy instruction for middle and high schools.* Pp. 18–65. Cambridge, MA: Brookline Books.

9. Scruggs & Mastropierri, above.

10. Weinstein, C. E., & Mayer, R. E. (1986). *The teaching of learning strategies.* New York: Macmillan.

11. Butler, D. L., & Winne, P. H. (1995). Feedback and self-regulated learning: A theoretical synthesis. *Review of Educational Research, 65, (3)* 245–282.

12. Schunk, D. H., & Zimmerman, B. J. (Eds.). (1994). *Self-regulation of learning and performance.* Hillsdale, NJ: Earlbaum.

13. Garavalia, L. S. (1998). Dealing with students' bad grades. Personal communication.

Part VII

Introduction

1. Elbow, P. (1973). *Writing without teachers.* Oxford University Press. P. iii.

Chapter 18

1. Sitko, B. M., (1998). Knowing how to write: Metacognition and writing instruction. In D. J. Hacker, J. Dunlosky, & A. C. Graesser (Eds.), *Metacognition in educational theory and practice.* Pp. 93–116. Mahway, NJ: Erlbaum.

2. B. J., Zimmerman, & Risemberg, R. (1997). Self-regulating dimensions of academic learning and motivation. In G. D. Phye (Ed.), *Handbook of academic learning.* Pp. 105–125. San Diego, CA: Academic Press.

3. Graham, S. & Harris, K. R. (1993). Self-regulated strategy development: Helping students with learning problems develop as writers. *The Elementary School Journal, 94, 2,* 160–181.

4. Harris, K. R., & Graham, S. (1996). *Making the writing process work: Strategies for composition and self-regulation.* Cambridge, MA: Brookline Books.

5. B. J. Zimmerman & R. Risemberrg, above.

6. El-Dinary, P. B., Brown, R., & Van Meter, P. (1995). Strategy instruction for improving writing. In E. Wood, V. Woloshyn, & T. Willoughby (Eds.), *Cognitive strategy instruction for middle and high schools.* Pp. 88–116. Cambridge, MA: Brookline Books. Pressley, M., McGoldrick, J. A., Carigulia-Bull, T., & Symons, S., (1995). Writing. In M. Pressley & V. E. Woloshyn (Eds.), *Cognitive strategy instruction that really improves children's academic performance.* Pp. 153–183. Cambridge, MA: Brookline Books.

7. Flower, L. S., & Hayes J. R., (1980). Identifying the organization of writing processes. In L. W. Gregg & E. R. Steinberg (Eds.), *Cognitive processes in writing.* Pp. 3–30. Hillsdale, NJ: Earlbaum.

8. El-Dinary, Brown, & Van Meter, above.

9. Sitko, above.

10. Hidi, S., & Anderson, V., (1992). Situational interest and its impact on reading and expository writing. In K. A. Renninger, S. Hidi, & A. Krapp (Eds.), *The role of interest in learning and development.* Pp. 215–238. Hillsdale, NJ: Earlbaum.

11. Graham & Harris; Harris & Graham, above.

12. Above.

13. Pressley, McGoldrick, Carigula-Bull, & Symons, above.

14. El-Dinary, Brown, & Van Meter, above.

15. Watkins, L., (1991). *The critical standards used by college students in evaluating narrative and argumentative essays.* Unpublished master's thesis, University of Hawai'i.

16. Pressley, McGoldrick, Carigula-Bull, & Symons, above

17. El-Dinary, Brown, & Van Meter, above.

18. Pressley, McGoldrick, Carigula-Bull, & Symons, above.

19. Above.

Chapter 19

1. Watson, D., DeBortali-Tregerthan, G., & Frank, J. (1984). *Social psychology*. Glenview, IL.: Scott, Foresman.

Chapter 20

1. Sternberg, R. J. (1997). The concept of intelligence and its role in lifelong learning and success. *American Psychologist, 52,* 1030–1037.

2. Pressley, M., & Lysynchuk, L. (1995). Vocabulary. In M. Pressley & V. E. Woloshyn (Eds.), *Cognitive strategy instruction that really improves children's academic performance.* Pp. 101–115. Cambridge, MA: Brookline Books.

3. Pressley & Lysynchuk, above.

4. Above.

5. Above.

Chapter 21

1. Woloshyn, V. E., & Pressley, M. (1995). Spelling. In M. Pressley & V. E. Woloshyn (Eds.), *Cognitive strategy instruction that really improves children's academic performance.* Pp. 116–152. Cambridge, MA: Brookline Books.

2. Graduates can't spell, bosses say. (November 1998). *Honolulu Advertiser.*

3. Hillerick, R. (1982). That's teaching spelling??? *Educational Leadership, 39,* 615–617.

4. Above, p. 116.

5. Allred, R. (1984). *What research says to the teacher: Spelling, trends, content and methods.* Washington, DC: National Education Association.

6. Brown, A. S. (1990). A review of recent research in spelling. *Educational Psychology Review, 2,* 365–397.

7. Woloshyn & Pressley, above.
Graham, S., & Miller, L. (1979). Spelling research and practice: A unified approach. *Focus on Exceptional Children, 12,* 1–16.
Fitzgerald, J. (1951). *A basic life spelling vocabulary.* Milwaukee: Bruce Publishing Co.

8. Woloshyn & Pressley, above.
   ~~Radaker, above.~~

9. Above.

10. Woloshyn & Pressley, above.

Part VIII

Chapter 22

1. Tough, A. (1990). Encouraging self-planned learning. In R. M. Smith (Ed.), *Learning to learn across the life span.* Pp. 289–304. San Francisco: Jossey-Bass.

2. Ditterman, D. K., & Sternberg, R. (1993). *Transfer on trial.* Norwood, NJ: Ablex.

3. Perkins, D. N., & Salomon, G. (1996). Learning transfer. In E. DeCorte & F. Weinert (Eds.), *International handbook of developmental and instructional psychology.* Pp. 483–487. Oxford, England: Pergamon Press.
   Meichenbaum, D., & Biemiller, A. (1998). *Nurturing independent learners.* Cambridge, MA: Brookline Books.

4. Schunk, D. H. (1998). Teaching elementary students to self-regulate practice of mathematical skills with modeling. In D. H. Schunk & B. J. Zimmerman (Eds.), *Self-Regulated Learning.* Pp. 137–159. New York: Guilford Press.
   Watson, D., & Tharp, R. (1997). *Self-Directed Behavior* (7th ed.). Pacific Grove, CA: Brooks/Cole.

5. Murnane, R., & Levy, F. (1997). *Teaching the new basic skills.* New York: The Reff Press.

6. Gibbons, M. (1984). Walkabout ten years later: Searching for a renewed view of education. *Phi Delta Kappan, 65 (9)* 591–607.

Index